The Holy Spirit and Reformed Spirituality

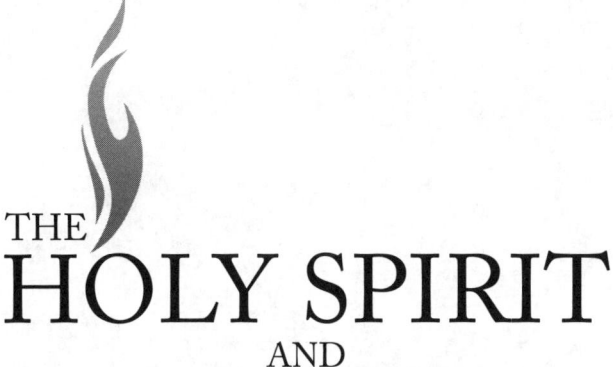

THE HOLY SPIRIT
AND REFORMED SPIRITUALITY

A Tribute to Geoffrey Thomas

Edited by
Joel R. Beeke and
Derek W. H. Thomas

REFORMATION HERITAGE BOOKS
Grand Rapids, Michigan

The Holy Spirit and Reformed Spirituality
© 2013 by Joel R. Beeke and Derek W. H. Thomas

All rights reserved. No part of this book may be used or reproduced in any manner whatsoever without written permission except in the case of brief quotations embodied in critical articles and reviews. Direct your requests to the publisher at the following address:

Reformation Heritage Books
2965 Leonard Street NE
Grand Rapids, MI 49525
616-977-0889 / Fax 616-285-3246
orders@heritagebooks.org
www.heritagebooks.org

Printed in the United States of America
13 14 15 16 17 18/10 9 8 7 6 5 4 3 2 1

Library of Congress Control Number: 2013949270

For additional Reformed literature, request a free book list from Reformation Heritage Books at the above regular or e-mail address.

Table of Contents

Preface... vii

I. Geoff Thomas: A Faithful Instrument of the Spirit

1. Hugh Geoffrey Thomas: A Biographical
   Appreciation — *Gary Brady*............................... 3
2. A Minister Who Has Produced Ministers — *Paul Levy*......... 18

II. Salvation and the Spirit of Christ

3. The Spirit and the Word Incarnate: John Owen's
   Trinitarian Christology — *Carl Trueman*................... 29
4. The Relation of the Righteousness of God and the
   Spirit of God in Romans 1–8 — *Sam Waldron*................ 39
5. The Illumination of the Holy Spirit — *Joel Beeke*.......... 52
6. The Holy Spirit and Human Responsibility — *Fred Malone*.... 70

III. Growth and the Spirit of Holiness

7. A Gracious, Willing Guest: The Indwelling
   Holy Spirit — *David Jones*............................... 85
8. Living by the Spirit's Sanctifying Ministry — *Ian Hamilton*..... 93
9. Some Reflections on the "First Title" of the
   Holy Spirit — *Sinclair B. Ferguson*...................... 104

10. John Owen on the Spirit's Ministry in Guarding
    the Believer's Heart — *Michael A. G. Haykin* 115
11. John Owen and Spiritual-Mindedness: A Reflection
    on Reformed Spirituality — *Derek W. H. Thomas*.............. 127
12. Professor John Murray and the Godly Life — *John J. Murray* 138
13. "The Spirit of God in the People of God":
    A Celtic Spirituality — *Iain D. Campbell*..................... 152

IV. Ministry and the Spirit of Counsel and Might

14. The Holy Spirit and the Call to the Ministry
    of the Gospel — *Stephen Turner* 167
15. The Empowering Work of the Holy Spirit — *Conrad Mbewe* 177
16. The Supply of the Spirit of Jesus Christ and
    Apostolic Ministry (Phil. 1:19) —*Austin Walker* 189
17. An Elizabethan Cameo: The Ministry of
    Edward Dering — *Robert Oliver* 201
18. Passion and the Spirit's Sovereignty in the Thinking and
    Evangelistic Preaching of Martyn Lloyd-Jones — *Gary Benfold*.... 220

Contributors 235

Preface

Having known Geoffrey Thomas for decades, we can say that, like Barnabas, "he was a good man, and full of the Holy Ghost and of faith" (Acts 11:24). Together with the other contributors to this book, we give public thanks for this brother's life and ministry on the occasion of his 75th birthday. He has been a rich blessing to us and many more. Yet we know that the blessing did not come from him, but only by means of him. Another graciously stood with our brother and dwells in him: the Spirit of the living God. Though this book is dedicated to Geoff, it is about Someone far more majestic and awe-inspiring than any mere man.

Geoff Thomas has preached and written often on the Holy Spirit and His saving work. In his recent book on the Holy Spirit, Geoff reminds us that the Spirit knows everything, is everywhere, and created everything; He is absolutely holy and completely sovereign—"the infinite-almighty and yet personal God."[1] The Bible exalts the Spirit. He is the Spirit of glory (1 Peter 4:14). He is the Spirit of counsel and might (Isa. 11:2). He is able to do what no human or angelic power can do: "Not by might, nor by power, but by my spirit, saith the LORD of hosts" (Zech. 4:6). Therefore we do not merely analyze the Spirit. We worship the Spirit.

The chapters in this book seek to honor the Holy Spirit and expound on His rich ministry of filling sinners with Himself and His graces. As Geoff's friends, we thought that our contributions on the subject of the Spirit and Reformed spirituality would excite and move him, and be a page-turner

---

1. Geoffrey Thomas, *The Holy Spirit* (Grand Rapids: Reformation Heritage Books, 2011), 8–11.

for him. Thus it is fitting that parts of this book are biography, the first of which will no doubt embarrass him a bit. Gary Brady and Paul Levy explore the life and influence of Geoff Thomas as an example, by grace, of a Spirit-filled minister. John J. Murray offers a tribute to the Spirit's fruit in the great Reformed theologian-exegete, Professor John Murray. Robert Oliver takes us back to the sixteenth century to the Spirit-worked boldness of Edward Dering, who rebuked Queen Elizabeth to her face.

The Holy Spirit carried along the prophets to write the Holy Scriptures. He inspired each stroke of the pen upon the ancient scrolls. The Holy Spirit opens our minds to receive the truth. He is the Spirit of truth. Therefore we honor the Spirit by studying the Word and reflecting on theology. Carl Trueman studies the work of the Spirit in the life of Christ, Sam Waldron the righteousness of Christ as the basis of the Spirit's work in us, Fred Malone the relationship between the Spirit's sovereignty and human responsibility in conversion and spiritual growth, and Gary Benfold the intersection of sovereignty and responsibility in evangelism.

The Holy Spirit stirs our hearts to trust and love Christ. Reformed Christianity emphasizes the experiential dimension of the Spirit's work. Joel Beeke considers the Spirit's illumination of the heart, David Jones the Spirit's indwelling in the believer, Sinclair Ferguson the primacy of the Spirit in His adopting and witnessing work, and Derek Thomas the nature of spiritual-mindedness.

The Holy Spirit builds Christ's church. We must never separate the Spirit from the body of Christ, for we are His temple. Iain Campbell, Ian Hamilton, Michael Haykin, Stephen Turner, Conrad Mbewe, and Austin Walker each contribute chapters on the Spirit's indwelling God's people and sanctifying them, His guarding their heart, His calling men into pastoral ministry, and His empowering and supporting them.

We have arranged these chapters under four headings reflecting the Spirit's various works: Part I focuses on Geoff Thomas as a faithful instrument of the Spirit, Part II on Christ and salvation, Part III on growth in holiness, and Part IV on ministry.

It should come as no surprise that this book repeatedly leans on the insight of the Reformers and the Puritans. The Spirit of God shone brightly in such men, and they in turn intently studied the work of the Spirit in applying the redemption purchased by Christ.

All quotations from the Scripture are from the King James or New King James versions. Many thanks go to Gary Brady, Geoff's son-in-law, who is the original inspiration behind this book. What a joy he and all of Geoff's happy children and their spouses are to him! Thanks too to dear Iola for being such a wonderful support to her husband over the decades, so that he could be who God made him to be as a friend and as a minister. And thanks, too, to all who have contributed to this volume in honor of our mutual friend.

It is our hope that God will use this book to pour out the Spirit once again upon His church, and raise up more men who, like Geoff, love to honor the person and ministry of the Spirit of Christ. But ultimately this book and its authors look beyond man to the ultimate goal and end of all things, the Lord Himself. May the Spirit use this effort to bring the kingdom of Christ to earth for the glory of the Father forever!

—Joel R. Beeke and Derek Thomas

PART I

Geoff Thomas: A Faithful Instrument of the Spirit

Chapter 1
by Gary Brady

Hugh Geoffrey Thomas: A Biographical Appreciation

On October 15, 2013, Hugh Geoffrey Thomas—Geoff, as he is known to all—will be seventy-five years old. Shortly after that, he will mark the forty-eighth year since he became pastor of Alfred Place Baptist Church in Aberystwyth, Wales.

The move to Aberystwyth took place late in October 1965, when Geoff and Iola, who had married the previous year (along with their six-week old baby girl, Eleri), moved up from Swansea, where Geoff had been working for the National Coal Board and Iola had been teaching in a secondary school.

That move marks the meridian line of Geoff's life, dividing it neatly, if somewhat asymmetrically, in two. First is the relatively varied and peripatetic twenty-seven years before Aberystwyth, then comes the more than forty, less varied but in many ways equally peripatetic, years based at the Buarth Road manse.

Being in Mid Wales, Aberystwyth can be thought of as a kind of compromise location, as Geoff was raised in South Wales and Iola Williams in Blaenau Ffestiniog, North Wales. They have much in common. In both homes, one parent was Congregationalist and the other Baptist. Both have relatives who have been university professors of the Welsh language. Both had uncles who were ministers trained in liberal theology. "We were both brands plucked from the burnt-over churches modernism had destroyed," Geoff once commented.

Two more girls were born in 1968 and 1972. I married Eleri in 1988, and her sisters married in 1994. There are nine grandchildren altogether, born between 1989 and 2008.¹ All eighteen of us get together from time to time, and those are occasions of great joy.

I first met Geoff in 1977 when I came, as an eighteen-year-old, to study at the university. He had then been a pastor some twelve years.² So I have known Geoff for well over half my life and nearly half of his. In writing about him, then, I have advantages and disadvantages.

Before Aberystwyth, 1938–1965

Perhaps the best way to cover this ground is to consider the chief influences, cultural and theological, that, under God, prepared Geoff for ministry. One can detect at least four strands.

The English-speaking South Wales valleys

First, there is the largely English-speaking milieu of industrial South Wales in which Geoff grew up and which was reinforced chiefly by his parents and by his schooling. Harry Eastaway Thomas (1905–1978) and Elizabeth Francis (1906–1995) married in the early 1930s. Geoff was born in 1938 and was their only surviving child. Harry's twin brother became a Congregational minister and, under liberal influence, was apparently afraid to preach the apostle Paul for years. Harry's sister was also married to a Congregational minister.

Harry worked for the railways, serving as stationmaster in various places and latterly at Hengoed. Geoff often says that his mother was always singing hymns. He assumed that was how every mother went about her housework! Both parents were churchgoers, but for many years attended different chapels, his father the Congregational and his mother, the Baptist. Geoff once described his father's church this way:

---

1. Catrin and Ian live with their son, Osian, in Wiltshire; Fflur and Glyn with their children, Iwan, Lydia, and Tomos, in Cardiff. Ian and Glyn are deacons; I pastor in London. Our five boys are Rhodri, Dylan, Dewi, Gwion, and Owain; Rhodri and his wife, Sibyl, live in Aber.

2. In 1976, Geoff preached at the church I attended. I have to confess to not recalling the occasion until reminded of it when we first met. How sleepy we can be when significant things are happening under our noses!

One of the most dynamic Congregationalist churches in the world a century ago, Bethania, Dowlais. A thousand strong congregation, its membership then was overwhelmingly evangelical but its ministers steadily and secretly moved into humanism in the old familiar way, becoming Arminian, bolstering man's free will as the pivot for every step in religion, abandoning the Old Testament in huge chunks, and soon after such a momentous step of defiance of Jesus' convictions, they turned against the apostle Paul in the New Testament. So they gave up Jesus' view of Scripture and Jesus' greatest spokesman and they imagined they could still be loyal to this living person and not grieve him deeply. The brotherhood of man and the fatherhood of God became for them the message of the Christian religion.[3]

Geoff passed the 11-plus examination for high school and qualified to attend one of the best state schools in the area, Lewis School, Pengam. Years before, David Lloyd George had described it as the Eton of the South Wales valleys. Geoff remained there for seven years and did well academically, athletically, and in other ways.[4] Not required to do national service and having some thoughts of entering the ministry, he continued to live at home when he went on to do university-level work in biblical studies with Greek and philosophy at the nearby Baptist College in Cardiff.

South Wales in the 1950s was still dominated by the coal industry and the left-wing politics the industry tended to foment. The 1904–1905 revival was something of a dim and distant memory for most. Geoff speaks very warmly of his mother's uncle, Oliver Bound, an antiques dealer and evangelist who had been touched by the revival. However, the chapels where Geoff's parents attended and the biblical studies department in Cardiff were alike affected by the ravages of liberalism.

---

3. Quotations in this chapter are mainly from two online articles: http://www.alfredplacechurch.org.uk/?page_id=3593 and http://www.banneroftruth.co.uk/pages/articles/article_detail.php?932. Quotations not footnoted can be located in one of these articles.

4. It is perhaps no surprise to learn of his prowess at long jump and triple jump. He was also part of a record-breaking relay team with John Dawes, later Wales and British Lions rugby coach. A younger contemporary, Neil Kinnock, would become Labour Party leader and Lord Bedwellty. "I only remember him drawing tanks," Geoff once said.

The Welsh-speaking milieu of North and South Wales

The Welsh-speaking milieu is found chiefly in North and West Wales, but also to some extent in the South. In ancient times, Cymric or Welsh (as the English call it) was spoken throughout the British Isles. With the coming of the Anglo-Saxons, early forms of English began to predominate and the native language was driven into the hills and far corners of the British Isles. England formally conquered Wales in 1282, with the two countries being united practically in 1485 and officially in 1536. Throughout the nineteenth century, the London government pursued an aggressive policy of promoting English so that by the twentieth century, only 20 percent of people in Wales spoke Welsh.

Geoff's father could speak Welsh, but because his mother could not, Welsh was rarely used at home. His cousin, Robert Maynard Jones (Bobi Jones), was brought up in a similar way but became proficient in the Welsh language while still at school, going on to be professor of Welsh in Aberystwyth University. He has published more works in the Welsh language than anyone before him. Some will be familiar with his translations of hymns by William Williams and others. Geoff himself had some Welsh, but was not at home with the language until marrying Iola, whom he met while studying in Cardiff. A Welsh speaker from birth, her passion for the language is boundless. Her parents were keen nationalists and lovers of the ancient but then apparently dying tongue. Iola's only sister, Rhiain, also lives in Aberystwyth, with her husband, Keith. Like Bobi and his wife, Beti, they are long-serving members of the town's Welsh-speaking evangelical church. Geoff's English has always been better than his Welsh, but he is able to listen to, and benefit from, preaching in Welsh, and on rare occasions he even has opportunity to preach in what some call the language of heaven.

Westminster Seminary and the United States

A further strand was added in 1961 when Geoff sailed in a cargo ship from Liverpool, England, to Newport, Virginia. (He read Jonathan Edwards's *Religious Affections* en route.) He went to spend three years studying theology in the institution founded by J. Gresham Machen in 1929, Westminster Theological Seminary, Philadelphia. Geoff's professors included John Murray, E. J. Young, Cornelius Van Til, and Ed Clowney. The formative influences of American Reformed theology and the American way of life on Geoff cannot be underestimated. I personally believe that his ideas of distance and of how to use a telephone were formed in those now far-off days when America was a much different place from Britain. These ideas do not conform to those of many British people of his age, for whom telephones are for emergencies and who consider covering three hundred miles in one day excessive.

Geoff has continued to travel quite extensively in the United States, speaking at various churches and conferences year after year, and has a pretty good idea of what is going on theologically on the American side of the pond.

The resurgence of Reformed theology in the United Kingdom
The fourth strand is partly personified in Banner of Truth Trust founder Iain Murray, but it includes a host of influences, such as London Welshman, Dr. Martyn Lloyd-Jones, the Strict and Particular (or Grace Baptists) of England, and the various shades of evangelical Presbyterianism found in Scotland, Ireland, and America, countries where Geoff has often preached.

To understand Geoffrey Thomas properly and what has made him the pastor and preacher he has been over these last forty-eight years, these four elements at least must be taken into account. Alongside these there is a genuine openness to all sorts of influences, secular and religious, too numerous to identify individually. Geoff is something of a culture vulture; in his home, he can be found listening to classical music, especially Mahler. On the walls of the manse are original paintings by local artists and prints by Vermeer and others. A subscription to *The Spectator* magazine betrays a conservative position politically (although it is probably the socialists of Plaid Cymru who usually get his vote). Favorite secular authors include Philip Johnson and Roger Scruton. There is also a warm glow of pride prompted by the family connection to the war poet Edward Eastaway Thomas. Living in a university town and often travelling to London, Geoff always has concerts, dramas, films, and exhibitions to enjoy. He carefully keeps up with reviews of the latest offerings.

Conversion and call to preach

In an interview in 2007, Geoff was asked about his conversion. He explained how his mother was a Baptist and how, influenced by her Uncle Oliver, she "gave her heart to the Lord Jesus" some time during the First World War period. He said warmly that "she maintained a sweet love for the Savior all her life." He spoke of her as "tender, modest, self-effacing to a degree, wonderfully kind and loving." He confessed, "I am like a mouse before an elephant when measured by her graces."[5]

He went on to say:

> I went with my mother to church (the lamb follows the ewe) and in 1951 we moved to Hengoed where the Tabernacle Baptist church had been erected a hundred yards from our house almost fifty years earlier. It had started as a split-away from the Mount Pleasant Baptist Church across the other side of the valley in Maesycwmmer when the 1904 revival affected that church and bifurcated the congregation. It was made impossible for those who had "entered into the blessing" to remain in the church and so they resigned and set up the Tabernacle half a mile away. Unfortunately they remained linked naïvely to the Baptist Union and so received into their pulpits the students and ministers who rejected the appallingly pessimistic evaluation of the human condition found in the Bible, one which could be relieved only by the incarnation, righteous life and atonement of the Son of God. Bland universalism and bourgeois ethics became the message of the day, disguised under traditional hymns and God words. Such insipid views depended largely on "personalities" to keep the wagons trundling on.

Geoff was brought to Christ when a young minister came to the church and began earnestly preaching for a decision. This was in 1954. He was soon baptized and joined to the church. Sadly, the young minister, infected by liberal teaching, lost his way, and the church shrank and shrank. It was eventually disbanded and the building demolished.

Geoff says that he sought fellowship wherever he could find it—in summer camps and then at university in the Inter-Varsity Christian Fellowship. In 1958, he heard Dr. Lloyd-Jones preach for the first time. That summer,

---

5. http://www.banneroftruth.org/pages/articles/article_print.php?1335

he also read two books that influenced him greatly. One was Lloyd-Jones's *Studies in the Sermon on the Mount*. Geoff says of that book that it "will show you the beauty of a righteous life and make you want to live it, and it will also show you what consecutive biblical preaching can achieve." The other book was Dr. J. I. Packer's crucial *Fundamentalism and the Word of God*. He also read around this time J. C. Ryle's *Holiness* and George Whitefield's *Journals*, and subscribed to a new magazine called *The Banner of Truth*.

By such means—even finding good books in the local library—he began to discover good theology. "God brought these things before me," he recalls, "His hand was upon me." He discovered "a growing group of role models, the 'sons' of Dr. Lloyd-Jones, some of them my contemporaries at University, and others who were younger Welsh ministers." These would include such men as Eifion Evans, Hugh Morgan, and a man who was to die tragically young but who would have a big influence on Geoff as a young man, J. B. Thomas of Swansea.

In 1959, Geoff preached for the first time. However, he confesses:

> It was only during the last months of my course at Seminary that I was assured of a call to preach, though I guess there was nothing else I ever wanted to do or was fit to do. It seemed a huge step to announce that I was going to be a preacher, but the counsels of Edmund P. Clowney, the most approachable, kindly and prayerful of teachers, were crucial in prodding me to come out with the inevitable decision.

Meeting Professor Clowney years later, Geoff was moved to be told, "Geoff, I have prayed for you every day."

Aberystwyth, 1965 to the present

Following his return from America and marriage, there was a period of about fifteen months before Geoff took up a pastorate. Convinced that the Lord wanted him to minister in Wales, he was drawn to Aberystwyth partly by the presence of a university in the town. Ministry among students was to prove an important part of his future work. The other big factor was the presence of evangelical believers keen to be taught.

If you stand in the tiny street called Alfred Place in Aberystwyth, you can see two Baptist churches diagonally opposite each other. Over the road is Bethel Baptist, a Welsh-speaking church, and in Alfred Place itself is the English Baptist Church put up by the Bethel folk in 1870 for the benefit of holidaymakers unable to understand Welsh. Over the years, the churches have led a fairly separate existence.

By the time Geoff came to Alfred Place in 1965, there was some confusion about the gospel. However, some of the people were to prove to be great supporters. Geoff was very grateful for one particular deacon, recently departed to glory, who was an enormous support when he arrived. He commented, "A minister needs only one man like that and in a sense he is home and dry." That man's son and one of his grandsons are deacons in the church today. Within seven years, it was possible, in what was then an innovation, to appoint three elders, two of whom remain in the church to this day. There were also godly women in the church, for all of whom Geoff has publicly expressed his deepest gratitude. He says:

> [The people were] patient with me in my early learning to be a pastor-preacher, checking and encouraging me. For them, Christians everywhere are also most appreciative. They know that I could never have survived in a church for so long without the support of older wise men who would rise up and be counted during the inevitable battles.

Even the strong believers were in need of sound teaching, and that is exactly what they got from the young seminary graduate. From the beginning, he was determined to preach the Word. He confesses to having come "back from three years at Westminster Seminary full of graduate theology," which had its drawbacks. He had spent six years—"those long years from 18 to 24"—with students, "that narrow spectrum of age and communication and interest. It was not the most helpful approach to preaching popularly to my fellow countrymen." Not that he despised the teaching of Murray, Van Til, and the others. "How can I demean such training?" he asks. Of Professor Murray, Geoff always speaks only in the most respectful, even reverential tones.

Preaching

From the beginning, Geoff's pattern was to preach systematically through the books of the Bible. He began with Genesis 1:1 and Matthew 1:1, but difficulties with plowing through the whole book of Genesis led to a modification of his original plan, so that he has not dealt with books in any particular order. He spoke once of how "modernism has shrunk the sermon to a comment on current affairs and book reviews." In Geoff's ministry, expository preaching has always been central. He has written:

> The preacher can minister to an entire congregation with all the differing needs of that gathering. The Word of God opened up and applied to the hearers can come upon them from all 360 degrees. The lines at which it comes running to you make sinners utterly defenceless to resist. This wisdom comes unexpectedly, from whence they least expect such truths to be dealing with them, from passages that seemed, when first announced, remote to their own needs, but by them God worked and elevated and inspired and reassured and directed. Hope was rekindled; conviction was experienced; love was reborn. When I look back to my own peak Christian experiences then so many of them have been when I was under the Word of God as it was preached to me and I melted, or again when it was I who was the spokesman and mouthpiece of God, and the congregation was still during the sermon, motionless after the service was over, knowing God was in this place. I have felt after such meetings that saving power was present though I might never hear of any specific individuals converted that day.

As for early influences, he once said:

> I found Al Martin[6] and Donald Macleod invaluable helps in preaching in the 1970s. I preached their sermons and envied their clear outlines and passion in delivery. Such men helped me to build on the Doctor and my Welsh role models to form me. I have also had Iain Murray as my most consistently helpful counsellor, and consider his friendship and advice the most single blessed support. If there is one man whose books I must read as they appear it has to be…Iain Murray.[7]

Geoff is not oblivious to the difficulties of systematic preaching. A few years back he wrote:

> But to do what I set out to do, preach through all the Bible, is inevitably to end in failure. All ministry ends in failure, of course. The plan

---

6. Geoff did a six-week pulpit exchange with Al Martin in the 1970s. The moving of the Alfred Place morning service from 11 a.m. to 10:30 a.m. can be dated to this period.

7. http://menforministry.blogspot.co.uk/2007/10/men-for-ministry-interview-series-geoff.html.

and the noble attempt to accomplish it was simply mine; God's plan for me was different. But I believe it was praiseworthy to try to preach through it all.

He speaks of having painted himself into a corner with several difficult books still to be tackled. He has said:

> I am not sure whether I will ever "finish" the task God gave me to preach the Word. Sometimes I feel I have left for myself some of the more demanding books of the Old Testament (as far as a preacher is concerned), or the second halves of books once started which after a year or two were abandoned as, alas, wearying to myself and the congregation. Generally I have felt an unease about a number of books before I commenced them, or about verses and passages looming up ahead, wondering how I could preach on such passages. Yet in the discipline of study and meditation those chapters and books have come alive; they have been a delight. I wish I had had more role models of preachers and preaching through Old Testament books. I have proved to be an uncertain guide myself in that department.

Tradition

If you came to Alfred Place one Sunday, you would find it quite traditional. Wooden pews face a raised platform (which conceals a baptistery beneath) with a square pipe organ to the preacher's left. For many years, the largely conservative *Grace Hymns* has been the main hymnbook. For a few less years, Scripture readings have all been from the 1984 New International Version, which slowly superseded the King James Version in the 1980s. The service follows the pattern of what has somewhat derogatorily been called "the hymn sandwich," including four carefully chosen hymns, notices or announcements, a reading, a long prayer, and a sermon of around forty-five minutes. Geoff loves to speak from the pulpit to any children present. A gifted storyteller, he usually has a nice one to share. Capitalizing on a Welsh tradition, there is usually a verse of Scripture to learn. (In earlier days, children would each stand up and repeat the verse learned from the previous week.) Since 1977, no collection has been taken up, but people are invited to place their gifts in boxes near the entrance. A cup of tea is served downstairs after the evening service.

Geoff does it all. He comments:

I have led the Sunday services myself. I announce the hymns, and I publicly read the Scriptures—I whose life uniquely in the congregation is spent in the Word. The pastoral prayer must be mine whose time is spent in healing, encouraging and correcting the people of God. All this is very acceptable to a congregation who accept one tremendous reality, that the Creator of the whole cosmos has summoned this man to bring his message to bear on these people, and it would be utterly woeful for me if they did not hear the Creator's servant and I did not preach to them in a way that was most suitable to his glory. "Why do you take the entire service?" I am asked. "Because I have this calling from God and no one else in the congregation has it," is my reply. People then can think about the God I am speaking of and not about a parade of personalities. At the midweek meeting opportunity is given to anyone to share something with the gathering, though rarely do people speak.

With regard to the hymns, a careful record is kept so that most hymns are sung only once or twice a year. The congregation is quite musical, and Geoff is keen to introduce new tunes from time to time. He has written of his preference for great hymns, old and new. Old hymns often come "from an era more filled with both the Spirit and great poets than our forlorn age," Geoff says.

The midweek meeting is usually on Tuesday in the basement below the church. One arrives to find photocopies of the prayer letters and e-mails from the past week set out on the chairs. The pattern is to begin with unaccompanied hymns, while a reading and message take up the next half an hour. There is then some discussion—rarely about what has been said but mostly about prayer topics—followed by half an hour or so of prayer. If things are a little slow, Geoff will call on one of the men to lead.

Ever changing
Over the years, there have been inevitable changes in the life of the congregation. While its core remains stable, the population of Aberystwyth is fairly mobile, as in most places today. The coming and going of students adds to this flux, as does the fact that Aberystwyth is a holiday destination. The smallest congregations are usually just before Christmas, when few

students or holidaymakers are about. Geoff has commented that an enduring ministry is helped by this factor:

> If a church is set in an area where there is some economic stability or in a city, or the place has a history of an earlier grace then there is more expectation of growth. If our building had been set in a valley miles outside Aberystwyth then the impact of the pulpit would have been muted, and the duration of my ministry would have been considerably briefer. However, our church was situated ideally, in the middle of town, a block from the sea, in a community of 13,000 people where today an additional 8,000 students are attending the university. The discipleship and consecration of 40 years of students have been an inspiration both to myself and the congregation. They have warmed the wintry months of the year.

Pastoral visiting is made easier by the fact that the town is fairly compact and it is possible to walk from the manse to the local hospital. However, because the town is on the edge of a rural community, some live in the outlying villages and, from time to time, some are hospitalized elsewhere.

On his fortieth anniversary of ministry, Geoff was able to write:

> I am as much committed to change today as I was forty years ago, to change myself, and the entire congregation, the churches of the town, the community of which we are a part and Wales as a whole. The Christian wants to change the world, and the one great instrument for change which we have been given is the Bible.

Given that Geoff has remained in one place and has changed little with regard to the services over the years, this may sound surprising to some. A number of people have left Alfred Place over the years because of a perceived unwillingness to change. One thing that has often struck me, however, is Geoff's willingness to try something new. For instance, in sermon preparation, Geoff continues to write out all he has to say, though he is never tied to his notes. Over the years, however, like others, he has moved from handwritten manuscripts to word-processed documents, and in more recent years has had the manuscripts printed and copied for the use of those who may find a written sermon easier to absorb. In a similar way, he has co-operated with others to produce not only audio but also written sermons on the Internet.

Church life

The Alfred Place church left the Baptist Union shortly after Geoff's arrival, owing to the mixed nature of that denomination. It has remained independent but has not become isolated, interacting with other churches in the town and throughout the area whenever possible.

One early initiative was the establishment of a bookshop, now adjacent to the church building and a major asset. For many years, the church has sought to support the preaching of Bud Mort to the deaf. The church was also able to establish a home for those with learning difficulties at Plas Lluest, which opened in 1975.

One of the most encouraging works with which the church has been involved over the years is the Reformed Baptist work in Kenya started by Keith Underhill. Keith was converted while studying in Aberystwyth and then worked as a schoolteacher in Kenya. After he completed his ministerial training at Westminster Seminary, the church sent him to begin church planting in Nairobi. Since then, the number of Reformed Baptist churches in that part of East Africa has mushroomed, and Keith has been greatly used to convert and teach a large number of people. Geoff has often visited Nairobi and the more remote parts where gospel work goes on to this day.

In each of the areas mentioned, there have been many difficulties and much heartache as work has developed, difficulties have been encountered, and sometimes serious division faced. Through it all, the Lord has continued to sustain the work and to use His servant.

Men in the ministry

One gratifying feature of the work has been that several men have either been called to the ministry while in the congregation or strengthened in their convictions under Geoff's ministry. Keith Underhill is an obvious example. Derek Thomas, Austin Walker, Graham Heaps, and Chris Peggington are others from the early period. We might also mention Ed Collier, Spencer Cunnah, Alan Davey, Malcolm Firth, Keith Hoare, Luke Jenner, Ian Middlemist, Tim Mills, Dan Peters, Mark Picket and Mark Rowcroft. I personally felt a call to the ministry before going to Aberystwyth, but sitting under Geoff's ministry, observing him both out of the pulpit and in it, and on occasion turning to him for pastoral counsel, was an invaluable blessing.

Conferences

In the second week of August each year, the Evangelical Movement of Wales Conference takes place in Aberystwyth. Geoff has been a great friend of the conference over the years, often speaking at evening meetings and seminars. In 1997, he was the main speaker. His book *Daniel: Servant of God under Four Kings* grew out of addresses given at that time.

Since Geoff ministered in Aberystwyth, people arriving for the conference on the preceding Sunday naturally gravitated to Alfred Place. As the conference grew, more elaborate arrangements were necessary, including the changing of times and venue. Enthusiasm for the ministry eventually led to what has become a virtual mini-conference, wherein the Sunday ministry is supplemented by a third well-attended but no-frills Monday morning sermon.

The UK is well blessed with conferences of a Reformed persuasion and similar gatherings. There can be few at which Geoff has not spoken more than once, either preaching or giving a historical paper. These include the Carey Ministers Conference, the Westminster Conference, and Grace Assembly. Geoff is a great believer in conferences, noting that loners in the ministry often defect from it by one means or another.

Books and articles

Mention of the book on Daniel also prompts us to note Geoff's written ministry. Geoff is an inveterate writer. He has kept a daily diary of events for decades and has written increasingly over the years for publication, first chiefly in magazines and newspapers, then in compilations, and, in time, in books of his own. His books include *The Life of Ernest Reisinger*, *Philip and the Great Revival in Samaria*, *The Sure Word of God*, and *The Holy Spirit*.

Conclusion

For Geoff, life has been and continues to be very full. Besides the demands of regular ministry, there are frequent preaching trips throughout the British Isles and overseas. Over the years, besides making regular trips to America and Canada, he has travelled to many other countries, including Albania, Brazil, Russia, and South Korea.

I am sometimes asked how he manages to do so much. People sometimes assume Geoff must be in a constant whirr. In fact, the secret, it seems to me, lies chiefly in his ability to relax. There are times when he is unable to sleep well, but otherwise he seems to have a rare ability both to work hard at one time and to sit back and relax at another, something some preachers find difficult to do.

Geoff himself would also point out that he has been blessed with a wife of consistent godliness and prayerfulness. "She accepted my absences and kept me in the pulpit," he once wrote. With her training in biblical studies and her skill in teaching the Scriptures, she has also worked faithfully over many years.

Beyond all this, of course, is the wonderful sustaining grace of God that both have known. Some years ago, Geoff reflected on the question, "Have you lost the wonder of the gospel of Jesus Christ?" His answer was an honest and resounding no. He said:

> I still have a passion for ministry, and pastoring, and officers' meetings, and the struggle of the two sermons each Sunday. The message is still wonderfully life-enhancing; the changes in the lives of men and women are still deeply encouraging. I shall be happy to give myself for another year or so if God wills preaching 84 sermons on Sundays and more than 40 during the week. The gospel of Jesus Christ is the power of God unto salvation to all who believe.

No one goes on ministering on earth forever, but we are thankful that the Lord has spared His servant these many years and pray that God will continue to make him a faithful instrument of the Spirit.

Chapter 2
by Paul Levy

A Minister Who Has Produced Ministers

In 2 Timothy, the apostle Paul gives Timothy a blueprint for the gospel to continue long after Paul has gone. The apostles are dying out. Those first eyewitnesses will not be around much longer. Paul himself is about to lose his head, so he writes to Timothy, his young apprentice, and gives him and every generation of ministers following him directions as to how gospel ministry is to be preserved and passed on, that is, how he is to guard the good deposit that was entrusted to him "by the Holy Spirit who dwells in us" (2 Tim 1:14).

Having instructed Timothy in chapter 1 about what is involved in staying loyal to the gospel, Paul moves on in 2:2 to tell Timothy and us that to merely finish one's ministry is not enough. Paul places an apostolic imperative on Timothy to train others, to hand the gospel baton on so that work will continue for generation after generation. At the start of chapter 2, Paul's commands could not be clearer: Timothy must "stay strong in the grace that is in Christ Jesus"; he must not give up, but must make sure to pass it on to faithful men "who will be able to teach others also" (2 Tim. 2:2).

Geoff Thomas has stayed strong, spending a lifetime ministering in a small university town, which, at its peak, when the students are around, has about fifteen thousand residents. He has served the same congregation for forty-eight years. While the congregation has normally been around the 150 mark, it has sometimes been near 200. To do the same job for forty-eight years, working for the same company, is remarkable by anyone's standards, but to do so in a church environment where one preaches to many of the same people, week in and week out, year in and year out, decade after decade, is a wonderful achievement. In the past fifty years in the UK, at best a handful of men have had such long pastorates.

However, I think even more powerful and admirable than Geoff's longevity is that he has passed the gospel baton to others. Out of this congregation and under his ministry, God has raised up scores of ministers and preachers of the gospel.

In 2000, Geoff delivered the John Reed Miller Lectures at Reformed Theological Seminary in Jackson, Mississippi. He began with these words:

> The full-time gospel ministry is still a protected oasis. We are relieved of so many of the tensions and temptations that the men to whom we minister are meeting each day. They work with their minds and bodies in this evil world and give their hard-earned money to us so generously that we may spend our days—think of it—in the quiet of our studies, in the Bible, in evangelism, and in pastoring God's people. I hope you will never join with those ministers who sit around grumbling in their fraternals about all the alleged hardships of being preachers. What a marvellously privileged life we lead. I trust that you earnestly believe that if it be God's will for you to spend the rest of your life caring for this particular congregation you will happily do so and thank the Lord at the end of each day for such blessings.[1]

Most of us reading this volume have never visited Alfred Place Baptist Church. We may have read Geoff's sermons online or heard him speak at a conference or as a visiting speaker. Alfred Place does not run a student ministry. There are two services on the Lord's Day and a midweek Bible study and prayer meeting. Geoff occasionally has had assistants, but no student workers or small army of apprentices. In short, no special student track has been put in place. The simple means of grace have been practiced, and I think it is fair to say that the combination of Geoff's preaching, enthusiasm for the Christian ministry, and unique personality under God has made the ministry attractive to many young men.

Longtime friend, Iain Murray of the Banner of Truth Trust, says:

> I have often been a witness of how Geoff's ministry has shaped lives around the world and, more particularly, the lives of successive

---

1. Geoff Thomas, *Preaching—The Man, the Message, the Method* (n.p.: Reformed Academic Press, 2003), 9.

generations of pastors. I believe the extent of that influence has come from the example of the ministry which men have seen in him, together with the warm interest and affection they have experienced in his presence. Preacher, reader and writer though he is, the time he has given to individuals must be one of the most significant features of his life. He is both admired and loved. His life has illustrated the saying, "He that multiplies the workers does more than the worker."[2]

So I hope to explore how Geoff's ministry has multiplied itself in producing workers. I have interviewed a number of men who attended Alfred Place in their student days, and I will offer their reflections as I try to give a picture of a minister who has produced ministers.[3]

In the pulpit

The first thing that people talk about when they speak of studying in Aberystwyth and attending Alfred Place is the preaching. Geoff felt called to preach in his early 20s and wept when he received the call to preach in Alfred Place Baptist Church. Since then, he has committed himself to an expository, "*lectio continua*," ministry, preaching through books of the Bible. At the close of forty-eight years, he has nearly preached on the whole of the canon.

Derek Thomas (no relation) was converted as a freshman, coming to Aberystwyth and arriving at Alfred Place in 1972 after dabbling in Anglicanism. Geoff was preaching on Matthew 11:28: "Come to Me, all you who labor and are heavy laden, and I will give you rest." Derek says: "I can see him now, arms outstretched, pleading with his listeners to heed the Word of Christ and bow to it. His eloquence, his passion, his Calvinism, his evangelicalism—these testified of a man in love with preaching, who believed in preaching."[4]

---

2. Email to the author, October 31, 2012.

3. I am grateful to the following men for allowing me to interview them regarding their time in Aberystwyth: Alan Davey, UFM missionary in France; Mark Rowcroft, pastor, Grace Baptist Church, Darlington; Luke Jenner, pastor, Grace Baptist Church, Halifax; Dan Peters, pastor, Newcastle Evangelical Reformed Church; Derek Thomas, senior minister, First Presbyterian Church, Columbia, South Carolina, and professor of systematic theology, Reformed Theological Seminary; and David N. Jones, pastor, Mount Stuart Presbyterian Church, Tasmania, Australia, and moderator, Presbyterian Church of Australia, 2009–2012. Unless otherwise stated, all quotes are taken from these interviews.

4. Geoff Thomas, *Preaching*, 6.

Derek joined the congregation, served as a deacon, and lived with Geoff and his wife, Iola, before going to Reformed Theological Seminary in Jackson. He writes:

> Geoff's preaching showed me that every word of the text is important, that preaching is not about you or your personality (even though he had a larger-than-life personality); preaching is about expounding Scripture. He had a great view of God and in his preaching he managed to convey that God is great and glorious. That is why I have always felt that my own call to be a preacher was an important vocation. His energy and enthusiasm for preaching made a generation of preachers feel that the ministry was the highest calling a man could receive.

The danger for many of us preachers, as we seek to follow expository preaching as a pattern for our ministries, is that our sermons become commentaries on passages, context becomes king, and we mistake Bible study for preaching. We forget that in preaching God's Word we are seeking to bring our listeners into an encounter with God in Christ. True preaching is a confrontation between God and man. Geoff never forgot this.

The Christ-centeredness that characterizes so much of Geoff's preaching flows in many ways from his training at Westminster Theological Seminary under Ed Clowney, John Murray, Cornelius Van Til, and others. He took the discipline of preaching Christ from all of Scripture with him to Aberystwyth and has determinedly tried to magnify the Savior in his preaching.

Luke Jenner writes:

> The one thing that will always live with me from my time in Alfred Place was that Geoff so clearly had such a glowing admiration for his Lord that it came out in his preaching without him even trying, I think. I had heard preachers preach the gospel before, but never before had I heard someone who loved and preached Christ simply because He was just so great. The character and beauty and majesty of Jesus would come across so powerfully in his preaching.... On one occasion I remember him saying, "I was talking to a Jehovah's Witness this week, and at one point I said something about Jesus that caused the man on my door to reply, 'Oh, but we mustn't put him on a pedestal, must we?' 'Oh, but we must,' I said." And the gravity and earnestness with which he said those words—as he leaned over the pulpit in his

typical way—will never leave me. He couldn't stand to see his lovely Savior so dishonoured.

Geoff preached God and the Bible, and proclaimed the loveliness of Christ. He preached in Aberystwyth to a congregation of mainly students in a university that was hostile to the gospel in its teaching, and so in his preaching of the Word he sought to equip students to live out the Christian faith in their settings.

Dan Peters, who studied English literature in Aberystwyth in the late 1990s, says:

> I learnt that students, and others particularly engaged in the marketplace of ideas, need to be hearing preaching that is deep, serious, logically coherent and intellectually credible. The fiercest assaults my Christian faith has ever faced were in the lecture theatres at Aberystwyth, and its survival through that period was due in no small part to the weekly preaching at Alfred Place. It's not that Geoff self-consciously preached "apologetics," or that he necessarily addressed the specific issues that were being raised on my university course, but that he preached a Christian faith that was every bit as robust and reasonable as the ideologies to which I was being exposed. The gospel, as it was preached at Alfred Place, didn't look flimsy alongside the sophisticated hypotheses of Jacques Derrida and Michel Foucault. Geoff set forth the doctrines of original sin and the incarnation and justification by faith just as carefully and rigorously as my lecturers set forth post-structuralist literary theory.

The preacher's job is to preach God from His Word and proclaim Christ in all His glory, but also to challenge the culture, to proclaim the lordship of Christ over every area, and to show God's people that the Christian faith is true and stands up to scrutiny. This, too, has characterized Geoff's ministry.

Of course, nearly all preachers in the Reformed tradition would aspire to preach in the ways I have tried to outline above, but tragically, seeking to put these things into practice, we too often become boring. To hear Geoff is to hear descriptive, interesting preaching. Those who have heard him preach recognize the importance of using language well; that familiar doctrines can be brought to life when expressed freshly and imaginatively rather than in rigid, Berkhofian terms. Stories Geoff has read, accounts of family members, sketches of characters he has met—all of these are recounted with a rhetorical artistry. New students arriving in church realize that they are going to use their dictionaries a bit more. A preacher's vocabulary is important. Geoff uses the tools of language that are available to him, including vivid words and illustrations.

It would be wrong to speak of Geoff's preaching with regard to technique, his engagement with culture, and his rhetorical ability without speaking of those times during the preaching of the Word when there is the tangible presence of the living God. No amount of training or mastery of a preacher's skills can make up for that. Each of the men I interviewed spoke about times when, as Geoff was preaching, they became conscious that the living God was addressing them by His Word through His Spirit. There is nothing more powerful than the Word of God preached. Question 89 of the Westminster Shorter Catechism says it well: "The Spirit of God maketh the reading, but especially the preaching of the Word, an effectual means of convincing and converting sinners, and of building them up in holiness and comfort, through faith, unto salvation."

The truths that Geoff has preached these forty-eight years have thrilled him, and that is one of the reasons why many of his hearers speak of the warmth of his ministry. His reading of the Puritans and involvement with the Banner of Truth Trust since its early days have led to a very Puritan understanding of the affections in preaching. There is a right and proper emotional response to biblical preaching—our hearts should be warmed within us. In all Geoff's writing, preaching, and teaching, there is not a hint of a cerebral, dry Christianity. He has preached the truths of Reformed Christianity and preached them warmly. He wrote in 1986:

> One of the great perils that face preachers of the Reformed faith is the problem of Hyper-Intellectualism, that is, the constant danger of lapsing into a cerebral form of proclamation which falls exclusively upon the intellect. Men become obsessed with doctrine and end up as brain-oriented preachers. There is consequently a fearful impoverishment in their hearers emotionally, devotionally and practically. Such pastors are men of books and not men of people; they know the doctrines, but they know nothing of the emotional side of religion. They set little store upon experience or upon constant fellowship and interaction with almighty God. It is one thing to explain the truth of Christianity to men and women; it is another thing to feel the

overwhelming power of the sheer loveliness and enthrallment of Jesus Christ and communicate that dynamically to the whole person who listens so that there is a change of such dimensions that he loves Him with all his heart and soul and mind and strength.[5]

David N. Jones, a student at Aberystwyth in the 1970s and now ministering in Australia, speaks of his time at Alfred Place: "[I was] struck not only by the consistent standard of preaching content but by the searching application and the rapt attention of the congregation. His preaching is Christ-centered, doctrinal, expository, warm, accessible, challenging, God-glorifying and always fresh."

Preaching is a glorious calling, and Geoff has modelled that. He has enjoyed the challenges of preaching, but it would be wrong to give the impression that all that Geoff has done is preach in order to raise up scores of ministers from this congregation. God has graciously used his example, warmth, and unique personality in the lives of others.

Out of the pulpit

Geoff writes: "To be a pastor, the preacher must be in love with his people, and he must like people and be interested in them. He must be approachable and not defensive in his attitudes. He must welcome and not resent people who want to ask him questions about his preaching."[6]

What aspects of Geoff's ministry outside of the pulpit has God used in the lives of others?

The manse has been an informal meeting place for students on Sunday nights. Every Sunday night is different; sometimes psalms are set to tunes, those from overseas are subjected to long and embarrassing interviews, *Reader's Digest* articles are read and discussed, or, more normally, some topic is introduced for discussion. Geoff will then pray and disappear into the kitchen to make the students popcorn in a saucepan. Each of the students I spoke to recounted warmly tales of the manse, how Geoff would treat students as equals and nurture what was good in them.

---

5. Geoff Thomas, "Powerful Preaching," in *The Preacher and Preaching: Reviving the Art in the Twentieth Century*, ed. Samuel Logan (Phillipsburg, N.J.: P&R, 2011), 369.
6. Thomas, *Preaching*, 33.

The midweek prayer meeting has been an opportunity to see the gifts of students in prayer. Geoff would "pick on" a student to open the meeting. The open-air preaching service on the promenade provided another opportunity to give young men "a go at preaching" while Geoff stood close by, smiling encouragingly as more often than not the student died on his feet.

The manse was always open, and those men who took courage in both hands to go and see Geoff about the possibility of going into the ministry were greeted with encouragement. Jenner describes his experience:

> [I remember] rather cautiously going to speak to him about my very early, nervous thoughts about going into the ministry. It was halfway through my second year. I tentatively brought the subject up, expecting him to give some measured, careful advice to keep pushing doors, keep exploring possibilities, don't dive in too quickly, etc. Instead, he just said, "Of course it's the only thing for you."

Others were given Clowney's *Called to the Ministry* or Al Martin's set of tapes, some were told to wait and get a secular job and throw themselves into church life. One of the students remarked, "Geoff would sit in his chair at such an angle he was almost horizontal—that just added to the sense that he was there for you, ready to listen, as an old friend despite the age gap. And then, once what was needed to be said had been said, he would suddenly sit bolt upright and launch into prayer. Then it was time to go—clear as anything."

Conclusion

As we pay tribute to Geoff and his influence that has gone out from a small town in Mid Wales to the entire world, we should also be thankful for a congregation that has prayed for him and elders who have supported him. In the providence of God, Geoff and Iola found their lifetime work in a university town. A student congregation has numerous blessings—fresh recruits every September and the encouragement of having a young, eager, willing, teachable group eager to reach out to their peers and serve—but students come and students go. There are those who have been in Aberystwyth and have served, prayed, and given for decades, and behind every man used of God is a congregation that has supported him—in this case, for forty-eight years.

Often today, our culture views ministers as men who are incapable of doing anything else and so end up in the church. The media relentlessly portrays those who work in the church as weak, indecisive, effeminate, and generally useless. Geoff could not be more different; in his love for God's Word and God's people, he showed generations of students how very important the ministry is. He showed them that it is the most important thing they will ever do in life. He brought a sense of energy and vitality to it, a robust manliness, and so those who heard and saw that desired to join him. Geoff continues to be a happy pastor; he genuinely loves pastoral ministry. He does not think he is the best pastor in the world or the best preacher. But he thinks he has the best calling in the world; he sees himself as enormously blessed to be a pastor.

Geoff, although possessing an enormous personality and being great fun, is not trivial, but once you have seen him preaching, and seen what preaching can be, you want to do it. As in all great preaching, there is something infectious about Geoff's pulpit ministry, and therein lies the secret, if it is a secret, as to why so many men have gone into the Christian ministry from Alfred Place. Geoff has so enjoyed being a minister and preaching the glorious gospel, and he still feels a sense of awe and wonder forty-eight years on. God has been gracious and kind, overlooking faults and using this servant to bring many other servants into His vineyard.

Of course, Geoff is not a perfect man; I once heard him lead a session at a ministers conference on his regrets in the ministry.[7] But Geoff shows us that if one is willing to faithfully plod, preaching the Word in season and out of season, loving people, being ourselves, not pretending to be someone else or taking ourselves too seriously, God can multiply our usefulness and raise up a generation of preachers of the gospel.

2 Timothy 2:1–2 is then fulfilled once more: "You therefore, my son, be strong in the grace that is in Christ Jesus. And the things that you have heard from me among many witnesses, commit these to faithful men who will be able to teach others also." *Soli Deo gloria!*

---

7. http://alfredplace.simbahosting.co.uk/pages/sermons/preaching/in-retrospect-a-minister-looks-around-and-back.php

PART II

Salvation and the Spirit of Christ

Chapter 3
by Carl Trueman

The Spirit and the Word Incarnate: John Owen's Trinitarian Christology

The phrase "Just preach the text" is, like a number of other evangelical catchphrases (such as "No creed but the Bible!"), both true and false at the same time. It is surely the aspiration of every preacher "just" to preach the text in terms of remaining faithful to the chosen text's divine intention and revelational scope. Yet anyone who has ever preached with any regularity knows that just preaching an isolated text can be a problem. To preach a text properly, the preacher must always set the chosen passage into the context not only of the book in which it occurs but also that of the whole of biblical revelation. This means that, whether we like the terminology or not, we have to take into account the contours and constraints of systematic theology even as we exegete and apply individual passages. No preacher can afford to expound any single passage or text in a way that would lead to a twisted or imbalanced reading of any other part of Scripture.

Of course, the debate over the relationship between exegesis, biblical theology, and systematic theology has been rumbling for centuries and shows no sign of abating. The purpose of this chapter is thus not to undertake the fool's errand of attempting to resolve or even to describe all of the points at issue. My primary task is the far more delightful one of honoring Geoffrey Thomas, a man whose faithful exposition of the Word of God has touched many lives, including my own. Thus, I wish to outline in brief compass one area in which the preaching of the biblical text is helped by the systematic theological constructions of the Reformed faith. In so doing, I hope to show the happy marriage of two of Geoff's great loves.

Perhaps some of the most acute passages in which the biblical text seems to run up against the conclusions of classical orthodox systematics are those that speak of development and struggle in the life of Christ. Indeed, the Incarnation accounts are surely those places in Scripture where the need to connect the eternal God to the temporal creation becomes most acute. The Christian preacher wants to defend the absolute priority, transcendence, and independence of God. At the same time, he wants to do justice to the reality of the Incarnation and to the fact that a docetic Christ who merely seems to be human is inadequate as a means of giving an account of the biblical data. The humanity of the Incarnation is vital, yet this very humanity throws up key challenges to the preacher every time he speaks of Jesus.

For example, Luke 2:40 and 52 speak of Jesus growing and maturing, and increasing in favor with both God and man. There is movement, drama, and development here that the preacher must not only acknowledge but also make a constitutive part of his message. Then there are the accounts of Jesus' temptations in the wilderness, His struggle in the garden of Gethsemane, and, of course, His death on the cross, with its powerful and mysterious cry of dereliction. In each case, the challenge for the preacher is to draw out the reality of the development, change, or struggle that is described in the text while at the same time respecting systematic concerns over divine simplicity, immutability, and impassibility.

These passages are not describing some piece of playacting on the part of Christ. Surely anyone who has ever seen a great drama on the stage will acknowledge that such has a direct emotional power that vanishes when the same is mediated via television. Yet the struggles of the incarnate Christ are not the equivalent of a theater production; their significance does not lie merely in eliciting an emotional response from the audience. It is not that Jesus is simply going through the motions like an actor on stage while yet being personally detached from what is happening. The growth is real; the temptations are real; the agonizing struggle in the garden is real; and the cry on the cross is real. To say less than this would be to turn Christ into a docetic phantasm and to reduce His significance to that of provoking an audience reaction. Neither is the significance of such struggle restricted to the Gospel narratives. The writer of Hebrews makes it quite clear that the dynamism of Christ's life is essential to His role as the believer's heavenly High Priest (Heb. 2:18; 5:14–16). The struggle is real and its significance is deeply theological.

One strategy with such texts is simply to abandon the classical understanding of God as simple and take the texts at face value. This has proved a popular move in recent theology, though it is often driven less by concerns about the biblical passages than by the problem of suffering as it occurs in secular history. I am not concerned to refute such moves here, though I would agree with critics who see such an approach as collapsing the distinction between the Creator and His creatures. In this chapter, I wish simply to highlight how one leading representative of Reformed Orthodoxy, John Owen (1616–83), developed a Christology that is quite capable of handling the textual issues from the perspective of classical doctrine.

The classical christological background

Like so many of his contemporaries, Owen had little interest in innovating in the area of theology. He was content to use the concepts and categories that had been forged by the church over a millennium and a half to articulate, elaborate, and, where necessary, defend orthodoxy. When it came to Christology, the basic terms of debate had been set by the Nicene Creed, as formulated at the Council of Constantinople in 381 and (for Western theologians) modified at a council in Toledo in 589 with the addition of the "and from the Son" clause with respect to the procession of the Holy Spirit; and also by the formula ratified at the Council of Chalcedon in 451. In short, these councils established basic parameters for future christological discussion: God is eternally one God, in one substance and three subsistences or persons; Christ is fully God and fully man, one person with two natures; and His natures are to be neither so separated that the unity of His person is undermined (the heresy of Nestorianism) nor so mixed that He is neither God nor man but a third something, an amalgam of the two (the heresy of Eutychianism). Neither Nestorianism nor Eutychianism described a Christ who could act as Savior.

The Chalcedonian Formula solved one set of problems but raised another. New christological questions emerged: for example, how many wills does Christ have? The answer—two—need not detain us here but points toward the need for theologians (and thus preachers) always to have some understanding of historical theology and the genealogy of doctrine in order to be able to operate with theological competence in the study and the pulpit. Only thus can apparently bizarre answers to such questions be seen as coherent and, indeed, the only viable ones.

One important question was this: Where does the "incarnate One's" personhood originate? Once the church established the language of nature and person as normative for discussing God and Christology, this question was bound to arise. If the Incarnation was the union of a divine person with a human person, then one had Nestorianism, two persons occupying one space. Thus, in the sixth century, theologian Leontius of Byzantium proposed that the human nature of Christ should be considered as having no personhood in and of itself but receiving such only upon its union with the divine person of the Logos. This notion is called that of anhypostatic human nature, literally human nature without hypostasis or personhood. It is an odd formula, but it solved the problem generated by the Nicene and Chalcedonian approaches to God and Christology.

Owen on the Incarnation

All of this might seem like so much angels dancing on pinheads to those who simply want to "preach the text," but it is actually of great significance to the problem noted above, that of doing justice to the dynamic of Christ's earthly life. Indeed, the anhypostasis theory provided Owen with the key to understanding Christ in a manner that allowed him to preach the biblical text in a way that preserved both divine transcendence and the reality of incarnate development and struggle. His major exposition of the significance of this for his Christology occurs in his treatise on the Holy Spirit. Here is the key passage that lays down the basic principles:

> 1. The only singular immediate *act* of the person of the Son on the human nature was the *assumption* of it into subsistence with himself. Herein the Father and the Spirit had no interest nor concurrence, εἰ μὴ κατ' εὐδοκίαν καὶ βούλησιν, "but by approbation and consent," as Damascen speaks: for the Father did not assume the human nature, he was not incarnate; neither did the Holy Spirit do so; but this was the peculiar act and work of the Son. See John 1:14; Rom. 1:3; Gal. 4:4; Phil. 2:6, 7; Heb. 2:14, 16; which places, with many others to the

same purpose, I have elsewhere expounded, and vindicated from the exceptions of the Socinians.

2. That the only *necessary consequent* of this assumption of the human nature, or the incarnation of the Son of God, is the *personal union of Christ*, or the inseparable subsistence of the *assumed nature* in the person of the Son. This was necessary and indissoluble, so that it was not impeached nor shaken in the least by the temporary dissolution of that nature by the separation of the soul and body: for the union of the soul and body in Christ did not constitute him a person, that the dissolution of them should destroy his personality; but he was a person by the uniting of both unto the Son of God.

3. That all other actings of God in the *person of the Son* towards the human nature were *voluntary*, and did not necessarily ensue on the union mentioned; for there was no transfusion of the properties of one nature into the other, nor real physical communication of divine essential excellencies unto the humanity.[1]

Three things are important to note here. First, the only direct and necessary consequence of incarnational union is that the human nature of Christ receives personhood from the Son. This avoids Nestorianism, the view that Christ is two persons, since the human nature, neither logically nor chronologically, possesses personhood of itself or outside the union. From the moment of its existence, the human nature is in union with the divine; but it is utterly dependent upon the divine for its possession of personhood or subsistence.

Second, by stating that all other actions of the Son on the human nature are voluntary, Owen precludes any possibility that the human nature possesses divine attributes merely as a result of the union. Thus, Christ as human does not have infinite knowledge any more than He is ubiquitous. This preserves the basic Reformed axiom that the finite cannot comprehend the infinite, and also guards against the Lutheran notion of the direct communication of properties between the natures. Christ's human nature is like ours, sin excepted. His body is geographically circumscribed; it is subject to all of the same physical limitations as ours.

---

1. John Owen, *The Works of John Owen*, vol. 3, ed. W. H. Goold (Edinburgh: T&T Clark, 1862), 160–61.

Third, and most significant from the perspective of this chapter, this view creates space for addressing the dynamism of the Gospel narratives and the theological claims that the Incarnation involves real struggle and real temptation, and these are fundamental to Christ's work as Savior. This occurs in two particular ways that are of great value to the preacher.

The role of the Holy Spirit
First, Christ's struggles and temptations open up a significant place for the role of the Holy Spirit in the incarnate life of Christ. Christians are familiar with the Spirit's role in the conception of Christ by Mary, but the Gospel accounts contain many references to the Spirit beyond the birth narratives. The Spirit descends on Christ at His baptism and then immediately drives Him out into the wilderness. Christ is said to be "full of the Spirit" (Luke 4:1). Christ is also constantly withdrawing to pray. The life of Christ is, in other words, one of profound Trinitarian communion in which the Spirit plays an absolutely crucial role.

Thus, Owen's construction of the Incarnation has both a theological and an exegetical advantage. Theologically, it drives a view of Christ that is utterly Trinitarian. One of the notorious weaknesses among the inhabitants of evangelical pews is the difficulty of many in articulating why the doctrine of the Trinity is important. They know that modalism and tritheism are wrong, but they cannot necessarily explain why that is the case. Owen's christological formulations dovetail beautifully with the Gospel narratives as they describe the growth of Christ to maturity and the role of the Spirit within that context.

Thus, we might take as an example the temptation story in Luke 4. This is framed (vv. 1 and 14) by references to the Spirit. The Spirit fills Christ and leads Him into the wilderness (Mark's language is stronger: the Spirit "hurls" Him into the wilderness, 1:12). Clearly the text demands christological nuance: if the Incarnation in and of itself is fully sufficient for Christ's mediation, why is the Spirit necessary here? With Owen's christological construction, the answer is obvious: Christ in His human nature cannot draw immediately on the divine attributes of the second person but must learn to depend on the work of the Trinitarian God as mediated to the created realm by the Spirit. So He must be filled with the Spirit, guided by the Spirit, and taught to depend upon the Spirit.

In one sense, this is entirely consistent with the general Trinitarian principle that governs God's relationship to the created realm—the Spirit is seen as the direct agent of, and in, creation. Christ's human nature is a creature; thus, the Spirit is the medium by which God acts upon it. This is not exceptional at all. In another sense, however, given Christ's existence as the incarnation of the Logos, we witness in the Spirit's ministry to Him an exceptional and unique role, given the uniqueness of the person and the mission involved.

This is a theological point that also has obvious practical implications. If Christ Himself, the incarnate Son of God, is dependent upon the Spirit, how much more should the church, corporately and individually, also be self-consciously dependent upon the same? The move from the history of salvation in Christ to the reality and experience of salvation in the church and the individual believer is thus a smooth and inevitable one. Further, the church is constituted by the indwelling of the Spirit through the Word. Like the human nature of Christ, she has no existence as the church prior to or outside of that relationship. Thus, she also needs to learn to be utterly dependent on the Spirit for guidance and strength. This safeguards the centrality of the Word, given that the Spirit proceeds from the Father and the Son, and roots the imperative of prayer in the indicative work of Christ as both paradigm and the One who has Himself prayed to the Father to send the Spirit.

Dramatic movement in Christ's life

The second advantage of Owen's approach is that it allows the preacher to do justice to the dramatic movement of Christ's life. The Gospels essentially tell the story of how the Logos humbled Himself to take human flesh. Anyone who preaches texts such as Luke 2:52 is going to be faced with questions from thoughtful congregants concerning how such verses can be reconciled with a robust doctrine of Christ as the incarnation of the transcendent God.

There are two obvious, and obviously inadequate, responses. One is that God is Himself transformed in the Incarnation, that the Logos becomes less than God as He is united with human flesh. Yet if Christ is less than

God, He cannot save. Further, such a change would raise serious questions about the reliability of the revelation embodied in Christ: if Christ is God manifest in the flesh, yet that God is somehow fundamentally less than God as He is in Himself, what kind of revelation is He? Such a view is lethal not only to salvation but to revelation as well.

The other inadequate response is to make the teaching of these verses merely docetic: for example, Christ only appears to grow in knowledge. Thus, when He wanders into Joseph's workshop, sees His earthly father using a chisel for the first time, and asks him what he is using, He is only pretending not to know in order to give an appearance of genuine humanity. Because He is God, and God presumably knows what a chisel is, the question is merely a piece of playacting. Such an approach does obvious violence to texts in Luke, but also empties a verse like Hebrews 5:8 of meaning.

Such an approach would also render the overall work of Christ to be one that is primarily didactic. Christ becomes a great example; the outward pattern of His deeds and sayings, not the constitution of His person, would be essential for understanding His work. Christ would be merely a great teacher. In fact, one might even raise the question of why it would be necessary for such a Christ to be a historical figure at all. Could not the work of a docetic Christ be done just as easily by a character in one of Aesop's fables? Clearly the biblical testimony demands a far different Christology.

Christ's growth in knowledge, like the temptations in the wilderness, the struggle in Gethsemane, and the agony of the cross, is real and an essential part of His work of salvation. It is not merely an inspiring story; neither is it the historical account of a mere man. At the center of the gospel is the Christ of the Gospels and of Philippians 2. The preacher must make that point without compromising either the Bible's doctrine of God or the Bible's narrative account of Christ.

Owen's Christology offers the preacher a way forward here. While there is often an impatience among preachers with systematic theology and particularly with some of the apparently more abstract concepts with which it operates, it should be clear from the above that such can actually help. The preacher without a fine grasp of Chalcedonian theology is likely to be doomed to commit again and again the christological heresies of the first four centuries. However, the preacher who has read Owen on the Incarnation is well equipped to do justice to Scripture's teaching in a manner that avoids elementary theological blunders.

The humanity receives its personhood or its subsistence from its union with the Logos, but the divine attributes are not communicated directly to the human nature. Instead, the human nature can receive knowledge through empirical means—education, observation, experience—and through the work of the Holy Spirit mediating such knowledge to the nature. Christ really learns obedience as an incarnate person because the human nature grows, develops, and learns throughout His earthly life. Christ really feels the devil's temptation because His humanity does not enjoy full access to divine power simply by virtue of the union. Christ's life is marked by prayer because, as a human, He, too, is dependent on God and demonstrates that dependence by constantly calling on the Father for help and assistance.

Owen's view of the Incarnation, of the anhypostatic human nature of Christ, and of the role of the Holy Spirit allow for a rich, dynamic, and Trinitarian foundation for preaching the texts that speak of Christ growing, learning, being tempted, and suffering.

Conclusion

Geoff Thomas belongs to a generation of preachers for whom there was no opposition between the great doctrinal constructions of systematic theology and the exposition of the biblical text. Sadly, the fragmentation of the theological discipline, the professionalized detachment of systematic theology and biblical exegesis from the life of the church, and the perennial human impatience with systems as cages that inhibit our creativity have all conspired to make sure that many preachers have an instinctive suspicion of anything that smacks of system or speculation. That is unfortunate. The Bible is not the assorted reflections of numerous individuals and communities on their religious experience; it is the revelation of the one God who is Himself truth and who has revealed Himself truly. That does not mean that there is no element of mystery in that revelation or that the whole can be safely comprehended in some set of finite categories, but it does mean that there is a consistency to the revelation that can find its expression in what we call systematic theology. Such theology arises out of the testimony of

Scripture as a whole and then regulates the interpretation of any particular passage or set of passages. The Gospel narratives in connection with the doctrine of God are perhaps only the most obvious of these.

I hope that what I have sketched briefly above reveals the usefulness of classical systematic categories, not in inhibiting the preacher in his exposition of the drama of the Gospel texts, but actually in enhancing it. Geoff Thomas has spent his life doing so. Here are the outlines of the conceptual foundations that will enable subsequent preachers to maintain this faith once for all delivered to the saints.

Chapter 4
by Sam Waldron

The Relation of the Righteousness of God and the Spirit of God in Romans 1–8

The thesis of this chapter is that in Paul's masterful exposition of "his gospel" in Romans 1–8, the Spirit of God is possessed by sinners in His saving influences only through and as a consequence of what Paul calls the righteousness of God, a righteousness that is revealed and created through the life and death of Jesus Christ. That is to say, it is only by means of the satisfaction of the wrath of God through the obedience of Christ that a way is made for the Spirit to come in His liberating power into the personal experience of the sinner. In yet other words, only the righteousness of God creates an avenue through the justice of God by which the Spirit of God may be released into the lives of sinners as the only power that can free them from the practical tyranny of sin over their hearts and conduct.

This statement, I hope, makes clear that I am not denying or even referring to the work of the Spirit in preparing and equipping the Mediator in His earthly life leading up to the cross. The Holy Spirit was active in Jesus' earthly life. The Bible bears witness to the fact that He was active in the conception and birth of Jesus (Luke 1:35), then in the growth of Jesus as the Spirit of wisdom (2:40, 52), yet more in the baptism and subsequent ministry of Jesus (3:22; 4:1, 14, 18), and finally in the sacrificial death of Jesus (Heb. 9:14).[1] In these ways, in the preparation of the Mediator, the Spirit

---

1. The 1689 Baptist Confession, in language substantially identical to the Westminster Confession, affirms this activity of the Spirit in chapter 8, paragraph 3: "The Lord Jesus, in his human nature thus united to the divine, in the person of the Son, was sanctified and anointed with the Holy Spirit above measure, having in him all the treasures of wisdom and knowledge; in whom it pleased the Father that all fullness should dwell, to the end that being holy, harmless, undefiled, and full of grace and truth, he might be thoroughly

of God was active both historically and causally prior to the revelation of the righteousness of God in the cross of Christ. My thesis is simply that the Spirit's saving influences (with regard to sinners whom God has elected to save) are logically and causally consequent to the righteousness of God revealed in the death of Jesus Christ.

This last remark also constrains me to make clear that I am not denying the saving work of the Holy Spirit in the Old Testament. The saving influences of the Spirit of God are logically and causally consequent to the righteousness of God created in Christ Jesus, but this does not mean that they are always historically or temporally consequent. This is an important distinction. While I believe it is significant that in redemptive history, or the *historia salutis*, the pouring out of the Spirit at Pentecost occurs after the crucifixion and resurrection of Christ, this does not mean—as is too often assumed—that the Spirit's saving influences with regard to individual believers were absent or different in the Old Testament period.

Consider a parallel. Justification and the forgiveness of sins plainly are logically and causally consequent upon the righteousness of God created by the life and death of Christ. Yet we know beyond any shadow of doubt that Old Testament saints were justified and forgiven prior to the historical revelation of the righteousness of God. Not only does the Old Testament frequently speak of the forgiveness of the sins of Old Testament believers (Pss. 103:3; 130:4), but the premier examples of justification by faith brought forward by Paul in Romans 4 are Abraham and David (Rom. 4:1ff.; Gen. 15:6; Ps. 32:1ff.).

In the same way, the saving influences of the Spirit of God to be poured out on the Day of Pentecost and in consequence of the righteousness of God accomplished in the cross of Christ were active and applied already in the Old Testament period. It may be granted that, just as with justification and forgiveness, the influences of the Spirit were more dimly revealed in the Old Testament. Hence, the evidence for the regeneration and indwelling of Old Testament saints by the Spirit of God may be somewhat obscure. Yet,

---

furnished to execute the office of mediator and surety; which office he took not upon himself, but was thereunto called by his Father; who also put all power and judgement in his hand, and gave him commandment to execute the same."

when it is remembered that it is only by the power of the Spirit of God that any sinner can be regenerated, sustained in the path of holiness, and assured of salvation, the fact of the Spirit's activity in the Old Testament must not be denied. The only alternative to this would be to adopt the heresy of Pelagianism, which asserts that men have the moral ability to renew and sanctify themselves. If one asserts that the Spirit of God was not active in the Old Testament as the Spirit of regeneration, indwelling, and adoption, then one virtually asserts a form of Pelagianism.

The logical structure of Romans 1–8

Exegetes across the ages have been impressed with the logical and systematic structure of Paul's epistle to the Romans. A chapter this length cannot provide historical support for my understanding of this structure. Indeed, the structure itself seems so self-evident that lengthy discussion of the views of expositors appears unnecessary.

The overall structure of the letter
Though my interest in this chapter is Romans 1–8 particularly, the structure of those chapters must be understood against the overall structure of the letter. This overall structure may be simply presented:

> *Introductory Matters (1:1–17)*
> *Part 1: The Doctrine of the Gospel—in Three Steps (1:18–8:39)*
> *Part 2: The Defense of the Gospel—against Jewish Unbelief (9:1–11:36)*
> *Part 3: The Demonstration of the Gospel—in Practical Life (12:1–15:13)*
> *Concluding Matters (15:14–16:27)*

Several comments on this outline of Romans may be helpful.

First, the theme of the letter seems to be well-established in its introduction. Four times in 1:1–17 Paul refers to the gospel (1:1, 9, 15, and 16). Particularly noteworthy are the occurrences of the word *gospel* in the very first verse of the letter and also in the passage that arguably states the theme of the letter (1:16–17).

Second, it needs to be noted that Romans 9–11 has an apologetic nature. Romans 9:1–11:36 is dominated by the problem that Jewish unbelief posed for the truth of the gospel. This was perhaps the premier objection to the gospel in Paul's day. Imagine the objection Paul must have heard many times as he preached in synagogues, schools, and marketplaces: "You say that Jesus is the Messiah promised to the Jews! Then why do not the mass of the Jews believe in Him?"

Third, the demonstration of the gospel in the practical living of Christians is clearly the theme begun in the famous imperative to present our bodies as living sacrifices to God (Rom. 12:1–2). This theme clearly continues through various permutations (the exercise of gifts, the priority of love, the relation to civil government, and the treatment of the weak) through 15:13.

Fourth, at 15:14, Paul clearly transitions to speaking of his own ministry and begins the division of the letter I have called "Concluding Matters." He goes on, in typical Pauline fashion, to conclude the book in chapter 16 with a commendation, greetings, and benedictions.

The particular structure of Romans 1–8

The description of Romans 1:18–8:39 given above should make it apparent why this chapter focuses on this section of Paul's epistle. These chapters are Paul's systematic exposition of the gospel he preached throughout the Roman Empire. Twice in Romans (2:16; 16:25), he describes the gospel as "my gospel." I noted above that I believe—I am certain with the support of many expositors—that Paul expounds "his gospel" in three simple steps. Here is the structure or outline—as I understand it—of this part of Romans:

> *Part 1: The Doctrine of the Gospel—in Three Steps (1:18–8:39)*
> *Section 1: The Ruin Addressed by the Gospel (1:18–3:20)*
> *Section 2: The Remedy Supplied by the Gospel (3:21–5:21)*
> *Section 3: The Result Achieved by the Gospel (6:1–8:39)*

This three-step presentation of Paul's gospel can also be aptly and succinctly described in a way that brings out more clearly the actual content of what Paul is saying. The doctrine of the gospel must be understood in terms of the problem addressed, the solution provided, and the result achieved:

> *Section 1: The Problem Is the Wrath of God (1:18–3:20)*
> *Section 2: The Solution Is the Righteousness of God (3:21–5:21)*
> *Section 3: The Result Is the Life (or Spirit) of God (6:1–8:39)*

Again, several comments will bring out the significance of this outline for our purposes.

Romans 1:18–3:20
First, there is, I think, general agreement with respect to the purpose and even movement of Romans 1:18–3:20. Paul has just stated the theme of his letter in 1:16–17. Having said that the gospel is the power of God unto salvation because in it the righteousness of God is revealed, Paul moves immediately to a discussion of the problem that makes that powerful gospel necessary. Romans 1:18 begins with the words, "For the wrath of God…." The problem addressed by the gospel is the wrath of God.

In our day and age, when the gospel is presented as the solution to many problems that it was never intended to address or intended to address only indirectly or secondarily, it is important to reflect carefully on the fact that the wrath of God is the issue that makes necessary the gospel as the solution to the problem that triggers that wrath. Indeed, a proper understanding of the gospel begins with an understanding of the problem it addresses.

There is, as I said, general agreement also as to the basic movement of thought in this section of Romans. Paul moves from God's wrath on the Gentiles or mankind in general to God's wrath on the Jews. He then summarizes the situation of mankind under sin. Here is my own take on how this section develops:

> *Section 1: The Problem Is the Wrath of God (1:18–3:20)*
> *I. The Ruin of All Men Generally (1:18–2:16)*
> *II. The Ruin of Jews Particularly (2:17–3:8)*
> *Conclusion: All Men Are Under Sin (3:9–20)*

Thus, Paul's thought moves in this section in terms of two concentric circles. He speaks first of the outer circle and God's wrath on all mankind in general. He speaks second of the inner circle and God's wrath on the Jews in particular. Then he summarizes the situation with regard to both Jews and Gentiles in 3:9–20.

Romans 3:21–5:21
Second, in 3:21–5:21, Paul moves to his pivotal discussion of the righteousness of God. Having made clear why men need the gospel, he returns to

the core of his understanding of the power of the gospel already mentioned in 1:16–17. The secret of the gospel's power is the righteousness of God. Paul, then, turns a crucial corner in his letter at 3:21: "But now the righteousness of God without the law is manifested, being witnessed by the law and the prophets." The development of thought, in my view, proceeds as follows in 3:21–5:21:

> Section 2: *The Solution Is the Righteousness of God (3:21–5:21)*
> I. *The Historical Revelation of the Righteousness of God (3:21–31)*
> II. *The Scriptural Confirmation of the Righteousness of God (4:1–25)*
> III. *The Reconciling Function of the Righteousness of God (5:1–11)*
> IV. *The Theological Foundation of the Righteousness of God (5:12–21)*

A brief word about each of the four divisions of thought in which Paul expounds his understanding of the righteousness of God may be helpful.

First, in Romans 3:21–31, Paul introduces his understanding of the righteousness of God by emphasizing five truths about it (vv. 21–26) and then answering three questions about it (vv. 27–31). Paul introduces the righteousness of God by speaking of (1) its paradoxical relation to the law, (2) its universal application to believers, (3) its special emphasis on grace, (4) its essential payment by Christ, and (5) its actual demonstration of justice.

Second, Romans 4 in its entirety is Paul's answer to an objection probably stated the following way: "I understand now what you are saying about the righteousness of God, Paul. I get it! The problem is that what you are teaching simply contradicts the Old Testament!" This is an objection that Paul could not ignore. His reply to it is overwhelming in its cogency. He appeals to the example of the father of the Jewish nation and shows that Abraham was justified exactly as Paul's teaching about the righteousness of God requires. According to the Old Testament, Abraham was justified by faith (4:1–8) while he was still an uncircumcised Gentile (4:9–12) and by God's promise, not by the law, which was given hundreds of years later (4:13–22).

Third, having introduced and defended from the Old Testament his understanding of the righteousness of God, Paul, in Romans 5:1–11, explains its main function, reconciliation. This theme is evident from the note on which Paul begins this passage (declaring in v. 1 that through the righteousness of God we have *peace* with God) and from the threefold reference to reconciliation in verses 10–11. The righteousness of God in the historical death of Christ satisfied the wrath of God (v. 9) against us while we were "still sinners" (v. 8) and "enemies" of God (v. 10). Now, through the heavenly life and intercession of the Mediator, this reconciliation objectively accomplished in the death of Christ is applied to us experientially and subjectively (v. 11).

Fourth, in 5:12–21, Paul steps back from his discussion of the righteousness of God and surveys the whole theological scene. It is as if he raises the question for himself and his readers: "What is going on here? What is the theological principle that underlies this whole, grand vision of the righteousness of God?" In this passage, Paul explains that the theological foundation of the righteousness of God is the idea of representative headship, and particularly the great and decisive representative headships of Adam and Christ. In verses 12–21, Paul says three things about representative headship. He speaks of:

A. *Representative Headship and the Entrance of Sin (5:12–14)*
B. *Representative Headship and the Righteousness of God (5:15–19)*
C. *Representative Headship and the Law of God (5:20–21)*

Romans 6:1–8:39
Third, in 6:1–8:39, Paul moves to a discussion of the experiential or moral results of the righteousness of God. As I noted in the outline given above, the point of this section can be described as follows:

Section 3: The Result Is the Life (or Spirit) of God (6:1–8:39)

It is important to keep in mind, first, that the theme of this section is the *result* of the righteousness of God. Too often today the moral renovation that takes place *as a result* of the righteousness of God and justification is made a part of justification itself. The confusion and ambiguity of saying that justification *entails* this moral renovation (or ethical sanctification) erases the sharp distinction between the Protestant doctrine of justification by imputed righteousness and the Roman Catholic doctrine of justification (at least in part) by infused or imparted righteousness.

Second, it is clear that the theme of this section of Romans is "the life of God." That is, it is concerned with the actual or subjective impartation of spiritual life to God's elect. The evidence for this in Romans 6:1–8:39 is pervasive (cf. 6:4–5, 10–11, 13, 22–23; 8:2, 6, 10–11, 13). Of course, the source of the life of God is the Spirit of God, as Romans 8:2 and 10 say explicitly.

Third, Paul's discussion of the moral consequences of his doctrine of the righteousness of God may be outlined as follows:

I. *The Questions about It (6:1–7:25)*
    A. *The Questions about Sinning (6:1–7:6)*
        1. *Are we to continue in sin? (6:1–14)*
        2. *Shall we sin because we are not under the law? (6:15–7:6)*
    B. *The Questions about the Law (7:7–25)*
        1. *Is the law sin? (7:7–12)*
        2. *Is the law death? (7:13–25)*
II. *The Conclusions from It (8:1–39)*

This outline makes clear that Romans 6 and 7 function as a defense of Paul's doctrine of salvation by Christ, grace, and faith alone against the antinomian conclusions it seems to entail. Paul's major response to these questions is that the righteousness of God, which Paul describes as dying to sin in Christ (Rom. 6:1–11), makes it impossible for the one embraced in Christ's saving work to continue in a lifestyle of rebellion against God (6:14 with 8:1–13).

Having cleared away the ethical objections to his doctrine of salvation by the righteousness of God, Paul positively celebrates its results in Romans 8. Before coming to his extended and climactic exaltation of the Father's electing love in Romans 8:28–39, Paul celebrates the gift of the Spirit that comes as a result of the righteousness of God in Romans 8:1–27. This assertion brings me to the striking and significant statistics with regard to the references to the Spirit of God in Romans 1–8.

The striking references to the Spirit of God in Romans 1–8

In Section 1 of Romans 1–8 (1:18–3:20), there is *one* reference to the Spirit of God. Romans 2:29 says, "But he *is* a Jew, which is one inwardly; and circumcision *is that* of the heart, in the spirit, *and* not in the letter; whose praise *is* not of men, but of God." I take this to be a reference to the Spirit of God's regenerating work that makes one a "true Jew."

In Section 2 (3:21–5:21), Paul's exposition of the righteousness of God, there is likewise only *one* reference to the Spirit. Romans 5:5 says, "The love of God is shed abroad in our hearts by the Holy Ghost which is given unto us."

In Section 3 (6:1–8:39), a striking change occurs with regard to Paul's references to the Spirit. In Paul's discussion of the moral results of the righteousness of God, there are *seventeen* references to the Spirit of God (if one counts the reference to the law being "spiritual" in 7:14). Fifteen of these references are in Romans 8:1–27, Paul's positive celebration of the results of the righteousness of God.

This statistic is remarkable. It strongly suggests that Paul regards the renewing work of the Spirit of God in the elect as the ethical consequence of the righteousness of God, which creates a way through the barrier of the justice and wrath of God for the Spirit to come in His liberating work into the hearts of God's elect. This suggestion is borne out by a study of particular references to the Spirit of God in Romans 1–8:

> Romans 1:3–4: "Concerning his Son Jesus Christ our Lord, which was made of the seed of David according to the flesh; and declared to be the Son of God with power, according to the spirit of holiness, by the resurrection from the dead."

This text occurs in the introduction to Romans. A common, older exegesis took the contrast evident in this passage to be a reference to the contrast between the divine and human natures of Christ. A better exegesis, in my opinion, sees a contrast between Christ's state of humiliation and His state of exaltation. In the older exegesis, "the spirit of holiness" referenced in verse 4 is seen as a reference to Christ's divine nature. The better exegesis understands it to be a reference to the Spirit of God who resurrected Christ from the dead (Rom. 8:11) and brought Him into the glorious state often described elsewhere in the New Testament (John 20:22; Acts 2:36; 1 Cor. 15:45; 2 Cor. 3:17–18; Rev. 5:6). If what I have called the better exegesis is correct, then this passage shows that the orbit of Paul's thought in Romans is not on the work of the Spirit in preparing the Mediator for His great redeeming work during the days of His flesh. Rather, it is on the work of the Spirit in the Mediator and His elect bride in His resurrection and its consequences for His people.

Furthermore, if the exegesis here adopted is correct, we may say that in the Mediator Himself the climactic expression of the Spirit's transforming power in His state of exaltation is a result of the work He accomplished in His state of humiliation. This is simply to say that—in confirmation of the thesis of this chapter—that even in the Mediator the full expression of the Spirit's power is the consequence of the righteousness of God. The righteousness of God worked out in the obedience of the last Adam is the cause and source of the resurrection of Jesus as "the Son of God with power." His obedience—the righteousness of God!—is the cause of His resurrection out of the death to which imputed guilt condemned Him. Of course, in the Mediator, this does not imply any cleansing from personal sin. He had no sin. It does imply, however, for Him as for His people, that the transforming power of the Spirit—including their deliverance from a lifestyle of sin—is the result of the righteousness of God.

> Romans 7:6: "But now we are delivered from the law, that being dead wherein we were held; that we should serve in newness of spirit, and not in the oldness of the letter."

This is the sole reference to the Spirit in Romans 6–7, where Paul is answering antinomian objections to his doctrine of the righteousness of God. While the KJV translates with the lower case, *spirit*, the contrast in this verse between the letter and the Spirit suggests that it is the Spirit of God in His renewing work in the believer that is in view. Both in Romans 2:27–29 and 2 Corinthians 3:6–7, the contrast between letter and spirit points to the regenerating work of the Spirit of God in God's elect. If this is correct, Romans 7:6 points to the fact that the power unleashed in the believer by the righteousness of God, which power makes it impossible for him to continue in sin (Rom. 6:1–23), is the Spirit of God.

> Romans 8:2: "For the law of the Spirit of life in Christ Jesus hath made me free from the law of sin and death."

This key reference to the Spirit of God is found in Paul's celebration of the results of the righteousness of God in Romans 8. No matter exactly how one understands the verse, one salient fact cannot be evaded. The sphere in which "the law of the Spirit of life" operates is in Christ Jesus. Nothing could make it clearer that it is only the righteousness of God created in the life and death of Christ that brings the life-giving power of the Spirit of God into the experience and life of God's elect.

> Romans 8:9–11: "But ye are not in the flesh, but in the Spirit, if so be that the Spirit of God dwell in you. Now if any man have not the Spirit of Christ, he is none of his. And if Christ be in you, the body is dead because of sin; but the Spirit is life because of righteousness. But if the Spirit of him that raised up Jesus from the dead dwell in you, he that raised up Christ from the dead shall also quicken your mortal bodies by his Spirit that dwelleth in you."

This key statement in Paul's continuing celebration of the work of the Spirit in believers makes several enlightening affirmations. First, it makes clear that to lack the life-giving presence of the Spirit of God marks someone as not belonging to Christ. To lack the Spirit is to lack (or be outside of) Christ. Second, the Spirit is strikingly described as the Spirit of Christ. No matter how the genitive is to be understood, this closely connects the Spirit of God to the being and work of the risen Mediator. Third, the commonality of Christ and the believer is strikingly affirmed by the assertion that the Spirit who raised Christ from the dead also dwells in us. Paul goes on to say that if the Spirit who raised Jesus from the dead dwells in us, then our own resurrection by the same Spirit is assured. Fourth, Paul makes the striking observation in verse 10 that "the Spirit is life because of righteousness." The righteousness in view here is the righteousness of God, which has been the theme of the previous chapters. This being the case, Paul here directly asserts that the life-giving operation of the Spirit in us is the result of—is on account or because of—the righteousness of God. John Murray remarks:

> The Holy Spirit is not life in the redemptive sphere apart from the accomplishment of redemption by Christ. Here again we have the same intimacy of interdependence. This is just saying that the Holy Spirit is not the life spoken of here apart from the righteousness which is the grand theme of this epistle. It is *on account of* the righteousness which the apostle calls "the righteousness of God" and which is the righteousness and obedience of Christ that the Holy Spirit is life in relation to and annulment of that death which conditions our sinful situation.[2]

---

2. John Murray, *The Epistle to the Romans* (Grand Rapids: Eerdmans, 1968), 1:290–91 (emphasis in original). For similar interpretations, see William Hendriksen, *Romans*

The application of the interpretation

As we seek to apply this interpretation of Romans 1–8 to the lives of the people of God, we must keep several points in mind.

First, we must maintain the priority of preaching the gospel as the objective righteousness of God over the subjectivism of preaching of the Spirit that forgets this priority. One danger that confronts those like myself committed to experiential Calvinism and applicatory preaching is that of becoming focused in an imbalanced way on the hearts of believers, their struggles with holiness and assurance of salvation, and the work of the Spirit in their souls. The result may be that we subtly forget to emphasize the objective gospel of the righteousness of God that is finally the only solution to such internal struggles. Another result may be a subjectivism in our preaching that is counterproductive to all that we hope to accomplish. Of course, we must preach about and to the subjective struggles of our people, but we must do so only with a strong and pervasive emphasis on the righteousness of God in the gospel, which is the source of those ministries of the Spirit that our people and we ourselves so much need.

Second, we must grasp the implication of the priority of the righteousness of God to the Spirit of God for particular redemption. If the thesis of this chapter is correct, then it follows immediately that the Spirit of God comes in the effectual call only to those for whom Christ died. Only those will experience the liberating power of the Spirit for whom, in God's mind, His righteousness satisfied His wrath. Union with Christ in His death on the cross is the necessary prelude to union with Christ in the life-giving power of the Spirit who raised Him from the dead.

Third, we must understand the implication of the priority of the righteousness of God to the Spirit of God for the distinction between different phases or dimensions of union with Christ. Beneath the argument of this chapter and assumed in all that it affirms is the distinction between three phases or dimensions of union with Christ. Elective union with Christ (Eph. 1:3–4), redemptive union with Christ (2 Cor. 5:14), and vital or experiential union with Christ (1 Cor. 1:9) must be distinguished but not separated. The

---

(Grand Rapids: Baker, 1980), 252; C. E. B. Cranfield, *The Epistle to the Romans* (Edinburgh: T. & T. Clark Limited, 1975), 390.

thesis of this chapter is that union with Christ in His historical redemptive work is the necessary prelude and means to union with Christ vitally or experientially. The righteousness of God creates the conduit by which the Spirit of God flows in life-giving power to God's elect. This is the significance of the fact that Pentecost follows the crucifixion and resurrection of Christ in the history of redemption, the *historia salutis* (Acts 2:33).

Fourth, we must see the implication of the priority of the righteousness of God to the Spirit of God for a distinction between the work of the regenerating Spirit uniting the sinner to Christ and the work of the Spirit after union with Christ as the Spirit of adoption and sanctification. The distinction between the Spirit's work of regeneration in uniting the sinner to Christ and the gift of the Spirit to the believing sinner as the Spirit of adoption and sanctification is a subject for another essay. Let me simply suggest here that just as the Spirit follows the righteousness of God in the *historia salutis*, so also there is a sense in which the Spirit follows the righteousness of God in the *ordo salutis*. Yes, effectual calling and regeneration logically and causally (though not temporally) precede faith, but there is a gift of the Spirit that logically and causally (though not temporally) follows the faith that unites the sinner to Christ.

There is broad evidence for such a distinction both in the Scriptures and in Reformed confessions. For the scriptural evidence, compare Proverbs 1:22–23; Acts 2:38; Galatians 3:2; 4:6; and Ephesians 1:13. Confessional evidence for this gift of the Spirit is found, among other places, in the Gallican Confession, which faithfully reflects the teaching of John Calvin:

> We believe that by this faith we are regenerated in newness of life, being by nature subject to sin. Now we receive by faith grace to live holily and in the fear of God, in accepting the promise which is given to us by the Gospel, namely: that God will give us his Holy Spirit.[3]

It is very important in our gospel preaching not only to offer men the forgiveness of sins that is found in Christ, but also through Him and the justification to be found in Him to offer men the power of the Holy Spirit to live holy lives and know that they are the children of God.

---

3. Gallican Confession, paragraph 22. For similar teaching, see the Augsburg Confession, Article 20, and the First Scottish Confession, chapter 13.

Chapter 5
by Joel R. Beeke

The Illumination of the Spirit

> *But if our gospel be hid, it is hid to them that are lost: in whom the god of this world hath blinded the minds of them which believe not, lest the light of the glorious gospel of Christ, who is the image of God, should shine unto them. For we preach not ourselves, but Christ Jesus the Lord; and ourselves your servants for Jesus' sake. For God, who commanded the light to shine out of darkness, hath shined in our hearts, to give the light of the knowledge of the glory of God in the face of Jesus Christ.*
> —2 CORINTHIANS 4:3–6

Some of the most remarkable miracles worked by our Lord Jesus involved the healing of the blind, and He healed many of them (Matt. 15:31; 21:14). Other prophets and apostles healed the sick and raised the dead, but God reserved to His Son the power to give sight to the blind.[1] The giving of sight was a sign accompanying the Servant of the Lord (Isa. 42:7; Luke 4:18; Matt. 11:5). It was a sign that God Himself had come in His glory to bring light, life, and joy to a fallen world (Isa. 29:18–19; 35:2, 5).

Our hearts are stirred when we hear how blind Bartimaeus learned that Jesus of Nazareth was passing by and began to shout, "Jesus, thou Son of David, have mercy on me!" (Mark 10:46–52). Many hushed him and told him to be quiet. But this man wanted to be healed. He cried out louder, "Son of David, have mercy on me!" He did not rest until Jesus said to him,

---

1. The Syrian army did recover its sight in answer to Elisha's prayer, but this blindness was a temporary judgment of God imposed just shortly beforehand, not a natural medical condition of blindness (2 Kings 6:18–20). Many thanks to Paul Smalley for his valuable assistance on this chapter.

"Thy faith hath made thee whole." Blindness is a serious handicap even today, but it was more so in the ancient world, when there were no laws and technologies to assist the disabled, and the healing of the blind was a supernatural and life-changing gift of mercy.

Yet when the Scriptures speak of blindness, something more disabling than a lack of physical vision is often in view. Isaiah spoke of those who were blind to the glory of God and His Word, and so turned to idols (Isa. 6:9; 42:16–25; 56:10; 59:10). The most terrible blindness belongs to those who have eyes but have no spiritual vision (Isa. 43:8). Though they may be highly educated in the Bible and be religious teachers, yet they are "blind leaders of the blind" and "blind guides."[2]

The good news of salvation is that Christ has the power to heal this blindness, opening the minds of His disciples "that they might understand the scriptures" (Luke 24:45). He heals our spiritual blindness because God gave Him as a light to the nations (Isa. 42:6; 49:6). Christ does this beautiful work of inner healing by the Holy Spirit, for He is anointed with "the Spirit of the Lord" to give "sight to the blind" (Luke 4:18; cf. Isa. 42:1, 7).

In this chapter, we will learn more about how the Spirit illuminates the minds and hearts of sinners so that they follow Christ. My teaching on this topic will follow 2 Corinthians 4:3–6, a classic text on the illumination of the Spirit; however, my intention is to do more than give an exposition of this text. I will bring in other biblical, confessional, and theological elements to help you understand the Reformed doctrine of spiritual illumination. I will draw from the great confessional statements of the Dutch Reformed[3] and Scottish Presbyterian[4] churches, as well as

---

2. Matt. 15:12–14; 23:16, 17, 19, 24, 26; cf. John 9:39–41.
3. For the Belgic Confession, Heidelberg Catechism, and Canons of Dort, see Joel R. Beeke, ed., *Doctrinal Standards, Liturgy, and Church Order* (Grand Rapids: Reformation Heritage Books, 2003).
4. For the Westminster Confession of Faith (WCF), Westminster Larger Catechism (WLC), and Westminster Shorter Catechism (WSC), see *Westminster Confession of Faith* (Glasgow: Free Presbyterian Publications, 1994).

the writings of John Calvin,[5] Richard Sibbes,[6] Thomas Goodwin,[7] John Owen,[8] and others.

Before we open the text, it may help to explain more clearly what we mean by illumination. Illumination is one dimension of our spiritual renewal in Christ that begins with regeneration and deepens as God grows us in maturity. Though we are focusing here on the mind as the object of illumination, we must remember that the Holy Spirit simultaneously works on the affections and will, addressing the whole man.[9]

We may define illumination as *supernatural light from God's Spirit producing experiential knowledge of God in Christ*. It is "a new, saving, supernatural light, to enable the mind unto spiritual actings,"[10] which is "the groundwork" for all the other operations of the Spirit.[11] Illumination produces experiential knowledge of the Lord. It goes beyond an understanding of the grammar and logic of the Bible to see the holiness and loveliness of God in Jesus Christ. It is a different kind of knowledge than unbelievers possess (Matt. 11:27; John 8:19; 17:3). Without the Spirit's illumination, a man knows God the way a blind man may study the properties of light but never sees the beautiful colors of a rainbow or sunset.[12]

The Westminster Shorter Catechism (Q. 31) says that one aspect of our effectual calling is "the work of God's Spirit...enlightening our minds in the knowledge of Christ" so that we are persuaded and enabled to "embrace

---

5. John Calvin, *Institutes of the Christian Religion*, ed. John T. McNeill, trans. Ford Lewis Battles (Philadelphia: Westminster Press, 1960); *Commentary on the Gospel according to John*, trans. William Pringle (Edinburgh: Calvin Translation Society, 1847); *Sermons on the Epistle to the Ephesians* (Edinburgh: Banner of Truth, 1973).

6. *Works of Richard Sibbes*, ed. Alexander B. Grosart (1862–1864; repr., Edinburgh: Banner of Truth, 1983).

7. *The Works of Thomas Goodwin* (1861–1866; repr., Grand Rapids: Reformation Heritage Books, 2006).

8. *The Works of John Owen*, ed. William H. Goold (1850–1853; repr., Edinburgh: Banner of Truth, 1965–1968).

9. Owen, *Pneumatologia, or, A Discourse Concerning the Holy Spirit*, in *Works*, 3:224.

10. Owen, *Discourse Concerning the Holy Spirit*, in *Works*, 3:221.

11. James Buchanan, *The Office and Work of the Holy Spirit* (1843; repr., London: Banner of Truth, 1966), 46.

12. William G. T. Shedd, *Dogmatic Theology*, ed. Alan W. Gomes (Phillipsburg, N.J.: P & R Publishing, 2003), 764–65.

Jesus Christ, freely offered to us in the gospel."[13] Calvin wrote that "the very nature and dispensation of the call…consists not only in the preaching of the Word but also in the illumination of the Spirit."[14]

Thus, saving illumination is *supernatural light from God's Spirit producing experiential knowledge of God in Christ*. We will unfold this doctrine in three steps: first, the need for illumination because of satanic blindness; second, the instrument of illumination by means of gospel preaching; and third, the power of illumination due to divine light.

Satanic blindness: the need for illumination

The reason we need illumination is found in 2 Corinthians 4:3–4: "But if our gospel be hid, it is hid to them that are lost: in whom the god of this world hath blinded the minds of them which believe not, lest the light of the glorious gospel of Christ, who is the image of God, should shine unto them." They heard the greatest missionary of all time preach the gospel, but it was hidden to them. They saw nothing of value in Christ crucified (1 Cor. 1:23). Calvin expressed it well: "Without the illumination of the Holy Spirit, the Word can do nothing."[15]

This text shows us something about our blindness with respect to our condition, the causes of this blindness, and particularly our blindness to Christ and the gospel.

The blind are in a desperate condition

The gospel is "hid to them that are lost," literally, those who are "perishing." Such blindness is not mere lack of information. Ephesians 4:17–18 says, "This I say therefore, and testify in the Lord, that ye henceforth walk not as other Gentiles walk, in the vanity of their mind, having the understanding darkened, being alienated from the life of God through the ignorance that is in them, because of the blindness of their heart." *Vanity* means "uselessness"; *alienated* means "hostile and prejudiced." No wonder Paul writes in

---

13. See also WCF 10.1, WLC Q. 67, and Canons of Dort III–IV, 11.
14. Calvin, *Institutes*, 3.24.2; cf. Edward A. Dowey, Jr., *The Knowledge of God in Calvin's Theology* (Grand Rapids: Eerdmans, 1994), 173.
15. Calvin, *Institutes*, 3.2.33.

Romans 3:11, "There is none that understandeth, there is none that seeketh after God." So here is a moral and spiritual darkness, described in the Canons of Dort (III/IV.1) as "blindness of mind, horrible darkness, vanity and perverseness of judgment." It is not just a lack of light, but a stubborn resistance to and proud rejection of light.[16]

God did not create us in this condition. He made man in the image of God (Gen. 1:26), which, as we see in Colossians 3:10, included knowledge. The mind was created to be the "candle of the Lord" (Prov. 20:27); Calvin called illumination "the light of the mind."[17] Jesus compared our minds to the "eye," which fills the whole soul with light if that eye is good, but with darkness if that eye is bad. The mind discerns what our true treasure is by what our heart follows after (Matt. 6:21–23; cf. 13:44).[18] We fell away from God's light by accepting the lies of the serpent, which distorted the way we perceived God and His creation (Gen. 3:1–6). We not only fell into darkness, but became darkness, as Paul says in Ephesians 5:8.

To understand the condition of fallen mankind, we need to see the difference between natural light and spiritual illumination. Natural light is human intelligence and conscience, which still distinguishes us from animals. Such remaining "rays of divine light" enable fallen human beings to do great works in the arts and sciences, and works of external morality.[19] Calvin distinguished "the light of nature" from "the grace of illumination."[20] The Westminster Confession of Faith likewise refers repeatedly to "the light of nature" (1.1; 10.4; 21.1, 7).

The light of nature gives all men some "glimmerings" of the knowledge of God, but natural man suppresses this knowledge, and in any case, it

---

16. Owen, *Discourse Concerning the Holy Spirit*, in *Works*, 3:252; Sibbes, *The Glorious Feast of the Gospel*, in *Works*, 2:465.

17. Calvin, *Institutes*, 1.15.4.

18. Goodwin, *An Exposition of the First Chapter of the Epistle to the Ephesians*, in *Works*, 1:299–300; Owen, *Discourse Concerning the Holy Spirit*, in *Works*, 3:281.

19. Gwyn Walters, *The Sovereign Spirit: The Doctrine of the Holy Spirit in the Writings of John Calvin*, ed. Eifon Evans and Lynn Quigley, Rutherford Studies in Historical Theology (Edinburgh: Rutherford House, 2009), 19.

20. Calvin, *Commentary on the Gospel according to John*, 1:38 [John 1:9]. On the "light of nature," see the WCF (1.1, 7; 10.4; 21.1) and WLC (Q. 2, 60, 121, 151.3). Owen also wrote of "sparks of celestial fire" remaining "under the ashes of our collapsed nature" (*Discourse Concerning the Holy Spirit*, in *Works*, 3:345).

cannot save him (Rom. 1:19–21).[21] What he knows he does not believe, but regards it with a secret contempt.[22] Though the universe surrounds him with "many burning lamps" showing the glory of the Creator, they only ignite tiny sparks in his mind, which his darkness quickly smothers.[23]

Without the Spirit, he cannot receive the truths revealed by the Spirit in the Word of God. Paul writes in 1 Corinthians 2:13–14: "Which things also we speak, not in the words which man's wisdom teacheth, but which the Holy Ghost teacheth; comparing spiritual things with spiritual. But the natural man receiveth not the things of the Spirit of God: for they are foolishness unto him: neither can he know them, because they are spiritually discerned." Note well those words: "neither can he know them." We need new "spiritual senses."[24]

Someone may object that if men are truly blind to spiritual things, then all the exhortations, commands, promises, and warnings of the Bible are useless. Owen anticipated this objection and replied to it. First, he said, even in sin's bondage, men are still rational beings with minds and wills, and therefore it is right for God to address them with words of law and promise. Second, commands tell us our duty, not our ability. If we believe that each command in Scripture implies the ability of all men to keep it with nothing more than a Christian education, then salvation ceases to be by grace alone, and we fall into the old Pelagian error.[25] Third, God is pleased to make His exhortations and promises into vehicles of grace, means by which the Holy Spirit sends power and life into blind and dead sinners so that they are born again through the Word (James 1:18; 1 Peter 1:23).[26]

If we would be faithful to Scripture, we must accept the grim reality that fallen men are blind and perishing in their blindness. Some of the most dreadful words of Scripture are found in Deuteronomy 29:4: "Yet the LORD hath not given you an heart to perceive, and eyes to see, and ears to

---

21. Canons of Dort III/IV.4.
22. Sibbes, *Glorious Feast*, in *Works*, 2:463–64.
23. Calvin, *Institutes*, 1.5.14.
24. Goodwin, *The Work of the Holy Ghost in Our Salvation*, in *Works*, 6:168.
25. Augustine, *On the Grace of Christ*, 1.8, in *A Select Library of the Nicene and Post-Nicene Fathers of the Christian Church*, ed. Philip Schaff (New York: Christian Literature Company, 1887), 5:220.
26. Owen, *Discourse Concerning the Holy Spirit*, in *Works*, 3:290; cf. 295.

hear, unto this day." Calvin said, "Our eyes are worse than put out until he enlightens them by his Holy Spirit."[27]

Blindness has a demonic cause
Why are we blind? It is because "the god of this world hath blinded the minds of them which believe not." There is a spiritual "power of darkness" that dominates the minds of all lost sinners (Luke 22:53; Col. 1:13). It is the power of Satan, who deceives the whole world (Rev. 12:9). Owen writes that men are blinded by "the efficacy of the temptations of suggestions of Satan, whereby their minds are filled with prejudices against the gospel and the doctrine of it."[28] The key word is *prejudice*—Satan works by building walls of prejudice or bias against the Lord.

Why is the devil called "the god of this world"? It may be because of the power he exerts over the souls of men. Christ called Satan "the prince of this world" (John 12:31; 14:30; 16:11). If the one who blinds men is so powerful, how great is this blindness! The Belgic Confession (Art. 14) says, "All the light which is in us is changed into darkness" (Eph. 5:8; Matt. 6:23).

Satan may also be called "the god of this world" because he especially rules it through idolatrous worship. He blinds humanity to the glory of God in Christ because he lusts after glory for himself. Ultimately, the devil is the object of the world's adoration (Deut. 32:17; 1 Cor. 10:20; Rev. 13:4). This fact reminds us that Satan has immeasurable power over the lost, and he uses it especially to corrupt worship. Nowhere does human blindness so blatantly appear as in man's worship of idols (Isa. 44:9–10). We should not be surprised, then, at how quickly the church's worship is corrupted away from the purity of spirit and truth commanded in Scripture.

Blinded to the declared Christ
What is it that men cannot see? They cannot see "the light of the glorious gospel of Christ, who is the image of God." You see, in a manner of speaking, they have God's light. Christ is shining on them through the Word.[29]

---

27. Calvin, *Sermons on the Epistle to the Ephesians*, 92.
28. Owen, *Causes, Ways, and Means of Understanding*, in *Works*, 4:169.
29. Calvin, *Institutes*, 3.24.2.

As "the image of God," Christ has perfectly represented God to man in His words and actions. Everything is plainly laid out before them. As they hear the preaching of the gospel, they are like blind men standing outdoors at noon on a cloudless summer day. The sun illuminates them with all its brilliance, but they are blind and cannot see it.[30]

Such is also the case for those who, like the ancient Israelites, have the Bible but not the Spirit. In the broader context of 2 Corinthians 3, Paul describes a light and glory that shone in God's revelation to Israel, and yet the Israelites were not changed by it. Instead "their minds were blinded" and a spiritual veil covered the eyes of their souls (2 Cor. 3:14). Thus, there is a light that comes to all who are exposed to the gospel and the church of Christ. The ministries of prophets and apostles shone with light (John 5:35; Acts 13:47); the Holy Scriptures continue to shine with light;[31] and God's people shine with light in the holiness of their lives.[32] However, this light evokes the natural reaction of hatred from sinners (John 3:19–20), causing them to love the darkness and refuse the light.

The "common operations of the Spirit" (WCF 10.4) may intensify the effects of the light of truth upon the mind and conscience. However, such common illumination is insufficient to transform the heart, though it may produce changes in outward behavior for a time.[33] It may bestow great gifts of teaching, but without spiritual light great teachers are nothing more than arrogant hypocrites.[34] Hebrews 6:4 tells us that the Holy Spirit can enlighten fallen men in this manner to the point that they experience something of the goodness of God's Word and manifest an outward repentance, and yet they ultimately fall away. Or perhaps they may continue as nominal Christians, but, as Owen said, over time they wither and "become walking and talking skeletons in religion—dry, sapless, useless, worldlings."[35]

Everything we need to know in order to trust and obey God is either set

---

30. Calvin, *Institutes*, 3.2.34.
31. Pss. 19:8; 119:105, 130; Isa. 8:20; 51:4; 2 Peter 1:19.
32. Prov. 4:18; Matt. 5:14–16; Phil. 2:15; Rev. 2:5.
33. Calvin, *Institutes*, 3.3.22–23; 3.24.8; Goodwin, *Work of the Holy Ghost*, book vi, in *Works*, 6:231–323; Owen, *Discourse Concerning the Holy Spirit*, in *Works*, 3:232–34, 346–62.
34. Sibbes, *A Glance of Heaven*, in *Works*, 4:161; Goodwin, *First Chapter of the Epistle to the Ephesians*, in *Works*, 1:284–85.
35. Owen, *Discourse Concerning the Holy Spirit*, in *Works*, 3:241.

down explicitly in Scripture or logically implied by it, but, as the Westminster Confession (1.6) says, "We acknowledge the inward illumination of the Spirit of God to be necessary for the saving understanding of such things as are revealed in the Word." Calvin wrote, "Wherever the Spirit does not cast his light, all is darkness."[36]

Gospel preaching: the instrument of illumination

So what is Paul's response to this situation of spiritual blindness? Does he give up? Does he retreat into a corner to pray and do nothing else? No, he believed that God uses means or instruments to overcome this blindness. We see this in 2 Corinthians 4:5: "For we preach not ourselves, but Christ Jesus the Lord; and ourselves your servants for Jesus' sake."

Paul is asserting that the fault of men's opposition to the gospel does not lie with him or his co-workers in mission. They have faithfully preached the gospel of Christ with honesty, openness, and "great plainness of speech" (2 Cor. 2:17; 3:12; 4:2). They are not discouraged (2 Cor. 3:4–5, 12; 4:1) because, as he explains in chapter 3, they believe that "the Spirit of the living God" works powerfully through their preaching of the Word of God as "ministers of the new testament" (2 Cor. 3:3, 6). They are content to preach the Word and trust in the Spirit.

See how they joined the Word and the Spirit. The Bible is the only means of supernatural illumination because it is the only source of supernatural revelation.[37] If we look for the Spirit to shine His light upon us through any other means, we dishonor the uniqueness of Scripture as the revealed truth of God.

Mystics and self-proclaimed prophets separate the Spirit from the Word and claim an inner light independent of and perhaps supreme over the Bible.[38] They build their faith on feelings and experiences. But illumination comes through objective truth. Jonathan Edwards said: "Nothing

---

36. Calvin, *Institutes*, 2.2.21.
37. Owen, *The Reason of Faith*, in *Works*, 4:12.
38. On the seventeenth-century Quakers in the Puritan context, see Joel R. Beeke and Mark Jones, *A Puritan Theology* (Grand Rapids: Reformation Heritage Books, 2012), 432–34; Geoffrey F. Nuttall, *The Holy Spirit in Puritan Faith and Experience* (Oxford: Basil Blackwell, 1946).

can come at the heart but through the door of understanding. And there can be no spiritual knowledge of that of which there is not first a rational knowledge."[39]

Roman Catholicism also separates the Spirit from the Bible, claiming that the Spirit gives the church traditions and revelations beyond the Bible, and led by the Spirit the church cannot err, though it goes beyond the Word. But God has joined the illumination of the Spirit to the written Word of God in what Calvin called "an inviolable bond" (Isa. 59:21).[40] Sinclair Ferguson writes, "The Spirit must never be separated from the Word, since the Spirit gives the Word so that He might illumine the Word, breaking down the stubborn prejudices of our nature."[41]

Some may say that it dishonors the Spirit to be subjected to a book. Calvin replied, "He is the Author of the Scriptures; he cannot vary and differ from himself."[42] The Bible is the external "instrument" or means by which the Spirit causes our illumination.[43] If men seek illumination apart from Scripture, then with Isaiah we say, "To the law and to the testimony: if they speak not according to this word, it is because there is no light in them" (Isa. 8:20).

In particular, 2 Corinthians 4 says that the *preaching* of the Word is God's

---

39. Quoted in John H. Gerstner, *The Rational Biblical Theology of Jonathan Edwards* (Powhatan, Va.: Berea/Orlando, Fla.: Ligonier, 1991), 1:186. For the views of Jonathan Edwards on saving illumination, see Jonathan Edwards, *A Spiritual Understanding of Divine Things Denied to the Unregenerate*, in *The Works of Jonathan Edwards, Volume 14, Sermons and Discourses, 1723–1729*, ed. Kenneth P. Minkema (New Haven: Yale University Press, 1997), 67–96; *A Divine and Supernatural Light*, in *The Works of Jonathan Edwards, Volume 17, Sermons and Discourses, 1730–1733*, ed. Mark Valeri (New Haven: Yale University Press, 1999), 405–26; *The Works of Jonathan Edwards, Volume 2, Religious Affections*, ed. John E. Smith (New Haven: Yale University Press, 1959), 266–91. The second and third of these are also found in *The Works of Jonathan Edwards*, ed. Edward Hickman (1834; repr., Edinburgh: Banner of Truth, 1974), 1:281–88; 2:12–17.

40. Calvin, *Institutes*, 1.9.1; cf. 4.8.11–13.

41. Sinclair B. Ferguson, "Calvin and Christian Experience," in *Calvin, Theologian and Reformer*, ed. Joel R. Beeke and Garry J. Williams (Grand Rapids: Reformation Heritage Books, 2010), 97.

42. Calvin, *Institutes*, 1.9.2.

43. Calvin, *Institutes*, 1.9.3; cf. 2.5.5; Owen, *Reason of Faith*, in *Works*, 4:94; *Discourse Concerning the Holy Spirit*, in *Works*, 3:363–64. Calvin also believed that the sacraments are means by which God illuminates people to strengthen faith, but only by the Spirit operating through them, not by any inherent power (4.14.8–12).

preferred means of illumination. The Westminster Larger Catechism (Q. 155) says, "The Spirit of God maketh the reading, but especially the preaching of the word, an effectual means of enlightening…sinners."[44] God uses the Word in various ways, but preaching is His primary means of grace.

Second Corinthians 4:5 tells us specifically what kind of preaching God ordinarily uses as a channel to illuminate sinners—preaching with lowliness: "We preach not ourselves, but Christ Jesus the Lord." The apostles also preached with love. In preaching Christ as Lord, they also presented themselves as "your servants for Jesus' sake." Though God is free to work even when men preach with wrong motives (Phil. 1:15–18), those whom He clothes with the Spirit of power and illumination He also fills with the Spirit of humility and love—the Spirit of Christ.

Let us honor our teachers and listen to them, but let us look to the divine Teacher to make their doctrine effective. James Buchanan wrote, "The Bible is the text-book, but the Spirit is himself the teacher."[45] Calvin said, "Nothing is accomplished by preaching him if the Spirit, as our inner teacher, does not show our minds the way."[46] Let us never think that "ministers and teachers penetrate into minds and hearts" to heal our blindness; God reserves to Himself the work of "illumination of mind and renewal of heart," and it is "sacrilege for man to claim any part of either for himself."[47] The Bible teaches us in 1 Corinthians 12:3b, "No man can say that Jesus is the Lord, but by the Holy Ghost."

Divine light: the power of illumination

The instrument of gospel preaching does not have power in itself to heal men's spiritual blindness. It is the wire but not the electrical current, the lens but not the light. God must add a divine and supernatural light to the gospel for men to be saved. We read of this in 2 Corinthians 4:6: "For God, who commanded the light to shine out of darkness, hath shined in

---

44. Cf. Augustine, *On Forgiveness of Sins, and Baptism*, 1.37, in *Nicene and Post-Nicene Fathers*, 5:29.
45. Buchanan, *Office and Work*, 50.
46. Calvin, *Institutes*, 2.2.20; cf. 4.14.8.
47. Calvin, *Institutes*, 4.1.6.

our hearts, to give the light of the knowledge of the glory of God in the face of Jesus Christ." Illumination is a work of the Trinity: the glory of God the Father shining through the mediation of God the Son, Jesus Christ, through God the Holy Spirit, who is the divine agent of it. Paul writes in 2 Corinthians 3:6 that God "hath made us able ministers of the new testament; not of the letter, but of the spirit."

Owen wrote of "the necessity of an internal, effectual work of the Holy Spirit, in the illumination of our minds, so enabling us to believe with faith divine and supernatural."[48] What does the Holy Spirit do in illumination? The words of 2 Corinthians 4:6 tell us about the Spirit's illumination using terms of a new creation, the innermost core of our being, and knowing Christ.

The Spirit forms a new creation

Paul describes the Maker of this divine light by saying, "God, who commanded the light to shine out of darkness." He alludes to Genesis 1:1–3: "In the beginning God created the heaven and the earth. And the earth was without form, and void; and darkness was upon the face of the deep. And the Spirit of God moved upon the face of the waters. And God said, Let there be light: and there was light." The illumination of lost sinners is a work of creating light where only darkness exists. God does not fan into flame some spark of spiritual light remaining in sinners; He must create this light out of nothing by the *fiat* of His power: "Let there be…and there was." Thus, Paul writes in 2 Corinthians 5:17, "Therefore if any man be in Christ, he is a new creature: old things are passed away; behold, all things are become new."

The Spirit is the divine agent who produces the new creation. Notice the presence of the Spirit in the work of creation in Genesis 1, hovering over the darkness and chaos to bring into effect what the Word calls forth. We find, too, that the Spirit of God is the agent of the new creation. Paul writes in 2 Corinthians 3:6 that "the Spirit giveth life." In Titus 3:5, we read of "regeneration" by "the Holy Ghost," literally, "genesis again."[49]

---

48. Owen, *Reason of Faith*, in *Works*, 4:53.
49. Greek *palingenesia*, from "again" (*palin*) and "generation" (*genesis;* thus the name of the book of Genesis, cf. Gen. 2:4; 5:1; 6:9, 10:1; etc.).

Creation is a supernatural work that requires the almighty power of the Creator.[50] Sibbes wrote, "There is no less work to shine in that dark heart of man, than to create the world, to create light out of darkness."[51] Owen wrote, "The act of God working faith in us is a creating act," which he calls "an act of omnipotent efficiency" and "divine, supernatural illumination."[52] Saving illumination is one dimension of our resurrection from spiritual death to become alive toward God; without it, we remain dead to the Word.[53] This new light gives new spiritual knowledge and new spiritual experience.[54] It's the difference between reading a book about China and actually traveling there and standing on the Great Wall.[55] God becomes real. The Spirit creates "a glorious supernatural light" and we see the "beauty and excellency" of the Lord.[56]

The Spirit shines in the innermost core of our being

God "hath shined in our hearts." This light does not merely shine *on* us; it shines *in* our hearts. The "heart" in the Bible is the place of our deepest feelings, thoughts, and purposes (2 Cor. 2:4; 9:7). Goodwin said: "My brethren, there is indeed a notional knowledge.... But then there is a real knowledge that bringeth down the things into a man's heart."[57] This divine light becomes a part of the innermost core of who we are. We not only receive light, but we *are* light (Eph. 5:8).

Again, it is the Holy Spirit who is the agent of the Trinity within the heart (2 Cor. 1:22). In 2 Corinthians 3:3, Paul compares Christians to a

---

50. Sibbes, *Glorious Feast*, in *Works*, 2:464.
51. Sibbes, *Exposition of Second Corinthians Chapter IV*, in *Works*, 4:320.
52. Owen, *Discourse Concerning the Holy Spirit*, in *Works*, 3:321, 333; *Reason of Faith*, in *Works*, 4:57.
53. Calvin, *Institutes*, 3.14.5; *Commentary on the Gospel according to John*, 1:74 (John 1:43).
54. Sibbes, *Glorious Feast*, in *Works*, 2:461–62; cf. Owen, *Sunesis Pneumatikē, or, The Causes, Ways, and Means of Understanding the Mind of God as Revealed in His Word, With Assurance Therein*, in *Works*, 4:156–57.
55. Sibbes, *Glorious Feast*, in *Works*, 2:463.
56. Owen, *Reason of Faith*, in *Works*, 4:98.
57. Goodwin, *First Chapter of the Epistle to the Ephesians*, in *Works*, 1:284; cf. Owen, *Discourse Concerning the Holy Spirit*, in *Works*, 3:260; *Causes, Ways, and Means of Understanding*, in *Works*, 4:170.

letter from Christ "written not with ink, but with the Spirit of the living God; not in tables of stone, but in fleshy tables of the heart."

Sibbes explained that an unbeliever's knowledge of Christ is "a mere outward light," but believers have a light rooted and incorporated into the soul so that it becomes a part of them just as light is a part of the sun. As a result, we see, taste, and feel this light; it is light with heat, "a blessed and gracious influence."[58] Sibbes wrote: "Light conveyeth life. All grace is dropped into the will through the understanding."[59] He added, "God's illumination goeth through the whole soul, alters the will and affection."[60] By nature, all men and women have minds; by illumination, those minds receive an embedded and living principle of spiritual knowledge.[61]

Paul speaks here of an experiential knowledge—a knowledge that engages the heart and brings "a sweetness to the soul."[62] Since the Spirit's illumination gives us "a spiritual sense of the power and reality of the things believed," the Bible often expresses it "by acts of sense, as tasting, seeing, [and] feeling."[63]

To say that God shines in our hearts is not to imply that believers have a clear and perfect understanding of all of God's Word from the moment of conversion; at best we see only dimly (1 Cor. 13:12), because our knowledge is only partial and imperfect.[64] Paul's prayer for the Ephesian saints, that "the eyes of your understanding [may be] enlightened" (Eph. 1:18), implies that we have much darkness remaining in us and need the Spirit to grant us ever-increasing light within our hearts.

The Spirit causes us to know Christ

What is this light? It is "the light of the knowledge of the glory of God

---

58. Sibbes, *Glorious Feast*, in *Works*, 2:462–63.
59. Sibbes, *Glorious Feast*, in *Works*, 2:470.
60. Sibbes, *Exposition of Second Corinthians Chapter IV*, in *Works*, 4:321.
61. The Puritans carefully distinguished between the mind as a faculty essential to the human soul and spiritual light as a living principle or power supernaturally added to that faculty. See Goodwin, *Work of the Holy Ghost*, in *Works*, 6:191–92; Owen, *Discourse Concerning the Holy Spirit*, in *Works*, 3:261–62.
62. Sibbes, *Bowels Opened*, in *Works*, 2:152; cf. *Glorious Feast*, in *Works*, 2:466.
63. Owen, *Reason of Faith*, in *Works*, 4:64; cf. Calvin, *Institutes*, 3.2.34.
64. Calvin, *Sermons on the Epistle to the Ephesians*, 93.

in the face of Jesus Christ." It is the same knowledge transmitted in the preaching of the Word (2 Cor. 4:4–5), not a new revelation of content. But it is another mode of knowing it, an inner sight of divine glory shining in the incarnate, crucified, and resurrected Lord. Owen said, "He irradiates the mind with a spiritual light, whereby it is enabled to discern the glory of spiritual things."[65] Edward Bickersteth wrote: "The eye of the soul is opened. They who were blind see. They see Christ."[66]

Such knowledge is the work of the Holy Spirit. Paul writes in 2 Corinthians 3:16–18: "Nevertheless when it [the heart] shall turn to the Lord, the vail shall be taken away. Now the Lord is that Spirit: and where the Spirit of the Lord is, there is liberty. But we all, with open face beholding as in a glass the glory of the Lord, are changed into the same image from glory to glory, even as by the Spirit of the Lord." The Spirit turns the heart, removes the blinding veil, and shines in the heart so that we see the Lord with a heart-transforming vision of His glory.

The manifestation of God's glory is the great goal of the gospel.[67] God will glorify Himself in the display of His mercy, love, wisdom, and justice in Jesus Christ.[68] Faith is a spiritual eye to see God's glory in Christ's humiliation and exaltation; in His offices as Prophet, Priest, and King; and especially in His death on the cross, bearing God's curse for our sins.[69] Since God reveals His glory to us in the Mediator, this is not the knowledge of a distant and terrifying God, but, as Goodwin said, "the intimate knowledge of God as of a friend."[70]

The spiritual sight of God's glory in Christ is the root of all our faith and holiness. Goodwin noted that it is not merely seeing that Christ is ours, but particularly seeing Christ Himself, that moves us to give ourselves to Him and never let Him go.[71] Once we see the glory of God in Christ, we will be satisfied with nothing less. God's glory becomes the North Star that

---

65. Owen, *Reason of Faith*, in *Works*, 4:57.
66. Edward H. Bickersteth, *The Holy Spirit: His Person and Work* (repr.; Grand Rapids: Kregel, 1959), 128.
67. Goodwin, *First Chapter of the Epistle to the Ephesians*, in *Works*, 1:287; cf. 289.
68. Sibbes, *Exposition of Second Corinthians Chapter IV*, in *Works*, 4:321.
69. Sibbes, *Exposition of Second Corinthians Chapter IV*, in *Works*, 4:323, 325.
70. Goodwin, *First Chapter of the Epistle to the Ephesians*, in *Works*, 1:288.
71. Goodwin, *First Chapter of the Epistle to the Ephesians*, in *Works*, 1:285–86.

guides us and the magnet that draws us, the chief good we desire and the chief end we purpose, the treasure where our heart is.[72]

Here, Owen tells us, is one of the great categorical differences between common illumination and saving illumination. Common illumination in the mind does not give "delight" and "satisfaction in the lively spiritual nature and excellencies" of God in Christ, but at best finds joy merely in "some benefit or advantage" one finds for himself from God.[73] In Paul's words, it does not cause us to see God's glory.

When the Spirit illuminates with the glory of God in Christ, He confers great benefits with it. Paul refers to this divine light later in 2 Corinthians 4 as "treasure" (v. 7), "power" (v. 7), the "life" of "Jesus" (vv. 10, 11), and the "spirit of faith" (v. 13). It produces lifelong fruit such as trust,[74] repentance,[75] peace,[76] joy,[77] study,[78] Christlikeness,[79] worship,[80] witness,[81] and hope.[82] In a word, "beholding as in a glass the glory of the Lord, [we] are changed into the same image from glory to glory" (2 Cor. 3:18).

How precious, then, is this gift of illumination by the Holy Spirit!

Conclusion: the pursuit of illumination

What does this mean for the unbeliever? It means that you should be smitten with grief over your willful blindness to Jesus Christ. You are guilty for

---

72. Goodwin, *Work of the Holy Ghost*, in *Works*, 6:459–64.
73. Owen, *Discourse Concerning the Holy Spirit*, in *Works*, 3:238.
74. Calvin, *Institutes*, 1.7.5; cf. Goodwin, *First Chapter of the Epistle to the Ephesians*, in *Works*, 1:285; Owen, *Reason of Faith*, in *Works*, 4:73, 91–94.
75. Arthur W. Pink, *The Holy Spirit* (Grand Rapids: Baker, 1970), 64.
76. Sibbes, *Exposition of Second Corinthians Chapter IV*, in *Works*, 4:322.
77. Sibbes, *Glorious Feast*, in *Works*, 2:466; *Exposition of Second Corinthians Chapter IV*, in *Works*, 4:324; Robert Philip, *The Love of the Spirit Traced in His Work* (1836; repr., Grand Rapids: Reformation Heritage Books, 2006), 95.
78. Calvin, *Institutes*, 1.17.2; Dowey, *Knowledge of God*, 179; Sibbes, *Glorious Feast*, in *Works*, 2:469; Owen, *Causes, Ways, and Means of Understanding*, in *Works*, 4:126, 199–234.
79. Sibbes, *Exposition of Second Corinthians Chapter IV*, in *Works*, 4:335; Buchanan, *Office and Work*, 55.
80. Sibbes, *Glorious Feast*, in *Works*, 2:469; Goodwin, *Work of the Holy Ghost*, in *Works*, 6:174; Jodocus van Lodenstein, "Divine Illumination in Conversion," in *A Spiritual Appeal to Christ's Bride*, trans. Bartel Elshout, ed. Joel R. Beeke (Grand Rapids: Reformation Heritage Books, 2010), 96–97.
81. Sibbes, *Exposition of Second Corinthians Chapter IV*, in *Works*, 4:314, 338.
82. Calvin, *Institutes*, 3.9.5; Sibbes, *Glance of Heaven*, in *Works*, 4:157.

your blindness, for your heart hates the light. You resist the Holy Spirit. You deserve for God to hand you over to Satan's strong delusions because you do not love the truth.

What should you do? You should cry out to the Lord just as blind Bartimaeus did when Jesus passed by: "Jesus, thou Son of David, have mercy on me!" No matter what might discourage you, keep crying out with desperate need, "Jesus, thou Son of David, have mercy on me!" Fix your eyes upon Jesus Christ and give Him your full attention with all the powers you have. Stop pretending that you have light in yourself so that Christ can be your only light. Even if you are still in darkness, go where the Sun usually shines—churches that preach the gospel of Christ.[83]

What does this mean for the believer? You should look back over your conversion with a sense of awe and wonder that God has granted you this spiritual illumination. It is good to give thanks to the Lord. Like the blind man who said, "I was blind, now I see" (John 9:25), give all glory to Jesus Christ who gave you illumination by His Holy Spirit. You were just as blind and dead in sin as anyone else, but God illuminated your heart solely on the basis of His free choice to save you.[84] If Christ gave thanks to God for saving His elect (Matt. 11:25–27), how much more should we who are saved?

But beyond looking back with gratitude and praise, does this doctrine have any relevance to your life today? Yes, it does. It calls you to pray for yourself, for the church, and for unbelievers, that God's light would shine in us. The Bible is full of prayers by believers for greater illumination. Owen observed, "What we pray for from God, we have not in and of ourselves."[85] Psalm 119:18 says, "Open thou mine eyes, that I may behold wondrous things out of thy law." Make Paul's prayers in Colossians 1 and Ephesians 1 your prayers, too (Col. 1:9–10; Eph. 1:17–19). Pray earnestly for an increase in your spiritual knowledge of God, for it is the great root of the increase of grace.[86] Calvin said that the Christian "needs continual direction at every

---

83. Ralph Robinson, *Christ All and in All* (repr., Ligonier, Pa.: Soli Deo Gloria, 1992), 273.
84. Calvin, *Institutes*, 3.22.10; 3.24.3, 17.
85. Owen, *Causes, Ways, and Means of Understanding*, in *Works*, 4:128.
86. Goodwin, *First Chapter of the Epistle to the Ephesians*, in *Works*, 1:283.

moment";[87] we should continually advance in illumination, and then God's truth will always appear new and fresh to us.[88]

So every time you open the Bible or go to a meeting of the church, pray, pray, pray for the illumination of the Spirit. Pray that God would increase the Spirit's supernatural light shining through Christ in the pages of the Bible. He will show you a true and rich treasure there. Spurgeon exclaimed: "Every letter glitters like a diamond. Oh! It is a blessed thing to read an illuminated Bible lit up by the radiance of the Holy Ghost."[89]

And pray for unbelievers, for without prayer, our witness is powerless.[90] But prayer for the illumination of the lost is powerful. William Tyndale poured out his life in the translation of the Bible into the English language. For this he was persecuted and finally martyred in 1536. Just before the executioner strangled him to death and then burned his body at the stake, Tyndale cried out, "Lord, open the eyes of the King of England."

There is no indication that King Henry VIII was converted. But just two years after Tyndale's death, the king approved the placing of the Great Bible, largely based on Tyndale's translation, in every church for everyone to read. When those Bibles were placed in the churches, there was an infant son in the household of King Henry. When that son became King Edward VI, the Bible and the Reformation were established in England. Tyndale's prayer for the illumination of the king ultimately lit up England, and from there shed light upon many nations. Who knows but that your prayers for God to open the blind eyes of a sinner might change the history of the world?

---

87. Calvin, *Institutes*, 2.2.25.

88. Calvin, *Institutes*, 3.2.19; Goodwin, *First Chapter of the Epistle to the Ephesians*, in *Works*, 1:290.

89. Charles H. Spurgeon, *Twelve Sermons on the Holy Spirit* (Grand Rapids: Baker, 1973), 37.

90. Edwin H. Palmer, *The Person and Ministry of the Holy Spirit: The Traditional Calvinistic Perspective* (Grand Rapids: Baker, 1958), 60–61.

Chapter 6
by Fred Malone

The Holy Spirit and Human Responsibility

I first met Geoff Thomas and heard him preach Christ in the late 1970s. Further exposure to Geoff's preaching caused me to wonder at God's sovereignty in salvation and sanctification in Christ, yet strangely moved me to take more responsibility to love Him and to keep His commandments under grace, to be more conformed to His image (Rom. 8:29–30). His book, *The Holy Spirit*, continues to proclaim this biblical balance: that man is fully responsible for his behavior and that God is fully sovereign in His work to conform man to the image of His dear Son.[1] Holding to both reformational truths, seemingly incompatible to man's puny reason, we find the glory of God both in Christian conversion and holiness.

In 1974, when I preached my senior sermon at Reformed Theological Seminary in Jackson, Mississippi, I chose this topic, expounding Philippians 2:12–13:

> Therefore, my beloved, as you have always obeyed, not as in my presence only, but now much more in my absence, work out your own salvation with fear and trembling; for it is God who works in you both to will and to do for *His* good pleasure.

Before seminary, I had been exposed to the various "higher life" movements. I found these teachings leading me to despair. Their emphasis on passivity in Christian effort, yet holding to the responsibility of a perfectionist "full surrender," could not explain to me why I still sinned as a Christian. Had I not surrendered enough? If Christ was living through me, why did

---

1. Geoffrey Thomas, *The Holy Spirit* (Grand Rapids: Reformation Heritage Books, 2011), 27.

I still sin? Further, the biblical emphasis on Christlike holiness in terms of loving Him and keeping His commandments was lacking (Matt. 28:18–20; John 14:15; Rom. 8:8–10; 1 John 2:3–6; Rev. 12:17; 14:12). I was confused.

While preparing for that senior sermon, I found a book by Edwin H. Palmer, *The Holy Spirit*, which contained two helpful chapters: "The Holy Spirit and Human Responsibility" and "The Holy Spirit and Sanctification."[2] Since then, I have continued to study this mystery in order to keep myself both from unbiblical passivity and from faithless self-dependence. I found that Scripture teaches that we are to work out our salvation in filial fear and trembling with all our might, yet knowing and believing that God is always at work in us (Phil. 2:12–13)!

In the recovery of "the doctrines of grace" during the past fifty years, the sovereignty of God in regeneration has been rightly emphasized as that which enables fallen man to respond to the gospel of grace. However, there has not always been a corresponding understanding about how the sovereignty of God and the responsibility of man work together in sanctification, the growth of the believer into Christlikeness and a holy life.

For some, salvation by sovereign grace alone through faith alone has spawned the erroneous idea of "sanctification by faith alone." Perhaps meaning well, some have misrepresented the truth that sanctification works by a living faith in Christ as a passive "faith alone" approach. In other words, Christians just have to keep believing in sovereign grace for salvation and wait upon the sovereign God to move one's will to obedience. In this error, the responsibility and duty of the Christian actively to work, fight, pray, and obey God's commandments has been diminished, leading to a passive higher-life mentality.

For others, the right emphasis on the responsibility of Christians to discipline themselves for the purpose of godliness has sometimes neglected a living faith in Christ's present love and grace. This error has occasionally resulted in a superficial conformity to the law without the empowering motive of love and worship to Christ in one's obedience. As a result, people

---

2. Edwin H. Palmer, *The Holy Spirit*, rev. ed. (Grand Rapids: Baker, 1971), 87–100, 175–84.

in the pew are often confused about God's sovereignty and their own responsibility in sanctification.

In spite of these errors, it is my belief that the historical Reformed faith has been very consistent in proclaiming the responsibility of man in both salvation and sanctification while at the same time giving all glory to the sovereign work of the Holy Spirit in both works.[3] This great mystery needs to be proclaimed even more today amidst the multitude of errors espoused through multiple media and conference venues. Conformity to the image of Christ for God's glory must rule our thinking as we approach this subject. It is for this holy goal that we work and God works in us.

My method in this chapter is, first, to outline the sovereignty of God and the responsibility of man in regeneration and conversion, and second, to explain these two great truths in sanctification. Only a right understanding of these two truths will bring about the miraculous transformation of the soul into Christlikeness—to God's glory alone!

The Holy Spirit and human responsibility in regeneration and conversion

Regeneration is one hundred percent the sovereign work of God in the heart of man; conversion is one hundred percent man's response of repentance and faith to that great work of God. Man does not regenerate himself; God does not repent and believe for man. God is responsible for His work of regeneration; man is responsible for his response of conversion. It is in these two great facts that we preach the gospel to every creature, calling for repentance and faith while praying for their regeneration by the Holy Spirit.

Regeneration by the Holy Spirit

When our Lord told Nicodemus that he must be born again to see or to enter the kingdom of God, He did not command Nicodemus to make

---

3. Sinclair B. Ferguson, *The Holy Spirit*, Contours of Christian Theology Series (Downers Grove, Ill.: InterVarsity Press, 1996), 139–73. See also George Smeaton, *The Doctrine of the Holy Spirit* (repr., Edinburgh: Banner of Truth Trust, 1974), 221–58; and Abraham Kuyper, *The Work of the Holy Spirit* (repr., Grand Rapids: Eerdmans, 1969), 431–507. These sample works reflect the Reformation's rediscovery of biblical justification and sanctification.

himself born again (John 3:3, 5). In fact, He told him that "that which is born of the flesh is flesh" (v. 6). No man can transform his fleshly nature to be born of the Spirit. He must *be* born from above by the sovereign work of the Holy Spirit to repent and believe if he is to go to heaven.

The need for regeneration. God commands spiritually fallen men everywhere to change—to repent and to believe the gospel (Mark 1:14–15; Acts 17:30–31). All men are under judgment and are responsible to turn from their fallenness to God (John 3:36; Rom. 2:1–16). Yet because of their fallenness in Adam and themselves (Rom. 5:12–19), they are spiritually unable to turn to God; this is part of God's curse (Gen. 6:5; Jer. 13:23; 1 Cor. 2:14; 2 Cor. 4:3–4; Eph. 2:1–3). There are none who seek God on their own (Rom. 3:9–12). As a result, only when God sovereignly restores spiritual ability to man in regeneration by the Holy Spirit can man respond to God in conversion and sanctification (John 3:3, 5; Acts 16:14).

This is why we must be born again by God to see or to enter the kingdom of God. We are responsible to repent, but we cannot. We are responsible to believe, but we cannot. Only a sovereign infusion of spiritual life from God, based on His electing grace, will enable sin-dominated sinners to respond to Jesus Christ as Savior and Lord. This is what happened to Lydia: "The Lord opened her heart to heed the things spoken by Paul" (Acts 16:14b). To God alone belongs the glory in the regeneration of the human soul by His sovereign electing grace (Acts 13:48b; Eph. 1:4–12).

The work of regeneration. But what exactly happened to Lydia and the believing Gentiles? How do unable sinners suddenly become able to repent and believe the gospel? Are they forced to Christ against their formerly stubborn will? Does this not make sinners robots whom God drags unwillingly to conversion? No, the answer of the Bible is that the miracle of regeneration brings new life to the souls of men by uniting them to Jesus Christ and His Spirit.

When God brings the Word of Christ to His elect (Rom. 10:17), in His time they are born again by the Holy Spirit and immediately joined to Christ, not only forensically but also experientially (Rom. 6:1–11). His Spirit, the Holy Spirit, the Spirit of the Father, regenerates spiritually dead sinners to become children of God, dwelling with and in believers' souls (Rom. 8:9–11).

Joined to Jesus Christ by the Holy Spirit, a person's nature is changed from loving sin to hating sin as He does (Heb. 1:9), from hating God to loving God as He does (Rom. 8:7), from Satan's child to Satan's enemy as He is (Col. 1:13). For this reason, the regenerated sinner desires to repent and believe in the Savior of his own free will. Louis Berkhof describes this change:

> The desire to resist has become the desire to obey, and the sinner yields to the persuasive influence of the Word through the operation of the Holy Spirit.[4]

God never saves sinners against their will. In grace and pity, He sovereignly conquers their sinful natures by joining them to Christ and changing their natures to desire and seek the things of God, to think like He thinks, to feel like He feels, and to will what He wills.

This earthly union with Christ in regeneration is but the foretaste, the earnest, of God's will to conform us fully to the image of His Son for eternity. The Holy Spirit's indwelling is only the down payment, the divine seal of things to come (Eph. 1:13–14). It is God's plan to bring us to glory, conformed completely to the image of Christ (Rom. 8:29–30; Heb. 12:23; 1 John 3:1).

In regeneration, man has no part. It is one hundred percent the work of God, zero percent the work of man. God alone receives the glory. But the first breath of the newborn soul is repentance and faith, converting to the Lord Jesus Christ (Acts 2:38–41).

Conversion by man

When an elect sinner hears the gospel call through the preaching of God's Word, God sovereignly regenerates him by His Holy Spirit. That sinner then responds willingly in repentance and faith. Joined to Christ by His Spirit, granted the repentance and faith that leads to life, the sinner repents and believes the gospel by his own will. He converts to Christ (2 Thess. 2:13–14; 1 Peter 1:1–2). He is justified once for all by faith alone in Christ

---

4. Louis Berkhof, *Systematic Theology* (Grand Rapids: Eerdmans, 1969), 471.

alone (Rom. 5:1–2). He enters into the state of standing grace before God (Rom. 6:14). He is adopted as a child of God. Regeneration is one hundred percent the work of God; conversion is one hundred percent the work of the new man.

This is why Paul exalted "the foolishness of the message preached" (1 Cor. 1:21) over the Jews' desire for signs and the Gentiles' desire for wisdom. It is only in the foolishness of preaching, and prayer for God's mercy (Rom. 9:1–4), that God alone receives the glory in the regeneration and conversion of the human soul to Christ.

The Holy Spirit and human responsibility in sanctification

Now we look into the mystery of the work of the Holy Spirit and human responsibility in sanctification. Sanctification is the process of being conformed to the holy image of Jesus Christ in this earthly life (Col. 3:9–11). It begins in regeneration, when God sanctifies us once and for all, setting us apart through union with Christ (2 Thess. 2:13; Titus 3:1–7; Heb. 10:10; 1 Peter 1:1–2). It continues progressively on earth until final glorification at death or His return (Rom. 8:29–30; 1 Thess. 5:23; Heb. 12:23). Only then will we be conformed fully to the image of Christ (1 John 3:1–5).

Philippians 2:12–13 presents the earthly pursuit of Christlikeness as one hundred percent a sovereign work of God the Holy Spirit who works within us and also as one hundred percent the work of man with his new God-given ability. If this two hundred percent sum sounds illogical, then we must bow to God's Word, not man's logic.

So if God is one hundred percent responsible for the will and strength by which we grow into Christlikeness, why is one Christian more holy than another? Cannot God's will and power overrule those who do not exert one hundred percent effort to grow in grace and Christlikeness? How does this mystery of sanctification work? We will assume the one hundred percent sovereign work of God and focus on the one hundred percent responsibility of man.

The responsibility of man in sanctification

When God regenerates our souls, He conquers our total dominance by depravity by joining us to Christ as new creatures. However, God has chosen that a remnant of depravity remains in each part of us when we become new creatures (Rom. 7:14–8:4). Our minds are still affected by sin and ignorance, our feelings are still tempted by sinful desires, and our wills sometimes choose unrighteousness by this remaining ignorance and sinful desires. This remnant of the sinful nature is sometimes called "the flesh" (Gal. 5:16–17). The best Christians still fall into sin (1 John 2:1–2).

So those who are regenerated immediately enter into a spiritual warfare between the flesh and the Spirit within (Gal. 5:16–17). We must put on the whole armor of God to fight the good fight of faith against the world, the flesh, and the devil (Eph. 6:10–18). It is here that this new ability to respond to God in conversion enables us and requires us to cooperate with God in a growing sanctification.

This new ability of repentance and faith in conversion must continue to be exercised as a living principle in progressive sanctification. This justifying faith works by love (Gal. 5:5–6; James 2:17). God calls Christians to take responsibility to cooperate with His inward work by pursuing the holiness without which no one shall see the Lord (Heb. 12:14).

How do Christians cooperate in sanctification? We must long for and seek God's Word as a newborn babe seeks milk (1 Peter 2:1–2). Using our new ability, we must daily set our minds on things above, where Christ is (Col. 3:1–3). We must look daily to Jesus, believing that we are truly in union with Him as the author and finisher of our faith (Heb. 12:1–4). We must respond daily to God's unchangeable love by loving Him and conforming our lives to His commandments (John 14:15; 1 John 2:4–6). We must repent of and confess our new sins and trust again in Christ alone for forgiveness and living fellowship (1 John 1:8–10). We must join ourselves faithfully to serve other believers in His church, not forsaking the assemblies (Heb. 10:23–25). We must work out our salvation in filial fear and trembling, knowing and believing that God has promised that He will never cease to work and will in us for His good pleasure, even when we fail Him (Phil. 1:6; 2:12–13; Jude 24–25).

Berkhof has spoken of the Christian's new ability and responsibility to cooperate with the Spirit's presence and work:

> It [sanctification] is a work of God in which believers co-operate. When it is said that man takes part in the work of sanctification, this

does not mean that man is an independent agent in the work, so as to make it partly the work of God and partly the work of man; but merely, that God effects the work in part through the instrumentality of man as a rational being, by requiring of him prayerful and intelligent co-operation with the Spirit. That man must co-operate with the Spirit of God follows: (a) from the repeated warnings against evils and temptations, which clearly imply that man must be active in avoiding the pitfalls of life, Rom. 12:9, 16, 17; 1 Cor. 6:9, 10; Gal. 5:16–23; and (b) from the constant exhortations to holy living. These imply that the believer must be diligent in the employment of the means at his command for the moral and spiritual improvement of his life, Micah 6:8; John 15:2, 8, 16; Rom. 8:12, 13; 12:1, 2, 17; Gal. 6:7, 8, 15.[5]

So for growth into Christlikeness, new creatures must take one hundred percent responsibility to employ their new ability of faith to use the means for spiritual growth given by God. We cannot blame God for our lack of conformity to Christ. God has given us His saving grace, the indwelling Holy Spirit, His Word, and a new nature to work out our salvation. Because of God's promise to will and work in His people, we walk by faith in God's faithfulness to that promise. He will help us because He is always helping us. Faith believes that. Every step we take forward in Christlikeness brings one hundred percent glory to God alone. However, if we are lacking in that conformity, we must take one hundred percent of the responsibility for that failure and press on by faith, believing that we live under grace (Rom. 6:14; Phil. 3:13–14).

The means that God has given for man to use responsibly
The "means of grace," as they are understood by Reformed theology, include the written and proclaimed Word of truth, our gift of faith, the privilege of prayer, and the biblically true church. Only God the sovereign Spirit can create and sustain spiritual life in the soul of man, but God the Father has ordained that believers are fully responsible to use the means He has determined to bless by His Spirit. This we must do "by faith."

---

5. Berkhof, *Systematic Theology*, 534.

For the sake of brevity in this chapter, I will focus only on the responsibility of the Christian to exercise his daily faith in using the means of God's Word.

His faithful Word. Our Lord Jesus Christ sanctified Himself unto His Father in order to sanctify His disciples (John 17:19). He also prayed to the Father: "Sanctify them by Your truth. Your word is truth" (John 17:17). Both in salvation and in sanctification, God works through His Word of truth, applied by His Spirit in the hearts of men. The Spirit never works contrary to the Word of God. This is impossible.

With regard to salvation, our Lord told His disciples that His words were spirit and life (John 6:63). Paul applied that truth to the Romans in salvation: "So then faith *comes* by hearing, and hearing by the word of God." (Rom. 10:17). It is the revelation of divine truth, God's Word, that the Father uses to enlighten the minds of men by the power of the Spirit. Faith comes and grows by the Spirit's application of divine truth to the souls of men.

In sanctification, too, God ordinarily uses His revealed Word and His Holy Spirit to further sanctify His people (2 Tim. 3:15–17; 1 Peter 1:1–2). So Christians must give full attention to learning the Word of God to grow thereby (1 Peter 2:1–2). As we read the inspired Word and hear it proclaimed, the Holy Spirit enlightens our minds to understand the things of God (Acts 20:32; 2 Cor. 4:5–6). As we grow in understanding God's Word of truth, our minds become more understanding of God and His thoughts (2 Cor. 10:5), conforming our thoughts to the mind of Christ (Rom. 12:1–2). The Word and the Spirit bring faith and life to our souls and enable us to grow into conformity to Christ. Christians must exercise responsibility to use the means of God's Word to grow thereby.

Our faith in His faithful Word. However, it is not enough just to expose ourselves to the Word of God (Heb. 4:1–2). Like newborn babes suckle the breast, we are called to embrace by faith the teachings of Scripture in order to grow (2 Tim. 3:14–17; 1 Peter 2:1–2). Peter called his readers to grow in the faith by continually believing the many and precious promises of God to believers (2 Peter 1:1–4). Justifying faith in the gospel of Christ is also the principle by which we love Him and work out our salvation in filial fear and trembling. Paul recorded the living faith in God's Word that enabled him to preach faithfully: "We also believe, therefore we also speak" (2 Cor. 4:13). We live by faith in a justifying God, and we walk by that same faith in obedience to His commands (Matt. 28:19–20). Faith works through love (Gal. 5:6).

Berkhof explains the relationship of a living faith to sanctification:

> Faith is the mediate or instrumental cause of sanctification as well as of justification. It does not merit sanctification any more than it does justification, but it unites us to Christ and keeps us in touch with Him as the Head of the new humanity, who is the source of the new life within us, and also of our progressive sanctification, through the operation of the Holy Spirit. The consciousness of the fact that sanctification is based on justification, and is impossible on any other basis, and that the constant exercise of faith is necessary, in order to advance in the way of holiness, will guard us against all self-righteousness in our striving to advance in godliness and holiness of life. It deserves particular attention that, while even the weakest faith mediates a perfect justification, the degree of sanctification is commensurate with the strength of the Christian's faith and the persistence with which he apprehends Christ.[6]

In other words, to the degree that we live believing the indicatives of grace revealed in the Word—the love of God for us in Christ's salvation, the unfailing faithfulness of God to His promises to work in us—so we grow in obeying the imperatives of the Word unto further sanctification and Christlikeness (John 14:15; 2 Cor. 5:14–15; 1 John 2:1–6). This is nothing else but the working out of the Reformation's great contribution: law and gospel theology. The condemnation of the law leads us to the Christ of the gospel, applied by the Holy Spirit in regeneration and conversion; the gospel believed and lived leads us to the law for greater conformity to Christlike thinking, feeling, and choosing. We are not sanctified by faith alone without the direction of the law. Neither are we sanctified by law without the empowering of faith. The indicatives of grace believed move the redeemed to live by that saving faith in loving obedience to the Christlike imperatives.

---

6. Berkhof, *Systematic Theology*, 537.

This is the key to the one hundred percent responsibility of Christians to pursue sanctification and conformity to Jesus Christ. As we believe in the effectual salvation of God through Christ, as we walk and live in believing His promises to work in and for us, as we look unto our justifying Jesus (Heb. 12:1–3), so we find the motive and power of the Holy Spirit strengthening us to grow in grace and in obedience to the stature of our Lord Jesus Christ. As Geoff says:

> Every true Christian is now able to defy sin and do what is righteous. But that does not make him sinless. On this side of heaven the virus of sin and its misdeeds will ever trouble us; they will make their presence known even on our deathbeds. What are we to do with the remaining sin that does not control us but yet is still within us?... We must keep looking to the Lord Jesus Christ, who is the source of our victory over sin, and constantly trust in Him. Paul tells us we must constantly put to death the misdeeds of the body, that is, to mortify the sin that remains within us. We are to weaken, starve, and murder anything evil that rises up within us and urges us to defy God and His law. We are to continue this work with the energy and under the direction of the Spirit of God. Regeneration is vain without the work of the Spirit. So is sanctification. We will never grow in Christlikeness without the Spirit. We also are impotent to put to death the misdeeds of the body without the Holy Spirit. All other ways of killing sin are vain; it can only be done by the Spirit....
>
> The Holy Spirit brings the Christian into communion with the crucified Christ. The Spirit brings the cross of Christ into the heart of the sinner by faith, and gives him fellowship with Christ in His death and sufferings. So the believer fights sin with the blood of Christ and by virtue of Christ's cross. Galatians 6:14 says, "But God forbid that I should glory, save in the cross of our Lord Jesus Christ, by whom the world is crucified unto me, and I unto the world." The Holy Spirit helps us fight sin with the mighty weapon of the cross.[7]

So a living faith in the Word of Christ who saved us and continues to save us is the working principle of progressive sanctification, just as it is the principle of initial sanctification at our conversion. As we attend the Word of God with believing hearts and pray for the Spirit's help (Eph. 1:19–23;

---

7. Thomas, *The Holy Spirit*, 158, 161.

3:13–21), God blesses His truth to conform us to the image of the Lord Jesus Christ.

This is why the saints are helped even by the preaching of the gospel of Christ to unsaved sinners. Our sanctifying faith must be Christ-centered to go beyond superficial obedience to the law in order to bear the Christlike fruit of the Holy Spirit, which is "love, joy, peace, longsuffering, kindness, goodness, faithfulness, gentleness, self-control" (Gal. 5:22–23). This is what it means to be Spirit-filled as a Christian (Eph. 5:18–6:9), to walk as He walked (Eph. 5:1–2), to be conformed to the image of Christ.

As Christians exert one hundred percent effort in faith to use all the means of sanctification (the Word, prayer, the church, etc.), the Holy Spirit of God blesses the means to conform believers more to the image of Christ. God has so promised (Phil. 2:12–13). Blessed with the promise of God's work within us, believing in His integrity and faithfulness, we actively embrace the responsibility to work out our promised salvation with filial fear and trembling, knowing all the time by faith that God is at work in us to will and to work for His good pleasure—to His glory alone.

Conclusion

I close this chapter with the good words of our brother Geoff. His preaching and teaching have captured the simplicity of the work of the Holy Spirit and human responsibility in conversion and sanctification well:

> You apply yourself to seriously working out what it means to please God as a saved person in every area of your life. If that responsibility crushes you, never forget that God the Spirit is working in you. He supplies you with power, motivating and encouraging you each day. That is how we are to understand the leading of the Spirit. "We do everything…the Spirit does everything, too."…
>
> What a consolation it is to know that we have been led by the Spirit of God to this very moment. Even when we find ourselves falling into sin, let us not despair as Christians because the indwelling Holy Spirit is far greater than all our sin. We would despair if we simply gave way to sin after sin, but we do not. We meet mercy after mercy while experiencing the energy to move forward in our journey. The Spirit of grace produces conflict in the believer against sin, and

He also spurs the believer to continue the fight. The victory is sure; the Spirit is within us, and we cannot fail. He will lead us home.[8]

As we look to Christ by faith each day, believing in His redemption and His promises of the Spirit's help to the justified, exerting full effort to use the means He has ordained, we grow in grace and holiness (Phil. 2:12–13). We become more and more conformed to the image of Christ.

Therefore, having these promises, beloved, let us cleanse ourselves from all filthiness of the flesh and spirit, perfecting holiness in the fear of God. (2 Cor. 7:1)

---

8. Thomas, *The Holy Spirit*, 156–57.

PART III

Growth and the Spirit of Holiness

Chapter 7
by David Jones

A Gracious, Willing Guest: The Indwelling Holy Spirit

The novelist Dorothy Sayers once said that for many Christians, the Holy Spirit, for all intents and purposes, has been removed from the Trinity. She wrote:

> There are those who would worship the Father, the Son & the Virgin Mary; those who believe in the Father, the Son and the Holy Scriptures; those who found their faith on the Father, the Son and the Church; and there are even those who seem to derive their spiritual power from the Father, the Son, and the minister.[1]

For many people, the Holy Spirit is the nameless, faceless person of the Godhead. Yet He is the one who brings the presence of God into our lives. Jesus said to His disciples in the upper room, "And I will pray the Father, and He will give you another Helper, that He may abide with you forever—the Spirit of truth.... He dwells with you and will be in you" (John 14:16–17). The hymn writer Harriet Auber called him "a gracious, willing guest."[2]

What are some attributes of the Spirit?

Personal

The Holy Spirit is a person, not a power. I suppose that for many, "the Spirit of truth" is much the same as "the spirit of Christmas" or the spirit to be found in a football team—an atmosphere, a force, an influence—and

---

1. Quoted in "Celebrating Pentecost," a blog post by Paul Beasley Murray, May 24, 2012; https://www.paulbeasleymurray.com/blog/2012/05/celebrating-pentecost/
2. From the hymn "Our Blest Redeemer, Ere He Breathed" by Harriet Auber, 1829.

nothing more. But Jesus says, "*He*...will be in you." John, who wrote these words, broke all the rules of grammar. The word translated as "Spirit" is neuter in Greek, but John calls Him "He," not "it." The Spirit is someone, not something.

He is not the comfort we get when we trust in Christ; He is the Comforter. He is not the help we receive when we become Christians; He is the Helper. Gottfried Osei-Mensah put it like this:

> If you received a package of explosives, you would have to decide what to do with it. But if you were favoured with the visit of a dignitary, he more or less decides what to do with you! You are at his disposal. The Lord Jesus promises his people not "parcels of power" but the powerful person of the Holy Spirit to stay with them.[3]

The Spirit is not at our disposal. We are at His. We receive Him, not by tapping into His power, but because the ascended Christ has sent Him into our hearts to live there as Lord. If you think of the Holy Spirit as a power rather than a person, your concern will be, "How can I have more of the Spirit?" But if you understand that He is a person, your concern will be, "How can the Holy Spirit have more of me?" Remember, it was the Holy Spirit who said to the church at Antioch as they worshiped, "Now separate to Me Barnabas and Saul for the work to which I have called them" (Acts 13:2).

We do not make use of the Spirit, He makes use of us. When Simon Magus offered money to buy the gift of the Spirit, Peter did not commend him for his spirituality; he rebuked him for his sin and warned him of God's judgment. As a result of this incident, a new word entered the dictionary: *simony*, which means trafficking for money in spiritual things (Acts 8:18–24).

A personality, not a personification

Jack Frost is the personification of cold weather, but the Holy Spirit is not the personification of Jesus. He is a distinct, divine person in His own right.

---

3. Gottfried Osei-Mensah, "The Holy Spirit in World Evangelization," in *Let the Earth Hear His Voice,* ed. J. D. Douglas, Lausanne Congress papers, 1974 (Minneapolis: World Wide Publications, 1975), 259.

He has all the qualities of a person. He knows me through and through. He knows when I sit and when I rise. He can read my thoughts from afar. He knows when I go out and when I come in. He knows what I am going to say before I say it.[4] He has individuality, intelligence, will, feeling, knowledge, and sympathy. He is able to love, see, think, hear, speak, desire, grieve, and rejoice. He teaches, guides, commissions, commands, and restrains. He can be obeyed, blasphemed, insulted, and outraged. He can be lied to.[5] When Ananias and Sapphira were removed from the Jerusalem church for their hypocrisy, it was for lying to the Holy Spirit. You cannot lie to an influence or a force field. You can lie only to a person. And this person is God. Peter told them, "You have not lied to men but to God" (Acts 5:3–5).

Distinct and divine

The Father, the Son, and the Holy Spirit are three distinct persons in the Godhead. The Father is not the Son and the Son is not the Father. The Son is not the Spirit and the Spirit is not the Son. Neither Son nor Spirit is the Father, and yet the three are one. Where one is, all three are. There is a kind of interpenetration.

Jesus describes this triunity in John 14:20–23. He promises His disciples that when He ascends to the Father and the Spirit is poured out, "you will know that I *am* in My Father, and you in Me, and I in you.... We will come...and make Our home [with you]." In other words, on that day the penny would drop, the lights would go on, and the disciples would realize, not so much intellectually as experientially, the mystery of the Trinity.

The early church fathers came up with a word to describe this, a composite of two Greek words, *peri*, which means "around," and *chorea*, which means "dance." *Perichoresis* has been called the "divine dance." It is a mutual indwelling without loss of personal identity. It is a fellowship of three coequal persons, perfectly embracing in love and harmony, and expressing an intimacy that no one on earth can humanly comprehend. By God's grace, we are caught up into it. The apostle John writes:

---

4. Ps. 139:1–4.
5. Gen. 6:3; Matt. 12:31; John 14:26; Acts 5:3–5; 8:24; 10:19–21; 13:4; Rom. 8:14; 1 Cor. 2:10–11; 12:11; Eph. 4:30; Heb. 10:29.

> That which was from the beginning, which we have heard, which we have seen with our eyes, which we have looked upon, and our hands have handled, concerning the Word of life—the life was manifested, and we have seen, and bear witness, and declare to you that eternal life which was with the Father and was manifested to us—that which we have seen and heard we declare to you, that you also may have fellowship with us; and truly our fellowship *is* with the Father and with His Son Jesus Christ. (1 John 1:1–3)

This is the fellowship of the Holy Spirit. It is a fellowship with the Father and the Son. It is by the indwelling Holy Spirit that we enter into this fellowship. Our hearts become His home.

Presence

Moses pleaded with God after the episode with the golden calf, "If Your Presence does not go with us, do not send us up from here" (Ex. 33:15). The disciples in the upper room must have felt the same. Jesus was going to be taken from them, and they dared not go forward without His presence. But Jesus reassured them: "I will not leave you as orphans; I will come to you" (John 14:18).

The Holy Spirit brings the presence of Jesus into our lives. When C. S. Lewis lost his wife to cancer, he struggled with the things people said to him. He is brutally frank and honest about his grief:

> What pitiable cant to say, "She will live forever in my memory!" Live? That is exactly what she won't do. You might as well think like the old Egyptians that you can keep the dead by embalming them. Will nothing persuade us that they are gone? What's left? A corpse, a memory... all mockeries...more ways of spelling the word dead. It was [she] I loved. As if I wanted to fall in love with my memory of her, an image in my own mind! It would be a sort of incest.[6]

These are strong words, but of course Lewis is right. It is the presence of the lost loved one we crave, not the memory. What a comfort it is, then, to hear Jesus say, "I will not leave you as orphans; I will come to you." Because of the indwelling of the Holy Spirit, Jesus is not just a distant memory but also a living presence in our lives. He is physically absent but spiritually

---

6. C. S. Lewis, *A Grief Observed* (New York: Bantam Books, 1976), 22.

present. Augustine said, "He departed from our eyes that we should return into our hearts and find Him there."[7]

As one of the Puritans put it, "The sun is at its hottest when it is at its highest." Our Jesus has gone up on high, for the highest place that heaven affords is His by sovereign right, and from heaven He pours out His Spirit into our hearts. This means He is nearer to us now than He was to the disciples when He walked the earth, for He dwells in us by His Spirit. That is why He could say to His astonished disciples, "It is to your advantage that I go away" (John 16:7). In a very real sense, we are better off in a twenty-first-century church where the gospel is preached than sitting in the crowd listening to the Sermon on the Mount.

Paraclete

Jesus called the Holy Spirit "another Comforter" (John 14:16). Some translations transliterate the Greek word and call Him the "Paraclete," which means literally "one who is called alongside." A "paramedic" is not a doctor but one who comes alongside a doctor. "Parachurch" organizations, such as missionary societies, come alongside the local church to help her with her mission to the world. Likewise, the Holy Spirit is the "called-alongside one."

For what purpose is He called alongside? The clue is to be found in the word *another*, which is used to translate two words in Greek: *heteros* and *allos*. *Heteros* means "different to," whereas *allos* means "more of the same." When Jesus called the Holy Spirit "another Comforter," He was promising us more of the same, another Comforter just like *Himself*. As the church father Tertullian pointed out, the title "vicar of Christ on earth" belongs to the Holy Spirit, not the pope.[8] The Holy Spirit is the One who stands in for Jesus.

In what ways does the Holy Spirit carry out this role?

He teaches us the truth

He is the Spirit of truth (John 14:17). He is another teacher just like Jesus. For three years, the disciples had been in the school of Christ, but now "the

---

7. Augustine, *Confessions*, trans. John K. Ryan (New York: Random House, 1960), 22 (4.12).
8. Tertullian, "On Prescription against Heretics," ch. 28, in *Ante-Nicene Fathers*, ed. Alexander Roberts and James Donaldson (New York: Charles Scribner's Sons, 1918), 3:256.

Helper, the Holy Spirit, whom the Father will send in My name, He will teach you all things, and bring to your remembrance all things that I said to you." (John 14:26). How does the Spirit do this?

First, He does it by inspiration. This is why we can be sure that the New Testament is the teaching of Jesus. He is speaking to the penmen of the New Testament Scriptures. According to Peter in 2 Peter 1:16–21, it is better to have the written Scriptures inspired by the Holy Spirit than to hear the audible voice of God on the Mount of Transfiguration. It is "a more sure word."

Second, He does it by illumination. Not only did He inspire these men to write down the teaching of Jesus, but He also enters our hearts; He gets into us. He illuminates the truth in our hearts and minds. He unpacks it and unlocks it for us. John says, "you do not need that anyone teach you; but as the same anointing teaches you concerning all things" (1 John 2:27). In other words, the author of Scripture Himself enters our hearts and minds, and switches on the lights for us, so that we see Jesus.

He transforms us

John Stott, in his book *The Radical Disciple*, cites William Temple,

> It's no good giving me a play like Hamlet or King Lear and telling me to write a play like that. Shakespeare could do it; I can't. And it is no good showing me a life like the life of Jesus and telling me to live a life like that. Jesus could do it; I can't. But if the genius of Shakespeare could come and live in me, then I could write plays like his. And if the Spirit of Jesus could come and live in me, then I could live a life like his.[9]

Stott concludes: "God's purpose is to make us like Christ, and God's way is to fill us with his Holy Spirit."[10] That is the kind of help we need. That is the fruit of the Holy Spirit. It is Christlikeness. The Spirit indwelling us produces the character of Jesus in us. It is not morality or legalism. It is the "beauty of Jesus" seen in us.

---

9. William Temple, cited in John Stott, *The Radical Disciple: Some Neglected Aspects of Our Calling* (Downers Grove, Ill.: InterVarsity, 2010), 37

10. Stott, *The Radical Disciple*, 37.

He talks up Jesus

The Holy Spirit is Jesus' cheerleader, if I can put it that way. He is a kind of motivational speaker: "But when the Helper comes, whom I shall send to you from the Father, the Spirit of truth who proceeds from the Father, He will testify of Me" (John 15:26). Imagine a Roman legion, stationed someplace where the figs are sour, the sun hot, and the bugs irritating. The soldiers become discouraged and morale sinks. The Roman army employed special personnel to deal with such situations. They were what we would call motivational speakers or cheerleaders, traveling about from cohort to cohort and giving pep talks to the troops. These dispellers of gloom, these dispensers of inspiration, were called "paracletes." The Spirit fulfills the role of Paraclete by strengthening us within and inspiring us to new hope by pointing us to Jesus.

So the Spirit is a distinct and divine person who brings the presence of Jesus into our lives. He is not Jesus, but He is so like Him as makes no difference. He is another Counselor, the Paraclete, the one called alongside. But what does a Paraclete do for us? Sometimes the term is used of a defense attorney to whom we call out for help. Sometimes it is used of an intercessor who calls out on our behalf. Sometimes it is used of a comforter who offers consolation in times of grief. Sometimes it is used of a cheerleader who yells encouragement from the sidelines. Sometimes it is used of a general rallying his troops and leading them into battle. The Holy Spirit is all of these and more.

Permanent

He is God's forever Spirit, with us and in us all the time: "And I will pray the Father, and He will give you another Helper, that He may abide with you forever" (John 14:16). When He comes, He comes to stay, every minute of every day, forever. He takes up permanent residence in our lives. David asks in Psalm 139:7, "Where can I go from Your Spirit? Or where can I flee from Your presence?" For the believer, the abiding presence of the Spirit is profoundly encouraging and reassuring, and not at all threatening. To have the Spirit permanently with us and in us is liberating, not claustrophobic.

Of course, we can offend and grieve this gracious, willing guest within us. We can grieve Him by ignoring Him, resisting Him, doubting Him, sinning against Him, spurning His love, refusing to obey Him, and turning our backs on Him. We can quench the fire of the Spirit. Have you ever been in a situation where you said something, only to have cold water poured on you? We quench the Holy Spirit by despising prophecies (1 Thess. 5:19–20), that is, by refusing to listen to what the Spirit says to the churches through the Word that He has inspired. When we step back from God's Word, when we refuse to allow the Word of Christ to furnish our meetings and enrich our fellowship, there will inevitably be a dampening-down of spiritual fervor. The Spirit is quenched (compare Eph. 5:18 and Col. 3:16). To be filled with the Spirit is to hang on His every word. It is to come completely under His influence. We should never take Him for granted. Paul exhorts us to keep in step with the Spirit in our lives, to be led by Him (Gal. 5:16, 18). This relationship between Word and Spirit is vital.

Present

Where does it all begin? How do you receive the Holy Spirit? How does He come into your life? Jesus says, "I will pray the Father, and He will give…" (John 14:16). The Holy Spirit is God's gift to all believers. Peter made that clear in his sermon on the Day of Pentecost: "Repent, and let every one of you be baptized in the name of Jesus Christ for the remission of sins; and you shall receive the gift of the Holy Spirit." (Acts 2:38). Everyone who receives the forgiveness of sins also receives the gift of the Spirit. There are no people who are forgiven whom the Holy Spirit does not indwell.

The Holy Spirit is not a reward to some. He is a present from God to all who believe in Jesus for the forgiveness of their sins. Charles Spurgeon puts it beautifully: "I looked at Christ, and the dove of peace flew into my heart, I looked at the dove, and it flew away."

The Holy Spirit is the shy member of the Trinity. He never draws attention to Himself. He always points us to Christ. As F. Dale Brunner has said: "The Holy Spirit does not mind being Cinderella outside the ballroom, if the Prince is honoured inside His kingdom!"[11]

---

11. Frederick Dale Bruner and William Hordern, *The Holy Spirit: Shy Member of the Trinity* (Minneapolis: Augsburg: 1984), 16.

Chapter 8
by Ian Hamilton

Living by the Spirit's Sanctifying Ministry

Paul writes in Romans 8:12–14: "Therefore, brethren, we are debtors, not to the flesh, to live after the flesh. For if ye live after the flesh, ye shall die: but if ye through the Spirit do mortify the deeds of the body, ye shall live. For as many as are led by the Spirit of God, they are the sons of God."

Today, many Christians—even Reformed Christians—do not think as much about the Holy Trinity as Christians did in earlier ages. John Calvin, for example, wrote magnificently about the Trinity in Book One of his *Institutes of the Christian Religion*, citing a passage from Gregory of Nazianzus, a fourth-century Greek father, which, he said, "vastly delights me."[1] That passage about the Trinity is taken from one of Gregory's baptismal orations, where he said, "No sooner do I conceive of the One [member of the Trinity] than I am illumined by the splendor of the Three. No sooner do I distinguish them than I am carried back to the one. When I think of any one of the three I think of Him as the whole, and my eyes are filled, and the greater part of what I am thinking escapes me."[2]

Can you identify with Gregory of Nazianzus's words or with Calvin's delight in reading them? Can the church today identify with the love for the Holy Trinity that was so obvious in the early church fathers and was replicated in the writings of Calvin, the other Reformers, and the Puritans?

---

1. John Calvin, *Institutes of the Christian Religion*, ed. John T. McNeill, trans. Ford Lewis Battles (Philadelphia: Westminster Press, 1960), 1.13.17.

2. Gregory Nazianzen, *Oration on Holy Baptism*, sec. 41, in *A Select Library of Nicene and Post-Nicene Fathers of the Christian Church, Second Series*, ed. Philip Schaff and Henry Wace (New York: The Christian Literature Co., 1894), 7:375.

What one does, all do

Let us begin to consider the work and ministry of the Holy Spirit by anchoring our thinking about the Spirit's sanctifying, beautifying work within the life and ministry of the Holy Trinity as a whole. A Latin phrase precisely captures what I am saying. It is *opera trinitatis ad extra indivisa sunt*, meaning "the works that are external to the Trinity are indivisible." What one does, all do. What one person does, the other persons do as well.

That does not mean that the Father and the Spirit died with the Son on Calvary's cross, but it does mean that through the eternal Spirit, our Savior, Jesus Christ, offered Himself to God the Father on the cross, as we read in Hebrews 9. Similarly, what the Holy Spirit does by way of eminency, as John Owen puts it, the Father and the Son also do.

Owen magnificently, movingly, and profoundly explains in Volume 2 of his *Collected Works* that, in the New Testament, love is almost always predicated of the Father; grace is almost always predicated of the Son; and comfort is almost always predicated of the Spirit. That does not mean the Lord Jesus Christ and the Spirit do not love, or that the Father and the Son do not comfort. But Owen gathers the testimony of Holy Scripture to help us understand that by way of eminency, the Father loves; by way of eminency, the Son pours out grace; and by way of eminency, the Spirit comforts.

Scripture tells us that the Spirit acts in the new covenant as the Spirit of the risen, reigning Jesus Christ, who was sent by Christ and His Father to apply the grace of Christ to the people of Christ. He does not act independently in His sanctifying, beautifying ministry, but is the agent by way of eminency of the Holy Trinity. What the Spirit does by way of eminency, the Father and the Son also do. They and their work are indivisible. When we think of one, we must then think of three. And when we think of the three, we must learn to understand the Trinitarian glory, the Trinitarian majesty, and the Trinitarian foundation of the Christian faith and of our personal union and communion with God in Christ by the bonding ministry of the Holy Spirit.

Conforming us to Christ

Let us begin this study of the Holy Spirit by asking: *What precisely is the Spirit's sanctifying, beautifying ministry?* We will examine this question first in general terms, then look at it more specifically.

In general terms, the Holy Spirit indwells believers as the Spirit of Christ to make us like Christ. The great purpose of God concerning His people is to make us like His Son. The Holy Spirit is sent by God's predestined grand design to conform us to the image and likeness of the Son of God.

This is so that Christ might be the firstborn among many brothers, because God's ultimate purpose does not terminate in us but in Jesus Christ, who has ever been His beloved Son. Even when God the Father was cursing His Son on Calvary, He was surely saying, "If ever I loved Thee, My Jesus 'tis now." The great burden of the Father's heart is to exalt His Son by conforming the people of His Son to His likeness, to the praise and glory of God.

Because the Holy Spirit comes as the Spirit of Christ, Calvin may then argue that the chief title of the Holy Spirit in the New Testament in His new covenant ministry is "the Spirit of adoption." Paul thus says in verses 15 and 16: "For ye have not received the spirit of bondage again to fear; but ye have received the Spirit of adoption, whereby we cry, Abba, Father. The Spirit itself beareth witness with our spirit, that we are the children of God." In other words, the Holy Spirit has come as the Spirit of Christ, and because He is the Spirit of Christ, He is the Spirit of adoption.

What is more, He indwells us to remove all the hindrances, barriers, and impediments to our experience of entering into what he calls in verse 21 "the glorious liberty of the children of God." Nothing hinders us from enjoying the glorious privilege of our adoption more than the presence of indwelling sin in us. The Holy Spirit comes as the Spirit of adoption to put sin to death in our lives so that we might experience more radically, more gloriously, more personally, more deeply, and more effectively what it means to be children of the living God.

So, in general terms, that is what the Holy Spirit's sanctifying beautifying ministry is. Jesus Christ is the firstborn among many brothers. And by the Spirit of adoption, we have been brought into that community of faith, into the family of the living God. We have been engrafted into Christ, the firstborn One, and have received the Spirit of adoption, whereby we cry, "Abba, Father."

Enabling us to mortify sin

But more particularly, what does the Holy Spirit, as the Spirit of Christ and of our adoption, actually do in our lives? What is His ongoing, new covenant ministry as the representative of the Holy Trinity?

Paul describes this ministry in verse 13, saying, "For if ye live after the flesh, ye shall die: but if ye through the Spirit do mortify the deeds of the body, ye shall live." This verse is often dislocated from its surrounding context. But note the words: "Ye shall live." In verse 14, Paul goes on to say, "For as many as are led by the Spirit of God, they are the sons of God." So what does it mean to be led by the Spirit of God? If only those who are led by the Spirit of God are the sons of God, how can they *not* be led by the Spirit of God?

That is a significant question. If we claim to be the sons of the living God, what credibility does our profession have? We might answer, "We are being led by the Spirit of God, and those who are led by the Spirit of God are the sons of God." But what is the distinguishing mark of the Spirit's leading that gives credibility to our profession that we truly are the sons of the living God? In verse 13, Paul says: "If ye live after the flesh, ye shall die: but if ye through the Spirit do mortify [put to death] the deeds of the body, ye shall live. For as many as are led by the Spirit of God" to mortify the deeds of the body, they shall live.

Thus, the distinguishing mark of the Holy Spirit's indwelling in us is that we, by the Spirit, are putting to death what Paul calls "the deeds of the body," or any sin that remains within us. By the grace of God, the atoning work of Christ, and the ministry of the Spirit, we who have believed in Christ have been set free from the guilt and power of sin. But the Lord has not yet set us free from every bit of the presence of sin. He thus gives us the Holy Spirit to help us remove everything in our lives that is not Jesus.

Greg Norman, a famous Australian golfer, was designing a golf course when he was asked, "What is in your mind when you look at this rough terrain and begin planning to create a golf course of it?" Norman said, "I look at the rough terrain and think, *I'll remove everything that isn't golf course.*" That is what the Holy Spirit does in us; He comes to remove everything that isn't Jesus from our lives. He comes to help us put to death the deeds of the body. Mortification of sin is the spiritual equivalent of uprooting and killing all of the weeds that threaten to overwhelm us and kill the flowers in our gardens. Without mortification, sin would overrun our lives and choke us to death.

Owen, the great Puritan writer, said: "Let not that man think he makes any progress in holiness who walks not over the bellies of his lusts. He who doth not kill sin in his way takes no steps towards his journey's end.... Be killing sin or it will be killing you."[3] Owen was stating in his own way what the apostle Paul tells us here: "If ye live after the flesh, ye shall die: but if ye through the Spirit do mortify the deeds of the body, ye shall live."

Paul makes at least three points in this statement. First, in saying, "ye shall live," he is telling us that the fullness of spiritual life, an ever-deepening fellowship with God, and the glorious liberty of the children of God are all impossible apart from mortification or putting sin to death in our bodies. As Owen wrote, "The vigour, and power, and comfort of our spiritual life depend on the mortification of the deeds of the flesh."[4]

Second, Paul is telling us that our usefulness to God and His church depends on our putting sin to death in our lives. He says, "But if ye through the Spirit do mortify the deeds of the body, ye shall live." In 2 Timothy 2:21, Paul says, "If a man therefore purge himself from these he shall be a vessel unto honour, sanctified, and meet for the master's use, and prepared unto every good work." If we purge ourselves from all that is dishonorable, sinful, and base, we shall be useful to the Master.

When Dan Edwards, a young theology student, was about to move to Germany, he received a letter from Robert Murray M'Cheyne, who was concerned that the young man might be affected by the infidelity that was beginning to raise its head within orthodox Christianity. M'Cheyne wrote: "Do not forget the culture of the inner man, I mean of the heart. How

---

3. John Owen, *The Mortification of Sin in Believers*, in *The Works of John Owen* (repr., Edinburgh: Banner of Truth, 1965), 6:14, 9.
4. Owen, *The Mortification of Sin in Believers*, 6:9.

diligently the cavalry officer keeps his sabre clean and sharp. Every stain he rubs off with the greatest care. Remember, you are God's sword, His instrument. In great measure, according to the purity and perfections of the instrument will be the success. It is not great talent God blesses so much as great likeness to Jesus."[5] The Holy Spirit comes to us to help us remove everything that isn't Jesus. Fullness of spiritual life and ever-deepening fellowship with God are impossible apart from mortification.

Third, Paul is reminding us that if we fail to mortify sin, we will cast a dark shadow over our profession to be children of God. Those who are led by the Spirit of God are the sons of God. If we are not led by the Spirit of God to put sin to death in our bodies, then our bodies will become the very instruments that sin uses to disseminate its heinousness, egregiousness, and wickedness.

Mortification does not earn us life in any way; only our Lord Jesus Christ does that. But mortification of sin is one thing we do that proves that our faith is alive. How can we claim to have a living, saving, uniting faith to Jesus Christ without day by day striving to kill the sin that once put our Savior to death?

Four aspects of mortification
Paul tells us four things about the Holy Spirit's beautifying, sanctifying discipline of mortification:

1. Mortification is the believer's obligation. Paul writes, "Therefore, brethren, we are debtors, not to the flesh, to live after the flesh. For if ye live after the flesh, ye shall die: but if ye through the Spirit do mortify the deeds of the body, ye shall live" (vv. 12–13). We are debtors to God, says Paul. We thus are obligated to God to put sin to death in our bodies. Paul also speaks of the believer as a debtor in 1:14—"I am debtor both to the Greeks, and to the Barbarians; both to the wise, and to the unwise." He is saying, in essence: "In order to preach to them, to proclaim to them, to make the

---

5. Robert Murray M'Cheyne, Letter to Daniel Edwards, Oct. 2, 1840, in *Memoirs and Remains of the Rev. Robert Murray M'Cheyne*, ed. Andrew A. Bonar (Dundee: William Middleton, 1845), 243.

gospel known to them, I have an obligation before God. I am a man who has received much, and therefore I must give much."

If you were to ask Paul, "Why do I have an obligation to put sin to death?" his answer might simply be, "the gospel." Mortification is our response to what the grace of God in Jesus Christ has done for us. We owe God everything. He has pardoned our sin. He has united us to His Son. By the grace of God in Jesus Christ, we are the bride of the Son of the Most High God. If our Savior died to put away sin, and if the Spirit has come into our lives to make us the dwelling place of God in the Spirit, then we have an obligation of gratitude to God to kill the sin that killed the Savior. It was for sin and sinners that Christ died.

Thomas Goodwin describes in a most remarkable way the particular and individual sins that were laid upon Christ by the Father. Goodwin may have been echoing Martin Luther's exposition of Galatians 3:13 in writing of the Father saying to the Son: "Be thou Peter that denyer; Paul that persecutor, blasphemer, and cruel oppressor; David that adulterer; that sinner that did eat the apple in paradise."[6] Goodwin was making the point that our sins in their "particularity" were laid on Christ. So when we are reminded of our particular sins, we must remember that it was those sins that killed our Savior and that our Savior atoned for all our particular sins.

If mortification is not rooted in the gospel, however, it becomes legalism at best and Romish superstition at worst. Only the gospel gives birth to true mortification. Owen wrote, "Not to be daily mortifying sin is to sin against the goodness, kindness, wisdom, grace, and love of God."[7]

Is mortification an evangelical obligation in your life? Do you find yourself a debtor to the grace of God that daily constrains you to put sin to death? Is this a grace and a duty that you daily seek to cultivate in your life? We have an obligation to do so.

2. Mortification is the believer's responsibility. Paul writes, "If ye live after the flesh, ye shall die: but if ye through the Spirit do mortify the deeds of the

---

6. Martin Luther, *Commentary on Saint Paul's Epistle to the Galatians* (New York: Robert Carter, 1844), 274–75.
7. Owen, *The Mortification of Sin in Believers*, 6:13.

body, ye shall live." Unlike justification, which is an act of God's free grace, mortification involves our efforts. We are to put to death the misdeeds of the body. We know that we cannot begin to do that without the enabling help of the Holy Spirit. But Paul stresses here that this soul-purifying work demands our activity, not our passivity. We are never to let go and assume that God will do this work for us, for God commands us to give ourselves to killing and rooting out this unwelcome, God-dishonoring, Christ-denying intruder in our lives. We are accountable for this. We are responsible before God.

3. Mortification is the believer's unceasing responsibility. Paul's verb tense here in verses 12–13 stresses that we are to keep on putting to death the deeds of the body. Mortification is not a once-for-all crisis experience; it is a daily and unceasing act. Our Lord Jesus Christ says in Luke 9:23, "If any man will come after me, let him deny himself, and take up his cross daily, and follow me." He did not excuse us from this ongoing work by saying, "You might be a fair-weather disciple or an immature disciple"; rather, the meaning of His words is clear: "If you do not take up your cross and nail yourself and all that you are to it every day, you cannot be My disciple."

That means that until the day we die, we are to wage war against sin in our lives. Sin "will no otherwise die," said Owen, "but by being gradually and constantly weakened; spare it, and it heals its wounds and recovers strength."[8] At times in your life, you might have thought: "Well, by the grace of God and by the goodness of His Spirit, I put that sin to death. I finally laid it in the dust." But soon after you ceased watching and praying about that sin, it began to rear its ugly head once again. Sanctification is a lifelong process; until you take your last breath, you must do battle against the world, the flesh, and the devil.

4. Mortification is carried out by the believer in dependence on the Spirit. "If ye through the Spirit do mortify the deeds of the body, ye shall live," says Paul. Any sin that remains in us has power. It has all the ingenuity of its master, Satan. We do not think enough about the malignant activity of Satan today.

---

8. Owen, *Pneumatologia: Or, A Discourse Concerning the Holy Spirit*, in *Works*, 3:545.

The Lord has given us the Holy Spirit to empower us to overcome any sin that remains within us, and the one who foments that remaining sin is Satan. Paul tells us in verse 26 that the Holy Spirit is our Helper. He is our *sunantilambanetai*, Paul says. That very complex word tells us the following about the Spirit:

The Holy Spirit is our *Sun*; He is together with us, in cooperation with us. He is also *anti*; over and against us. He is together with us and yet over and against us. What is Paul saying? He is telling us that we are actively involved in our mortification, but also that every virtue we possess, every victory we win, and every thought we have of holiness also belong to Him, for it is the Spirit who enables us. The glory is His as the representative of the Holy Trinity. We must cast all of our victories at His feet because they are His victories, not ours.

How the Spirit helps in mortification

How does the Holy Spirit help us put sin to death? We know that the Holy Spirit, by God's grace, has tied us to Jesus Christ. He brings into our lives a new, God-centered nature, a new heart characterized by love for the Lord and a desire to please Him and keep His commandments. But as our Helper, He also enables us to put sin to death and mortify the deeds of the body. There are four ways in which the Spirit does this.

First, He shows us the loveliness of our Savior, Jesus Christ. Through the Holy Scriptures, He reveals to us the greatness, the majesty, the glory, the tenderness, the kindness, the power, and the holiness of Christ. In John 16:14, Jesus promised that when He gave His Spirit to believers, His Spirit would bring glory to Christ. The churches that are most animated by the Spirit are those that bring glory to Jesus Christ.

I live in Cambridge, which is the home of King's College. At night, if you walk through the campus, you can see its magnificent chapel, illuminated by lights. I have never seen anyone walk along King's Parade in Cambridge with his head down, looking at the floodlights and saying, "My, what wonderful wattage." Most people look up at what the light is illuminating.

That is what the Holy Spirit does. He shows us the loveliness of Christ, the multifaceted grace and glory of the Savior, and the excellence of His merited and personal grace. Like Joseph, we say, "When sin rears its ugly, egregious head, how could I do such a thing and sin against such a God?" (see Gen. 39:9). The Holy Spirit helps us see the loveliness of Jesus Christ.

Samuel Rutherford makes this beautiful response to his Savior: "O fair sun, and fair moon, and fair stars, and fair flowers, fair roses, and fair lilies, and fair creatures; but O ten thousand thousand times fairer Lord Jesus!"[9] The Spirit helps us to see how great Christ is and how tawdry and fleeting are the attractions of this world.

Second, the Spirit convinces us of the sinfulness of sin by showing us sin's true colors, its great deceitfulness, and its tragic end. He does this supremely through the Scriptures (Rom. 7:9–11), for the great function of the Holy Law of God is to bring us face to face with God. Goodwin said, "If thou wouldst see what sin is, go to Mount Calvary."[10] Notice that He said Mount Calvary, not Mount Sinai. The Spirit shows us what sin is by leading us through the Scriptures. The Spirit confronts us with the Holy Word of God and the holy standards of a holy God.

Sometimes He comes to us through the loving words of true friends. Think, for example, of David's response to the prophet Nathan's story about a man who had killed his neighbor's only sheep (see 2 Samuel 12). David says in Psalm 51:4, "Against thee, thee only, have I sinned, and done this evil in thy sight." We might object, saying: "David, get a grip on yourself. You have sinned against your wife, your children, and your nation. But against God? What do you mean by that?" David knew what he was saying, for the Holy Spirit had shown him the horrors of his sin. Yes, David had sinned against his wife, children, and nation, but most of all, he had sinned against God. The Spirit comes to us to graciously show us the sinfulness of the sin we commit against our loving God.

Third, the Spirit causes His graces to take root in our lives. Owen wrote: "Growing, thriving, and improving in universal holiness, is the great way of the mortification of sin.... The more we abound in the 'fruits of the Spirit,' the less shall we be concerned in the 'works of the flesh.'... This is

---

9. Samuel Rutherford, "Letter to the Laird of Cally, 1637," in *Letters of Samuel Rutherford*, ed. Andrew A. Bonar (Edinburgh: Oliphant Anderson, 1891), 398.

10. Thomas Goodwin, *Christ the Mediator*, in *The Works of Thomas Goodwin* (repr., Grand Rapids: Reformation Heritage Books, 2006), 5:287.

that which will ruin sin, and without it nothing will contribute anything thereunto."¹¹ The Holy Spirit comes to plant the graces of Christ in our lives. He plants those graces in the inhospitable soil of our hearts where sin still lingers. As those graces are watered by the Word of God, by prayer, by the ministry of God's people, and by the fellowship of the saints, they flourish and squeeze sin out of our lives.

Last, the Spirit gives us courage to put righteousness before sin in our lives. Think of Daniel, Peter, the apostles, and Luther; the Holy Spirit gave each of those men the courage to put truth before consequences and to resist compromise. The Holy Spirit helps us by giving us the grace we need to say no to certain people, certain places, certain television programs, certain literature, and certain Internet sites. But in all of this, the Spirit does not mortify sin without our cooperation. He blesses or prospers our striving, but He does not bless our sloth.

Let us remember that we are not engaged in an unequal battle against sin today, for the One who is in us is greater than the one who is in the world. No remaining sin in us is so ingrained or troublesome that we cannot kill it or mortify it with the Spirit's help.

In conclusion, consider these words from Owen regarding sanctification: "Set faith at work on Christ for the killing of thy sin...and thou wilt die a conqueror; yea, thou wilt, through the good providence of God, live to see thy lust dead at thy feet."[12] Put your faith in Christ, for He is the great sin-killer. Then, too, trust the Spirit of Christ, for He comes and says: "Child of God, we can do it together. The Holy Trinity is for you, and I am here with all the resources of the Holy Trinity to help you."

---

11. Owen, *Pneumatologia*, 3:552–53.
12. Owen, *Mortification of Sin in Believers*, 6:79.

Chapter 9
by Sinclair B. Ferguson

Some Reflections on the "First Title" of the Holy Spirit

In his discussion of the ministry of the Holy Spirit in *The Institutes of the Christian Religion*, John Calvin surprises the reader by noting that "Spirit of adoption" is the "first title" of the Holy Spirit.[1] Calvin was biblical scholar enough to know that this was not true in a chronological sense. Nor can he have meant this in any statistical sense, since the title is *hapax legomenon* in Scripture, occurring only in Romans 8:15.

What Calvin evidently has in view is that "Spirit of adoption" is the supreme description of the Spirit's identity in terms of His ministry to the Christian. In all likelihood this reflects both his use of *adoptio* as the most comprehensive New Testament description of what it means to be a Christian, and also his sense that, to use an expression of John Murray, adoption itself is "the apex of grace and privilege."[2]

From the early centuries Christian theologians have insisted that the so called *opera ad extra Trinitatis* (the works of God the Trinity beyond His own inbeing) are always the actions of the whole Godhead, each person

---

1. John Calvin, *The Institutes of the Christian Religion*, ed. John T. McNeill, trans. Ford Lewis Battles (Philadelphia: Westminster Press, 1960), 3.1.3.

In contributing these brief reflections to this festschrift for Geoff Thomas, whose friendship and encouragement I have long prized, I share with other colleagues admiration for his long ministry at Alfred Place Baptist Church, Aberystwyth, Wales, and deep gratitude to God for his friendship and encouragement, and rejoice in the measure in which he himself has experienced and enjoyed life in the Son, the love of the heavenly Father, and the witness of the Spirit of sonship leading him to cry, "Abba, Father!"

2. John Murray, *Redemption—Accomplished and Applied* (1955; repr., Edinburgh: Banner of Truth, 2009), 127. Cf. the comments by James Buchanan, "The privilege of adoption presupposes pardon and acceptance, but is higher than either." James Buchanan, *The Doctrine of Justification* (Edinburgh: Banner of Truth, 1961), 263.

being involved in some dimension or aspect. This is doubtless also true of our adoption into God's family: it takes place in Christ, and is the fruit of the Spirit's work in us. But adoption itself is an act specifically appropriated to Himself by God the Father. He is the One who adopts. Like justification it is a legal act—the individual's status is changed. But this transition is not now from condemnation to justification by the pronouncement of a Judge. It is a transition from being a child of wrath and Satan to being regarded as a child of God—it is a familial action accomplished only by a Father.

The individual believer's adoption as a son (*huiothesia*: literally, being placed as a son) is a distinctively New Testament privilege. Jewish law did not quite possess this concept, since in some senses all that adoption might effect for the benefit of a child was already built into the nature of Old Testament family relationships. It is probable, therefore, that Paul derived his metaphor from Roman law where the concept did exist.[3] Significantly the occurrence of the term in the New Testament is restricted to letters written to Rome and Romanized areas, such as Galatia and Ephesus.

This said, Paul does see "adoption" as a lens through which the old covenant community as a whole can be described. To his kinsmen, the Israelites, "belong the adoption" (Rom. 9:4). In fact, it is mentioned first in the list of blessings they have received. And while it is the communal adoption of the people as a whole Paul has in view here,[4] it may well be that he uses it as a summation of all the blessings of God's people Israel. But the realization of individual adoption as such, with all of its privileges, awaited the full revelation of God in His triune nature as Father, Son, and Holy Spirit.[5] Only when the Father is known through the Son by the Holy Spirit is adoption a fully coherent notion.[6]

---

3. Cf., among others, Francis Lyall, *Slaves, Citizens and Sons: Legal Metaphors in the Epistles* (Grand Rapids: Academie Books, 1984), 81–99.

4. Cf. the picture Ezekiel paints in Ezekiel 16:1ff.

5. It is noteworthy that the few references to adoption (Rom. 8:15, 23; Gal. 4:5; Eph. 1:5) are all set within the context of letters and are not only addressed to areas under Roman rule, but are set within deeply trinitarian contexts.

6. A simple contrast supports this distinction. The three chapters of Matthew comprising the Sermon on the Mount contain many more references to the believer knowing God as his or her heavenly Father than the entire Old Testament.

Paul speaks about the "Spirit of sonship"[7] as such in only one place, Romans 8:14–17. But in Galatians 4:5–6 there is a clear parallelism to his later thought. If there is a difference it is that in Romans Paul's perspective deals with experiential situations and needs while in Galatians 3 and 4 his perspective is redemptive-historical.

Here we have space for only a few suggestive reflections.

The Spirit of Sonship and the "Spirit of Bondage"

The Spirit of sonship is contrasted with the "spirit of bondage" in Romans 8:15. The text presents several exegetical issues: (1) Is the reference to *pneuma* (spirit) the same in both expressions? (2) Are either or both references to the human spirit or to the Holy Spirit? In the Reformed tradition a considerable number of earlier pastor-theologians assumed that the reference was to the Holy Spirit (or at least to the fruit of His ministry) in both instances: the Spirit brings conviction of sin (the "spirit of bondage") and then freedom in the new sense of sonship enjoyed by the regenerate.[8] Before an individual becomes a believer the "(S)pirit of bondage" prevails: the internal disposition of the individual in relationship to God is one of fear and restrictiveness. It is well illustrated in different ways in each of the sons in the Parable of the Prodigal Son: first in the case of the younger son, in his rehearsed speech, "And [I] am no more worthy to be called thy son: make me as one of thy hired servants" (Luke 15:19). He sees slavery as his destiny, but is granted sonship as a gift. Similarly, the elder brother complains "These many years do I serve thee ('all these years I have been slaving for you,' NIV)…and yet thou never gavest me…" (Luke 15:29). Despite the fact that everything the father had to offer was his, he knew only a "spirit of bondage."

However this issue is resolved, in the act of adoption the believer is introduced into a wonderful new status in Christ and receives "the Spirit of

---

7. "Sonship" not because of any gender prejudice on the part of Paul, but because in antiquity—and indeed until relatively recently in English law, it was only sons (not daughters) who inherited—as the underlying plot-line of Jane Austen's famous *Pride and Prejudice* indicates.

8. See Sinclair B. Ferguson, "The Spirit of Bondage," *The Banner of Truth*, no. 156 (Sept. 1976): 1–10.

sonship." Through the Spirit (by way of analogy with Galatians 4:6) believers cry "Abba, Father."

But what are the implications of the Spirit's ministry to us in this capacity?

The Cry, "Abba, Father"

Some commentators take the believer's cry, "Abba, Father," to be to a corporate, liturgical, or charismatic moment in the life of the Christian assembly, suggesting that it is expressive of a charismatic outbreak of praise, an outburst of response to the gospel, or even a saying of the Lord's prayer, the "Our Father."

But Paul gives us an important clue to an interpretation more suited to the context. It lies in his use of the onomatopoeic verb *krazein*, expressing a loud cry, a sharp cry of pain and need. It is thus used in the Septuagint,[9] for example in Psalm 34:6, "This poor man cried, and the LORD heard...." It is later used in the Gospels of the cries for mercy of blind men (Matt. 9:27) and of our Lord's own loud cry on the cross (Matt. 27:50). Its context is certainly not limited to the liturgy of the church but extends to the experiences of misery, pain, shock, and need that may characterize the individual Christian life.

What Paul here underlines is that the consciousness that we are the children of God which comes to expression in this filial cry of need is not reserved for outstandingly mature believers at the height of their spiritual powers but for all believers, and it comes to expression not only in the heights of spiritual ecstasy but in the depths of their need. It is a cry *de profundis* (from the depths), which wonderfully, if paradoxically, expresses a subconscious, "deep-down" awareness of the heights of privilege and honor—"I am a child of God and call out to Him as my Father!"

The significance of this aspect of the Spirit's ministry should not be lost on us. Paul is here pointing to a deep experiential anchor of the believer's assurance. Just as a little boy who has tripped and fallen painfully instinctively cries "Daddy!" because of the deep consciousness of his relationship to his father, so it is with the believer. The emergence of the cry, "Abba,

---

9. The Greek translation of the Old Testament.

Father" is the supreme illustration of the deep-down knowledge the Christian has of his or her true status in Christ.

The non-Christian may be capable of reciting the Lord's Prayer, but will never instinctively cry out, "Abba, Father," in times of stress and pressure, of sorrow and pain. At best the words, "O God," or the like form on his lips.

In this sense, John Murray was right to say, "The consciousness of the believer differs by a whole diameter from that of the unbeliever. At the lowest ebb of faith and hope and love his consciousness never drops to the level of the unbeliever at its highest pitch of confidence and assurance."[10]

The reason is that God is the redeeming and adopting Father of the former and has a fatherly desire for His children to be conscious of the gracious relationship they have with Him. Rather than break the bruised reed or quench the dimly burning wick, the Lord grants an assurance—a consciousness that cannot be erased or finally destroyed by trials. And this consciousness comes to the surface precisely in the midst of trials in the manner in which the Christian's deepest cry of need gives clearest expression to his awareness that he is nothing less than a son of the heavenly Father.

The Witness of the Spirit

Paul provides a further analysis of this cry. In it the Spirit is bearing witness with our spirits that we are God's sons. Two interpretive issues arise here.

Who is said to cry "Abba, Father"?
In Galatians 4:6 Paul states that "Because ye are sons, God hath sent the *Spirit of his Son* into your hearts, *crying* Abba Father." Here it appears that the cry, "Abba, Father," is uttered by the Spirit. In the parallel passage in Romans 8:15 it is clearly the believer who cries, "Abba, Father": "ye have received the Spirit of adoption, whereby *we cry* Abba, Father."

Are there then two different cries? Or is there a resolution to this paradox? In my own view a hint towards the solution lies in Paul's parallel thinking in connection with our confession of Christ.

---

10. John Murray, *The Collected Writings of John Murray* (Edinburgh: Banner of Truth, 1976), 2:265.

"No man can say that Jesus is the Lord, but by the Holy Ghost" (1 Cor. 12:3). In this context the believer's confessional cry, "Jesus is Lord," is possible only through the concursive ministry of the Spirit in the believer. The Spirit bears His witness to Jesus as Lord (John 16:13–14), but I am the one who cries "Jesus is Lord." The witness of the Spirit is not distinguishable from my witness.

In the same way, the implicit confession, "I am your child," expressed in the cry, "Abba, Father!" is made by believers, but only through the concursive operation of the Spirit in their hearts. As Benjamin B. Warfield well puts it, "Distinct in its source, it is yet delivered confluently with the testimony of our human consciousness."[11]

Commentators have rightly noted the background to Paul's statement may lie in the principle that testimony needs to be established in the mouth of two witnesses if it is to be allowed in court.[12] Both the spirit of the believer and the Spirit who indwells the believer give conjoint testimony in the single cry of the believer, "Abba, Father." It is this that then confirms for the believer the assurance of being a child of God.

Does the Spirit bear witness "with" or "to" our spirits?
Some commentators have argued vigorously that Paul must here be thinking of the Spirit's witness *to* our spirits. That, after all, is the assurance we need—a testimony: "I authenticate you as a genuine child of God." Among modern scholars no one has argued this position more forcefully than C. E. B. Cranfield. He argues that the witness of the Spirit is not conjoint *with* our own witness but a witness given *to* our spirits by God's Spirit. He seems to view this exegesis as being theologically confirmed by his answer to the question: "What standing has our spirit in *this* matter? Of itself it surely has no right at all to testify to our being sons of God."[13]

But this surely confuses two things, namely (1) the authority of God by whom alone an individual is counted a son of God, and (2) the consciousness the believer has, on the basis of the gospel, that he or she is in fact a

---

11. B. B. Warfield, *Faith and Life* (New York: Longmans, Green, and Co., 1916), 185.
12. Deut. 19:15. Hence the significance in Jesus' trial of Matthew 26:60 and Mark 14:59.
13. C.E.B. Cranfield, *Commentary on Romans* (Edinburgh: T and T Clark, 1975), 1:403.

son of God. For if the believer has a properly grounded *consciousness* he is a son of God, and a recognition that this status is not based on his opinion but on God's promise, then he has in fact the God-given privilege of expressing this consciousness in saying, in whatever words, "I am a son of God." Indeed one might say that not to do so would be more an expression of unbelief than of faith.

Furthermore, throughout this section of Romans 8 Paul uses a series of compound words with the prefix *sun* (together with): *sugklēronomoi* (v. 17: heirs together with); *sustenazei kai sunōdinai* (v. 22: groaning together in the pains of childbirth—groaning and travailing together); *sunantilambanetai* (v. 26: helps together with); v. 28: *sunergai* (works together). It is likely therefore that this refrain of things happening or being accomplished "together with" should influence our understanding of the Spirit's witness and *summarturei* (v. 16: bears witness with) should be translated "witnesses *along with*" and not "witnesses *to*." Yes, our spirit's testimony may be shaky at times, especially in times of stress and pain. But in the moment of deepest weakness this cry, "Abba, Father," is both a summons for help and an expression of the deep-down conviction, "I am a child of the heavenly Father."

John Owen well captures what this means in practice when he writes:

> Now, sometimes the soul because it hath somewhat remaining in it of the principle that it had in its old condition, is put to the question whether it be a child of God or no; and thereupon, as in a thing of the greatest importance, puts in its claim, with all the evidences that it hath to make good its title. The Spirit comes and bears witness in this case.
>
> An allusion it is to judicial proceedings in points of titles and evidences. The judge being set, the person concerned lays his claim, produceth his evidences, and pleads them; his adversaries endeavouring all that in them lies to invalidate them, and disannul his pleas, and to cast him in his claim. In the midst of the trial, a person of known and approved integrity comes into the court, and gives testimony fully and directly on the behalf of the claimer; which stops the mouths of all his adversaries, and fills the man that pleaded with joy and satisfaction. So it is in this case.... When our spirits are pleading their right and title, he comes in and bears witness on our side; at the same time

enabling us to put forth acts of filial obedience, kind and childlike; which is called "crying, Abba, Father."[14]

And Charles Hodge, although he slips in stating that the Spirit is called Spirit of sonship "because he adopts" is surely right to say, "How this is done we cannot fully understand, any more than we can understand the mode in which he produces any other effect on our mind."[15]

The Spirit of the Son and the Spirit of Sonship

A final reflection is worth offering here. We have noted that Galatians 4:1–6 and Romans 8:14–17 are in several respects parallel to each other:

Galatians 4:1–6	**Romans 8:14–17**
We were *enslaved*	The *spirit of slavery* to fall back into fear
God has sent the Spirit of his Son	*You have received* the Spirit of adoption as sons
The *Spirit of his Son*	The *Spirit of adoption as sons* by whom
crying *"Abba, Father!"*	*we cry "Abba, Father!"*

Of interest here in these parallels is a further distinction: in Romans the Spirit is described as "the Spirit of adoption as sons" while earlier in Galatians Paul had called him "the Spirit of his Son." Through the Spirit of adoption/the Spirit of his Son comes the cry "Abba, Father!"

For Paul, it seems, the Spirit of adoption is to be thought of precisely as the Spirit of the Son. In other words, the Spirit of adoption in the believer who brings him a consciousness that he is a child of God is one and the same Spirit as the Spirit who exercised an indwelling and empowering ministry in the life of the Lord Jesus. Set against the background of the New Testament's insistence that there is "one Spirit," this, surely, is a truth of staggering proportions. He who enabled the Son to cry "Abba, Father!" is the one who

---

14. John Owen, *The Works of John Owen*, ed. W. H. Goold (Edinburgh: Johnstone & Hunter, 1850–1853), 2:241–42. Interestingly Owen goes on in this context to compare the Spirit's witness to Jesus' action in stilling the storm on Galilee, described in Matthew 8:25–27. This was the very passage which had been the means of his own assurance through the sermon of an unknown preacher who had substituted for the great Edmund Calamy whom he had gone to hear preach at Aldermanbury Chapel in London.

15. Charles Hodge, *Commentary on Romans* (1864; repr., Edinburgh: Banner of Truth, 1986), 266–67.

indwells believers as they cry "Abba, Father!" He is not merely sent *from* the Son; He comes to us in His specific identity as the Spirit of the Son.

What is implied here is that the Spirit who indwells believers is the One who first indwelled the incarnate Son, being constantly present with Him from the moment of His conception (Luke 1:35), through His growth in wisdom (Luke 2:52, cf. Isa. 11:1–2), His baptism (Luke 3:22), temptations (Luke 4:1), ministry in word and deed (Luke 4:18–19), in His joy (Luke 10:21), empowering His miracles (Luke 11:20—"finger of God" = Spirit [Matt. 12:28]). To this catena of Lukan passages we may add testimony to the Spirit's empowering in Jesus' death (Heb. 9:14) and His resurrection (Rom. 1:4).

This is the Spirit Jesus promised to send from the Father in order that His disciples would not be left as "orphans" (John 14:18). The new covenant identity of the Spirit, and therefore the specific identity and capacity in which He comes to believers now is that He is the Spirit of the incarnate, crucified, risen, reigning Son. Christ was not only empowered by Him, but on His ascension specifically asked the Father that He might be sent to us (John 14:16), and, in perhaps the least emphasized aspect of the work of Christ, "being by the right hand of God exalted, *and having received of the Father the promise of the Holy Ghost*, he hath shed forth this, which ye now see and hear" (Acts 2:33).[16] The Son's final "transaction" in fulfilling the mandate of His incarnation was to ask for, and to receive, the gifting of His own Spirit, His incarnation-companion, for all believers. We are therefore able to cry, "Abba, Father!" as He did, because we are possessed by the Spirit who possessed and was possessed by the Son. There is no deification implied here, but rather a glorious indwelling in which the believer's individual identity is never lost and the Creator-creature distinction never transgressed.

Earlier in Romans 8:9–11 Paul had set up the parameters of his thinking:

- You, however, are not in the flesh but in the Spirit, if in fact the Spirit of God dwells in you.

---

16. Doubtless here there is also a fulfillment of Ps. 2:8, "Ask of me, and I shall give thee the heathen for thine inheritance, and the uttermost parts of the earth for thy possession." But our interest here lies in the other aspect of the Pentecost event.

- Anyone who does not have the Spirit of Christ does not belong to Him.
- But if Christ is in you, the body is dead because of sin; the Spirit is life because of righteousness.
- If the Spirit of Him who raised Jesus from the dead dwells in you, He who raised Jesus from the dead will give life to your mortal bodies through the Spirit who dwells in you.

The Holy Spirit is the Spirit of God. As such He is the Spirit of the Father. He is also the Spirit of Christ the Son. As the Spirit of the One who raised Jesus from the dead He indwells us. This is one and the same reality as Christ indwelling us.[17]

Paul is not here confusing the persons of the Trinity, but rather indicating that the intimacy of the relationship between Christ and the Spirit in the course of the incarnation means that the Spirit who indwells the believer does so in a manner that is economically indistinguishable from the indwelling of Christ.

Moreover, He is the "one Spirit." There are not two Spirits, the one who indwelt the Son and the one who indwells believers. No, our spirits are one with Christ (1 Cor. 6:17) through the bond of union effected by the indwelling of the Spirit of the Son in those He has made sons and joint heirs with Him (Rom. 8:17).

Again, there are not many Spirits, the one who indwells one believer and the many who indwell other believers. This is why we are not only sons of God, brothers of Christ (John 20:17), but also in the deepest sense members of one another, children in the same family, indwelt by the Spirit by whom each of us cries, "Abba, Father!"

Here, then, is the reason why the title "Spirit of sonship" is truly "the first title" of the Holy Spirit. This is why we can sing with Charles Wesley, whose brother John was taught by their dying father, "The inward witness, son, the inward witness; this is the proof, the strongest proof, of Christianity".[18]

---

17. Further, it seems to be this that Christ has in view when He says, "If a man love me, he will keep my words: and my Father will love him, and we will come unto him, and make our abode with him" (John 14:23).

18. John Wesley, letter to John Smith, March 22, 1748, in *The Works of the Rev. John Wesley* (London: Wesleyan Conference Office, 1872), 12:98.

> *My God is reconciled; His pardoning voice I hear;*
> *He owns me for His child; I can no longer fear:*
> *With confidence I now draw nigh,*
> *With confidence I now draw nigh,*
> *And "Father, Abba, Father," cry.*

And with Henry Francis Lyte:

> *Think what Spirit dwells within thee,*
> *What a Father's smile is thine,*
> *What thy Saviour died to win thee,*
> *Child of heaven, should'st thou repine?*

Chapter 10
by Michael A. G. Haykin

John Owen on the Spirit's Ministry in Guarding the Believer's Heart

One of the most remarkable Christian ministries in the history of the church was that of the eighteenth-century evangelist George Whitefield (1714–1770).[1] In the thirty-five years between his conversion in Oxford, England, in 1735 and his death in Newburyport, Massachusetts, it is calculated that he preached around eighteen thousand sermons. That works out to about 514 sermons a year! Moreover, many of his sermons were delivered to congregations that numbered ten thousand or so, and some to audiences possibly as large as twenty thousand.[2] In addition to his preaching throughout the length and breadth of England, he regularly ministered in Wales, visited Ireland twice, and journeyed fourteen times to Scotland. He made seven trips to America and preached in virtually every major town on the Atlantic Seaboard.[3] And this was in a day when going on a twenty-mile excursion from one's home was considered a significant undertaking.

---

1. It is a distinct privilege to contribute this essay to a festschrift for my esteemed brother Geoff Thomas. The memory of fellowship with him over the years, going back to the Canadian Carey Conference in the 1980s, is precious. While the times we have seen one another have not been numerous, I can say that his ministry has given a different course to my life on two very distinct occasions, and I am deeply thankful to God for such a brother in the gospel.
   Portions of this essay will appear in Matthew Barrett and Michael A. G. Haykin, *Owen on the Christian Life: Living for the Glory of God in Christ* (Wheaton, Ill.: Crossway, 2014). Used by permission.
2. For the numbers, see Arnold Dallimore, *George Whitefield: The Life and Times of the Great Evangelist of the Eighteenth-Century Revival* (Westchester, Ill.: Cornerstone Books, 1979 and 1980), 1:263, 267, 295–96; 2:522–23.
3. He was in America in 1738, 1739–1741, 1744–1748, 1751–1752, 1754–1755, 1763–1765, and 1769–1770.

What did all of those words and all of that travel amount to? In the hands of the Holy Spirit, they were a catalyst for revival. Whitefield played a key role in the transformation of the British culture and society on both sides of the Atlantic during what is called the Evangelical Revival of the eighteenth century or the First Great Awakening. From a different vantage point, that of the individuals who listened to him, his preaching was used to bring about the personal conversion of tens of thousands of men and women. Among them was the Baptist preacher and hymnwriter Robert Robinson (1735–1790).

Awakened to his sinful state under Whitefield's preaching in the summer of 1752, Robinson became a Christian two weeks before Christmas 1755, and subsequently wrote that quintessential evangelical hymn, "Come, Thou Fount of Every Blessing," to celebrate God's work of grace in his life.[4] After a short career as a Methodist preacher, Robinson went on to build a thriving work at St. Andrew's Street Baptist Church, Cambridge, where he became known as one of the finest evangelical preachers in England.

Toward the end of his life, though, Robinson underwent a season of spiritual declension. The story is told about a certain occasion during this time when Robinson was travelling in a stagecoach with one other passenger who happened to be a lady. As Robinson and the lady began to converse, the subject of hymns came up. The woman started to testify to the great spiritual blessing that "Come, Thou Fount of Every Blessing" had been to her, little knowing that she was speaking to the author of the hymn. Suddenly Robinson burst out, "Madam, I am the unhappy man who composed that hymn many years ago, and I would give a thousand worlds, if I had them, to enjoy the feelings I had then!"[5]

---

4. For the story of his conversion, see Andrew Fuller, "Anecdote," *The Evangelical Magazine*, 2 (1794): 72–73. Fuller had received this account of Robinson's conversion from Robinson himself. The story was written under the name of "Gaius," a pen name that Fuller regularly used. For a study of "Come, Thou Fount of Every Blessing," see Michael A. G. Haykin, "'Come, Thou Fount of Every Blessing': Robert Robinson's Hymnic Celebration of Sovereign Grace," in Steve West, ed., *Ministry of Grace: Essays in Honor of John G. Reisinger* (Frederick, Md.: New Covenant Media, 2007), 31–43.

5. Cited in Graham W. Hughes, *With Freedom Fired: The Story of Robert Robinson, Cambridge Nonconformist* (London: Carey Kingsgate Press, 1955), 106.

There is some evidence, though not conclusive, that Robinson's thinking was impacted by the eighteenth-century's abounding confidence in human reason and, thus, in his final years, he began to entertain doubt about the veracity of that central tenet of the Christian faith, the doctrine of the Trinity. He also became deeply engrossed in various political debates of the day, which may well have had a negative effect on his spiritual life.

Keep your heart with all vigilance
Whatever the reasons for Robinson's declension, however, the ultimate place of failure in his life lay within his heart. As Proverbs 4:23 admonishes: "Keep thy heart with all diligence; for out of it are the issues of life." Our Lord Jesus similarly reminded His Jewish hearers during His earthly ministry—and us, through the inspired transcription of His reminder—that it is not the foods that go into a person that cause spiritual defilement, but what comes out of a person's heart, "for from within, out of the heart of men, proceed evil thoughts, adulteries, fornications, murders, thefts, covetousness, wickedness, deceit, lasciviousness, an evil eye, blasphemy, pride, [and] foolishness" (Mark 7:20–22). Quite differently from the popular parlance of modern Western culture, which depicts the heart primarily as the center of love and emotions, in biblical anthropology the heart is regarded as the source of a person's entire being and that which determines the total shape of his or her life.[6] The Puritan John Owen (1616–1683), whose teaching on the keeping of the heart will occupy much of what follows, noted that while the word *heart* is used in various ways in the Scriptures, "it denotes the whole soul of man and all the faculties of it, not absolutely, but as they are all one principle of moral operations."[7] Hence, it is vital to keep the heart pure, lest, it being defiled, it pollute the entirety of one's being and life.

---

6. For this understanding of the heart, see B. O. Banwell, "Heart," in D. R. W. Wood *et al*, eds., *New Bible Dictionary*, 3rd ed. (Leicester: InterVarsity Press/Downers Grove, Ill.: InterVarsity Press, 1996), 456, and J. M. Lower, "Heart," in Merrill C. Tenney and Moisés Silva, eds., *The Zondervan Encyclopedia of the Bible* (Grand Rapids: Zondervan, 2009), 3:71–72.

7. John Owen, *The Nature, Power, Deceit, and Prevalency of the Remainders of Indwelling Sin in Believers* in *The Works of John Owen*, ed. W. H. Goold (1850–1853; repr., London: Banner of Truth, 1967), 6:170. Subsequent references to the works of Owen are cited simply according to the volumes and page numbers of this edition.

From a biblical standpoint, the immediate causes of the spiritual pollution of the heart are numerous. For instance, in the parable of the sower, or the four soils, as it is sometimes now denominated, Jesus speaks of "the care of this world"—undue anxiety about the multitude of things that have to be done simply to live in this world—and "the deceitfulness of riches"— the unfettered and, frankly, idolatrous pursuit of wealth and possessions (Matt 13:22). In the narratives about the kings of Israel, it was pride—an utterly foolish sense of self-sufficiency—that led two good kings, Uzziah and Hezekiah, to stray from the Lord (see 2 Chron. 26:16; 32:25). One of the writers of Proverbs is concerned lest the one he is seeking to mentor entertains inappropriate thoughts about the wife of another man—"lust not after her beauty in thine heart," he warns him (Prov. 6:25). And the apostle Paul, in his advice to Timothy, urges him to "flee...youthful lusts," that is, the tendency of some young men to be strongly opinionated and argumentative due to their being enamored of their own views (2 Tim. 2:22). The Bible, of course, knows of numerous other reasons for spiritual declension and decline, as is evident in the sins that Jesus enumerates in Mark 7 and in other lists found in the Scriptures.[8]

The Holy Spirit works in us and with us

Thanks be to God, though, the Bible not only lists ways in which our hearts can be spiritually defiled, but it also describes means by which we can keep our hearts pure. In the history of the church, there have been various interpretations of these means of "heart-keeping," that is, various ways in which the disciplines of the Christian life have been understood. One of the best and most biblical is the tradition of the late sixteenth- and seventeenth-century Puritans—which our dear brother Geoff Thomas has done much to recommend.[9] In what follows, the thought of one of these Puritans,

---

8. See, for example, 1 Corinthians 6:9–10; Galatians 5:19–21; and Colossians 3:5–6, 8–9.

9. It is vital to realize that a concern for biblical piety lies at the very core of English Puritanism. See Irvonwy Morgan, *Puritan Spirituality* (London: Epworth Press, 1973), 53–65, especially 60; Dewey D. Wallace Jr., *The Spirituality of the Later English Puritans: An Anthology* (Macon, Ga.: Mercer University Press, 1987), xi–xiv; J. I. Packer, *A Quest for Godliness. The Puritan Vision of the Christian Life* (Wheaton, Ill.: Crossway Books, 1990), 37–38.

Owen, the "Calvin of England,"[10] is especially examined as it relates to the work of the Holy Spirit in keeping the believer's heart. Roger Nicole has described Owen as "the greatest divine who ever wrote in English," and J. I. Packer says of him that during his career as a Christian theologian he was "England's foremost bastion and champion of Reformed evangelical orthodoxy."[11] But, as will be seen, Owen's chief interest was not in producing theological treatises for their own sake, but to advance the personal holiness of God's people.[12]

After the close of the British Civil Wars (1642–1651), Owen was appointed to the oversight of Oxford University as its vice chancellor. From this position, Owen helped to reassemble the faculty, who had been dispersed by the wars, and sought to put the university back on its feet. He also had numerous opportunities to preach to the students at Oxford. Two important works on holiness came out of his preaching during this period.

Of Temptation, first published in 1658, is essentially an exposition of Matthew 26:41 ("Watch and pray, that ye enter not into temptation"). Owen enumerates four seasons in which believers must exercise special care that temptation not lead them away into sin: times of outward prosperity, times of spiritual coldness and formality, times when one has enjoyed rich fellowship with God, and times of self-confidence, as in Peter's affirmation to Christ, "I will not deny thee" (Mark 14:31). The remedy that Owen emphasizes is prayer. Typical of Puritan pithiness is his remark in this regard: "If we do not abide in prayer, we shall abide in cursed temptations."[13] The second work,

---

10. Allen C. Guelzo, "John Owen, Puritan Pacesetter," *Christianity Today*, 20, no. 17 (May 21, 1976):14. For a good account of Owen's life, see Peter Toon, *God's Statesman: The Life and Work of John Owen* (Exeter: Paternoster Press, 1971). For his theology, the best study is Carl R. Trueman, *The Claims of Truth: John Owen's Trinitarian Theology* (Carlisle, Cumbria: Paternoster Press, 1998). See also Sinclair B. Ferguson, *John Owen on the Christian Life* (Edinburgh: Banner of Truth, 1987); Robert W. Oliver, ed., *John Owen—The Man and His Theology. Papers Read at the Conference of the John Owen Centre for Theological Study September 2000* (Darlington: Evangelical Press, 2002); Kelly M. Kapic and Mark Jones, eds., *The Ashgate Companion to John Owen's Theology* (Farnham, Surrey/Burlington, Vt.: Ashgate Publishing, 2012).

11. Roger Nicole, cited in Guelzo, "John Owen," 14; Packer, *Quest for Godliness*, 81.

12. Guelzo, "John Owen," 15–16.

13. Owen, *Works*, 6:126.

The Mortification of Sin in Believers (1656), is based on Romans 8:13 and lays out a strategy for fighting indwelling sin and warding off temptation.

In 1667, a third treatise on this subject of keeping of the heart, *The Nature, Power, Deceit, and Prevalency of the Remainders of Indwelling Sin in Believers*, appeared. This volume was based on Romans 7:21 ("I find then a law, that, when I would do good, evil is present with me"). Owen shows how sin lies at the heart of even the best of believers' lives, and, if not resisted by prayer and meditation, slowly but surely eats away zeal for and delight in the things of God.

In some ways, *Of the Mortification of Sin in Believers* is the richest of Owen's treatises on this subject of holiness and "heart-keeping."[14] This book began life as a series of sermons in which Owen undertook a close analysis and explanation of Romans 8:13. For Owen, this text made it abundantly clear that the believer has a constant duty to put to death the sin that still indwells his mortal frame.[15] But equally important for Owen was the fact that this verse revealed that such a duty is possible only in the strength that the Holy Spirit supplies, for he alone is "sufficient for this work."[16] Just as regeneration and true intercession are impossible without the Spirit, so mortification of sin can be performed only by the Spirit.

> All other ways of mortification are vain, all helps leave us helpless; it must be done by the Spirit. Men, as the apostle intimates, Romans 9:30–32, may attempt this work on other principles, by means and advantages administered on other accounts, as they always have done, and do: but, saith he, "This is the work of the Spirit; by him alone is it to be wrought, and by no other power is it to be brought about."[17]

---

14. For a contemporary presentation of the same truths that Owen sets forth in this treatise, see Kris Lundgaard, *The Enemy Within: Straight Talk about the Power and Defeat of Sin* (Phillipsburg, N.J.: P&R Publishing, 1998). For studies of Owen on mortification, see especially Randall C. Gleason, *John Calvin and John Owen on Mortification: A Comparative Study in Reformed Spirituality* (New York: Peter Lang, 1995), especially 79–136; and the introduction and notes by Kelly M. Kapic and Justin Taylor in their edition of John Owen, *Overcoming Sin & Temptation* (Wheaton, Ill.: Crossway, 2006).
15. Owen, *Works*, 6:5, 8, 9–16.
16. Owen, *Works*, 6:16.
17. Owen, *Works*, 6:7.

Owen adduced two reasons for this assertion that the Spirit alone can mortify sin.[18] First, according to a number of Old Testament texts, such as Ezekiel 11:19 and 36:26, God the Father promised the gift of the Holy Spirit for the removal of "stubborn, proud, rebellious, unbelieving" hearts, which Owen saw as a description of the work of mortification. Second, the mortification of sin within the believer comes as a gift from Christ. But it is only through the Holy Spirit that any of Christ's gifts can be actually communicated to believers. As Owen wrote, "All communications of supplies and relief, in the beginnings, increasings, actings of any grace whatever, from him [i.e. Christ], are by the Spirit, by whom he alone works in and upon believers."[19] In support of this statement, Owen proceeded to cite Acts 5:31 and 2:33, which, when taken together, bring to light the fact that repentance (which Owen took to include mortification) issues from Christ and is made a reality by His Holy Spirit.

Owen's emphasis on the fact that only the Spirit is sufficient for the work of mortification should not be taken to mean, however, that he was of the opinion that the believer should be entirely passive with regard to mortification and expect the Spirit to sanctify him without any struggle on his part against sin. Owen took very seriously the reality of the exhortation "if *ye*...do mortify the deeds of the body" (Rom. 8:13). In his exposition of this Pauline text, Owen was thus careful to maintain that it is a duty laid upon every believer to make his daily business the putting to death of indwelling sin.[20]

Owen, however, was also concerned lest Christians fall into errors similar to those made by some in the monastic tradition, who supposed that mortification of the human body was equivalent to mortification of sin.[21] Some of the early monks, as well as the Roman Catholic Church of Owen's day and even some professing Protestants, not only adopted ways and means of mortification that God had not prescribed (for instance, hair shirts and penance), but also regarded those means appointed by God (such as prayer, fasting, and meditation) as an end in themselves. Consequently,

---

18. Owen, *Works*, 6:18.
19. Owen, *Works*, 6:19.
20. Owen, *Works*, 6:7–8, 9–16.
21. Owen, *Works*, 6:17–18.

they looked solely to these means to put sin to death, and in doing so, ignored the Spirit, the fountain of all holiness and the ultimate guardian of the hearts of God's people.[22] Against such a practice, Owen contended that without the Spirit "all ways and means…are as a thing of nought."[23] Rather, the truth of the matter is that:

> The Holy Spirit doth not so work our mortification in us as not to keep it still an act of our obedience. The Holy Ghost works in us and upon us, as we are fit to be wrought in and upon; that is, so as to preserve our own liberty and free obedience. He works upon our understandings, wills, consciences, and affections, agreeably to their own natures; he works in us and with us, not against us or without us; so that his assistance is an encouragement as to the facilitating of the work, and no occasion of neglect as to the work itself.[24]

From the same perspective, Owen later asserted in his magisterial work on the Holy Spirit that the "Holy Spirit is the author of this work [of mortification] in us, so that although it is our duty, it is his grace and strength whereby it is performed."[25] As proof of this assertion, Owen pointed to Romans 8:13.[26]

Nine directions to keep the heart

In typical Puritan fashion, Owen provided his readers with a concrete series of nine directions on how exactly Christians can best fight sin. First, he stated that the believer should consider whether the sin he or she is seeking to kill displays especially dangerous symptoms. For instance, the "frequency of success in sin's seduction, in obtaining the prevailing consent of the will," is indicative of spiritual ill health. Does the believer find himself or herself frequently and readily giving into the sin? Another dangerous symptom is that the believer avoids the sin only out of a fear of punishment. The

---

22. Owen, *Works*, 6:17–18. See also Owen, *Works*, 3:549: "The foundation of all mortification of sin is from the inhabitation of the Spirit in us."
23. Owen, *Works*, 5:16. See also Owen, *Works*, 5:34.
24. Owen, *Works*, 6:20. See also the comments of J. I. Packer, "'Keswick' and the Reformed Doctrine of Sanctification," *The Evangelical Quarterly*, 27 (1955):156.
25. Owen, *Works*, 3:547.
26. Owen, *Works*, 3:547–48.

believer should fight sin out of an abhorrence of sin *as sin* and a conviction that communion with God is too precious a treasure to be lost.[27] In other words, we are "to cultivate the same hatred of sin that God possesses."[28]

Second, Owen recommended that the believer get "a clear and abiding sense upon [the] mind of the guilt, danger, and evil" of the particular sin that he or she is fighting. For example, Owen urged Christians to think seriously about some of the evils entailed by allowing unmortified sin to exist in their lives. Christ is wounded afresh when believers harbor sin that He came to destroy. His "tender and loving Spirit, who hath chosen our hearts for a habitation to dwell in," is also grieved and deeply wounded "by our harbouring his enemies, and those whom he is to destroy, in our hearts with him." Such harboring of "spirit-devouring lusts" will cause God to "take away a man's usefulness in his generation."[29]

Third, Owen emphasized that the believer should reflect on the punishment that his or her sins deserve and how displeased God is with regard to them. He urged his readers to say to their souls: "What have I done? What love, what mercy, what blood, what grace have I despised and trampled on! Is this the return I make to the Father for his love, to the Son for his blood, to the Holy Ghost for his grace?"[30] In the fourth place, Owen encouraged the believer, being thus affected with the gravity of his or her sin, to get "a constant longing, breathing after deliverance from the power of it."[31] Owen rightly understood that key to the battle against sin are the affections: we are to loathe sin in the very same way that our great God finds it utterly repulsive and loathsome.

Fifth, the believer should consider whether there is a natural or temperamental proneness to the sin with which he or she is troubled. If so, Owen recommended that the fight against it be accompanied with fasting, by means of which "the Spirit may, and sometimes doth, put forth strength for the accomplishing of his own work" of mortification.[32] Owen's sixth

---

27. Owen, *Works*, 6:43–50.
28. Joel R. Beeke, *Holiness* (Pensacola, Fla.: Chapel Library, n.d.), 15.
29. Owen, *Works*, 6:55–56.
30. Owen, *Works*, 6:58.
31. Owen, *Works*, 6:59.
32. Owen, *Works*, 6:60–61.

direction is for the believer to be on guard for those occasions and situations that are conducive to giving in to temptation.[33] And if one does fall into temptation, then, seventh, Owen strongly encouraged the believer to "rise mightily against the first actings" of the sin: "suffer it not to get the least ground." If one allows it one step, it will certainly take another, for, Owen pointed out, it is "impossible to fix bounds to sin. It is like water in a channel,—if it once break out, it will have its course."[34]

In the eighth place, Christians should meditate regularly on the "inconceivable greatness of God" and His omnipresence as a way of fighting sin: "Will not a due apprehension of...that infinite distance wherein we stand from him," he asks, "fill the soul with a holy and awful fear of him, so as to keep it in a frame unsuited to the thriving or flourishing of any lust whatever?"[35] Finally, Owen urged believers to be careful not to speak peace to their souls before God does and to note that when "peace is spoken, if it be not attended with the detestation and abhorrency of that sin which was the wound and caused the disquietment, this is no peace of God's creating, but of our own purchasing."[36]

The Holy Spirit and the killing of sin

But exactly how does the Spirit effect the mortification of sin? Near the beginning of his treatise on mortification, Owen enumerated three general ways.

First, there is that which Kenneth Prior has described as strangling: the sinful nature, like a weed in a well-tended garden, is strangled by that which is good and beautiful.[37] The Spirit causes the believer to thrive in grace and the fruit of the Spirit, which are "destructive to all the fruits of the flesh."[38] Second, Owen observed that it is not without reason that the

---

33. Owen, *Works*, 6:61–62.
34. Owen, *Works*, 6:62.
35. Owen, *Works*, 6:70. The discussion of this "weapon" in the fight against sin takes up nearly seven and a half pages: Owen, *Works*, 6:63–70.
36. Owen, *Works*, 6:70, 73.
37. Kenneth Prior, *The Way of Holiness: A Study in Christian Growth*, rev. ed. (Downers Grove, Ill.: InterVarsity Press, 1982), 160.
38. Owen, *Works*, 6:19. See also Owen, *Works*, 3:551–53.

Spirit is described in Isaiah 4:4 as a "spirit of judgment and…burning." For "he is the fire which burns up the very root" and habit of sin.[39] This aspect of the Spirit's work in the mortification of sin also probably includes the convicting work of the Spirit, which Owen mentions at the end of his treatise.[40] Third, the Spirit brings the believer into communion with the crucified Christ: "He brings the cross of Christ into the heart of a sinner by faith, and gives us communion with Christ in his death, and fellowship in his sufferings."[41] As Sinclair Ferguson has noted, "It is in the death of Christ that we find the death of sin."[42]

At the end of his work on the mortification of sin, Owen expands this list to include the following:[43]

1. The Spirit reveals Christ's power over sin (1 Cor. 1:8): though the believer may fall and lose various skirmishes against sin, because of his or her union with Christ, ultimate victory is assured, which gives the believer hope and sustenance in the fight against sin.

2. Thus, the believer is encouraged to expect aid from Christ (2 Cor. 1:21).[44]

3. The Spirit constantly provides believers with the grace to undertake positive acts and duties of holiness (Eph. 3:16–18).[45]

4. The Spirit, as "the spirit of…supplications" (Zech. 12:10; see also Rom. 8:26), inspires the believer to pray and, in prayer, to find strength to overcome temptations.

For Owen, the enumeration of these various ways in which the Spirit mortifies indwelling sin is a clear demonstration that the work of

---

39. Owen, *Works*, 6:19.
40. Owen, *Works*, 6:85–86.
41. Owen, *Works*, 6:19. See also Owen, *Works*, 6:86: "The Spirit alone brings the cross of Christ into our hearts with its sin-killing power; for by the Spirit are we baptized into the death of Christ"; Owen, *Works*, 6:83: "Mortification of sin is peculiarly from the death of Christ…. He died to destroy the works of the devil."
42. Sinclair B. Ferguson, "John Owen on Christian Piety," *The Banner of Truth*, no. 191–192 (August-September 1979):58.
43. Owen, *Works*, 6:85–86.
44. See also Owen, *Works*, 3:553–54.
45. See also Owen, *Works*, 3:553.

mortification is "effected, carried on, and accomplished by the power of the Spirit, in all the parts and degrees of it."[46]

A coda

In an article on Owen's spirituality that was written just before the recent renaissance of interest in the Puritan theologian, Daniel E. Wray observed that Owen was very concerned "to maintain a balanced and biblical view of the Spirit's place in the Church."[47] This essay focused mainly on Owen's description of mortification as a work of the Holy Spirit, but a study of his exposition of Romans 8:13 bears out the truth of Wray's observation. On the basis of this Pauline text, Owen expounded the biblical truth that mortification is both a duty and a gift. As the believer undertakes this duty and sees moral change in his or her life, the Spirit enables him or her to carry it out to the glory of God from start to finish. Every true believer must thus concur with Owen: the Holy Spirit is indeed "the great beautifier of souls."[48]

---

46. Owen, *Works*, 6:85.
47. Daniel E. Wray, "The Spiritual Man in the Teachings of John Owen," *The Banner of Truth*, no. 182 (November 1978):11.
48. Owen, *Works*, 6:188.

Chapter 11
by Derek W. H. Thomas

John Owen and Spiritual-Mindedness: A Reflection on Reformed Spirituality

First, some personal words of recollection. In 1974, for several months, I lived with Geoff Thomas and his wife, Iola (along with his three children and a Houdini-like gerbil), at the manse on Buarth Road, Aberystwyth. We agreed that it would be profitable to rise early, Puritan-like, and read together John Owen's 250-page treatise, Phronēma tou Pneumatos, *or,* The Grace and Duty of Being Spiritually Minded. *Not being a "morning person" (then or now), I penciled comments on almost every margin of my copy (Volume 7 of* The Works of John Owen *in the 1965 Banner of Truth edition), largely in an effort to remain awake and focused in the face of tortuous Owenian prose and logic. There remain comments such as "N.B." and "good illustration here" on almost every page. There are occasional question marks when we lost traction on the logical flow of the great theologian's mind; and at one point a criticism, severe in its tone, to the effect that Owen lacked a "world-and-life" view.*

Needless to say, when asked to write a chapter in a festschrift honoring Geoff Thomas, I thought of this period of my life and the debt I owe to both Thomas and Owen.

Published in 1681, two years before John Owen's death, *The Grace and Duty of Being Spiritually Minded* is an exposition of Romans 8:6 and represents the mature Owen. The work was originally part of his private meditations during a time of illness when he feared he might not engage in public preaching again. After his recovery, he delivered the substance of it to his congregation at Leadenhall Street, subsequently preparing it for publication.[1] In a short preface, Owen writes something that suggests it could have been written yesterday:

> The world is at present in a mighty hurry, and being in many places cut off from all foundations of steadfastness, it makes the minds of men giddy with its revolutions, or disorderly in the expectations of them... hence men walk and talk as if the world were all, when comparatively it is nothing. And when men come with their warmed affections, reeking with thoughts of these things, unto the performance of or attendance unto any spiritual duty, it is very difficult for them, if not impossible, to stir up any grace unto a due and vigorous exercise.[2]

Owen's goal was to write a piece of experiential Calvinism, vindicating Reformed theology's robust nature in light of anemic detractors, whether Roman, Arminian, or Socinian. His style, as readers have always found, is formidable, adopting the Ciceronian-Quintilian manner of complex, argumentative sentences with too many subordinate clauses. As J. I. Packer comments, "At his best, Owen becomes stately; that is the height of his stylistic achievement; at his worst, he is simply cumbersome."[3] Even after having him as my guide for forty years, I love him in spite of these flaws, and I am grateful to the likes of Justin Taylor and Kelly Kapic for lightening the prose in more recent publications of his works.[4]

Theological foundations

As a Reformed theologian, Owen believed that when Scripture speaks, God speaks. Furthermore, he believed that the entire Bible is the product of God's *theopneustic* out-breathing (2 Tim. 3:16–17). Therefore, Owen

---

1. See William Orme, *The Life of the Rev. John Owen, D.D. abridged from Orme's Life of Owen* (Choteau, Montana: Gospel Mission Press, 1981), 200–1; Peter Toon, *God's Statesman: The Life and Work of John Owen* (Exeter: Paternoster Press, 1971), 168.
2. John Owen, *The Works of John Owen* (London: The Banner of Truth Trust, 1965), 7:264.
3. J. I. Packer, "A Puritan Perspective: Trinitarian Godliness according to John Owen," in *God the Holy Trinity: Reflections on Christian Faith and Practice*, ed. Timothy George (Grand Rapids: Baker Academic, 2007), 92.
4. John Owen, *Overcoming Sin and Temptation*, eds. Kelly Kapic and Justin Taylor (Wheaton, Ill.: Crossway, 2006); *Communion with the Triune God*, eds. Kelly Kapic and Justin Taylor (Wheaton, Ill.: Crossway, 2007).

contends, "That the whole authority of the Scripture in itself depends solely on its divine original, is confessed by all who acknowledge its authority."[5] Thus, Scripture must govern the course and content of our spiritual thoughts. Speaking of the affections in particular, Owen writes: "The rule of them is the Scripture. The way marked out therein is the only channel the stream of spiritual affections doth take its course unto God."[6] This commitment to Scripture's authority and the concomitant disciplines of thoroughgoing exegesis and application purges Owen's view of spiritual-mindedness from errant forms of mysticism and lyricism. The mind and the affections must be engaged by what Scripture teaches. That was Owen's starting point.

Additionally, if we may be forgiven an Owenian method of numbering, seven features of what we might call Owen's spiritual theology need highlighting.

First, Owen's theological perspective was at once biblically rigorous, theologically robust, and Calvinistic (he is sometimes referred to as "the Calvin of England"); at the same time it was essentially practical and experiential. Post-Enlightenment theological education has divided the disciplines of study in such a fashion as to produce exegetes who are ignorant of theology, theologians who are ignorant of exegesis, historians who are ill-acquainted with theological subtleties and, more to the point, practical specialists who are known for being at best theologically light and at worst pragmaticians who baptize secular theory so long as it produces results. Owen, as his volume on spiritual-mindedness eloquently displays, was a champion of every discipline.

Second, Owen (like the Puritans generally) was preoccupied with the need for holiness in all of life. "Holiness in everything" sums up his mindset, and the topic at hand, spiritual-mindedness, is typical of the kind of thing this magnificent theologian found energy to write about at great length. He wrote extensively about holiness because he practiced it *himself*.

Third, he wrote as a pastor who saw his calling as one of reinvigorating a moribund church, pressing home God's sovereignty in the totality of life and experience, urging Christians (individually) and churches (corporately)

---

5. Owen, *Works*, 16:297.
6. Owen, *Works*, 7:469.

to manifest godliness in thought as well as practice. Owen understood the Scriptures to be concerned as much with *motive* as with *effect*. He displayed a fear (to the point of near-paranoia) of nominalist expressions of Christianity (all head and no heart), as well as theologically anemic expressions of piety (all heart and no head).

Fourth, as a seventeenth-century Puritan, Owen operated according to a "faculty psychology" of his time. As created beings in God's image, we are naturally creatures of thought, affection, and will. Owen and his contemporaries believed that the way to the human heart is via the mind. Meditation (the rigorous and disciplined exercise of the mind) is therefore vital in producing spiritual affections (the ultimate goal). With a keen eye to the prevalence of idolatry, Owen therefore warns of how easily our affections are caught in the web of worldly desires. If we are to produce warm affections for the triune God, we must practice meditation in a discursive, disciplined, and dutiful manner. As Packer warns: "We today, who know to our cost that we have unclear minds, uncontrolled affections, and unstable wills when it comes to serving God, and who again and again find ourselves being imposed on by irrational, emotional romanticism disguised as super-spirituality, could profit much from the Puritans' example at this point too."[7]

Thus, the quality and disposition of our thoughts—the *inner* life—are, for Owen, the very parameters by which spirituality is judged; the exercise of spiritual-mindedness must be viewed as a litmus test of spiritual maturity. Such a thing ought to spring "naturally" from the renewed individual in Christ. To put it simply, we must ask ourselves this question: What do we think about when we are not thinking about anything in particular? As Owen writes, "ordinarily voluntary thoughts are the best measure and indication of the frame of our minds."[8]

Observing that the natural man may have occasional spiritual thoughts, Owen adds: "Where our affections unto spiritual things are sincere, where they are the true, genuine application of the soul and adherence unto them,

---

7. J. I. Packer, *A Quest for Godliness: The Puritan Vision of the Christian Life* (Wheaton, Ill.: Crossway, 1990), 24–25.
8. Owen, *Works*, 7:275.

they are firm and stable; love and delight are kept up unto such a constant exercise as renders them immovable."⁹

Having warned of preachers who are forced to think spiritual thoughts by virtue of their calling and responsibilities, and Christians who have particular habits of devotional exercises in the course of each day, Owen says: "There is a certain track and course of thoughts that men ordinarily betake themselves unto when not affected with present occasions. If these be vain and foolish, proud, ambitious, sensual, or filthy, such is the mind and its frame; if they be holy, spiritual, and heavenly, such may the frame of the mind be judged to be."¹⁰ He adds:

> For so it is with the principle of the new nature, the Spirit and his graces, in the hearts of them that do believe,—it doth of itself and from itself, without any external influence on it, incline and dispose the whole soul unto spiritual actings that tend unto eternal life.¹¹

In the end, he says, no greater evidence of spiritual renewal can be ascertained than "a change wrought in the *course of our thoughts*."¹²

Fifth, Owen's doctrine of sanctification, both in its positional (definitive) and progressive dimensions, formed a controlling mechanism on his understanding of the need for and nature of spiritual-mindedness. Relational sanctification, the condition of being permanently set apart for God (in the sense that Paul addresses the Corinthians as "sanctified in Christ Jesus" [1 Cor. 1:2]), flows from the cross, where Christ purchased us for Himself (Acts 20:28; Heb. 10:10). In principle, therefore, the Spirit effects a universal change in every believer involving a renewal of mind, will, and affections. From this new condition grows moral renovation whereby we are increasingly changed from what we once were. This progress is achieved, as with the totality of the Christian life, *by faith*: "We can *love nothing sincerely with divine love* but what we *believe savingly with divine faith*."¹³

Sixth, Owen treated spiritual-mindedness as part of his overall concern for the Christian's *perseverance*. Thus, Sinclair Ferguson, in summarizing

---

9. Owen, *Works*, 7:483.
10. Owen, *Works*, 7:276.
11. Owen, *Works*, 7:279.
12. Owen, *Works*, 7:299. Italics, here and elsewhere in direct quotes, are Owen's.
13. Owen, *Works*, 7:445.

Owen's *oeuvre* (work), places his treatment of spiritual-mindedness in a chapter titled "Apostasy and Its Prevention,"[14] along with such writings as *The Nature of Apostasy* (1676) (a spine-chilling exposition of Hebrews 6:4–6). As Ferguson concludes: "For all his emphasis on divine sovereignty and the certainty of final salvation, Owen's teaching emphasizes that the means God normally employs are Christian duties. There is no room here for our security becoming an excuse for moral laziness or license. For Owen, the Christian life demands the obedience of faith from the start to finish."[15]

Seventh, Owen viewed spiritual-mindedness as confirmatory of spiritual transformation and thus *assuring* in nature. Indeed, despite the imperatival nature of progressive sanctification (there are aspects of it that we are morally commanded to perform and held responsible in achieving), Owen underlines that the "life and peace" (Rom. 8:6, the text on which this entire discourse is based) attained through gospel-grounded, Christ-focused, Spirit-enabled spiritual-mindedness is ultimately a gift from God: "God communicates by an act of sovereign grace, for the most part without any preparation for it in ourselves."[16]

Focus on spiritual-mindedness

What is the focus of spiritual thought from a Reformed point of view? Indeed, is there a distinctive *Reformed spirituality*? In delineating this moral renovation, Owen focused on a variety of issues, employing a razor-sharp pastoral sensitivity to the machinations of the human spirit.

God Himself

Surprisingly, given his treatment of it elsewhere,[17] Owen does not explore the doctrine of the Trinity here. Instead, he singles out three aspects:

---

14. Sinclair B. Ferguson, *John Owen on the Christian Life* (Edinburgh: The Banner of Truth Trust, 1987), 248–61.
15. Ferguson, *John Owen on the Christian Life*, 248–61.
16. Owen, *Works*, 7:492.
17. See Owen's 1658, *Of Communion with the Father, Son and Holy Ghost, Each person Distinctly, in Love, Grace and Consolation; or, The Saints' Fellowship with the Father, Son and Holy Ghost Unfolded*. It is found in vol. 2 of the *Works*. Consisting of sermons preached some years earlier, the work explores (in asymmetrical fashion) communion with the Father (twenty-four sermons), the Son (182 sermons) and the Holy Spirit (fifty-two sermons).

God's *existence* (in the face of growing atheism),[18] His omnipresence and omniscience,[19] and His omnipotence.[20] In contemplating God, "we betake ourselves unto a *holy admiration* of what we *cannot comprehend*.... Infinite glory forbids us any near approach but only by faith."[21] At the conclusion of this section, Owen adds a typical exhortatory comment (one that is underlined in my account, signifying that Geoff and I must have talked about it in those early-morning readings together): "It is our hearts that he requireth, and we can no way give them unto him but by our affections and holy thoughts of him with delight. This is to be spiritually minded. This is to walk with God."[22]

Christ

"Think much of *him who unto us is the life and centre of all the glory of heaven; that is, Christ himself,*" Owen says.[23] Specifically, our thoughts should be of Christ's passion, on that which "pardon for sin, justification, and peace with God, do depend," namely, Christ's active and passive obedience on our behalf.[24] Also, we should think on the fact that "ere long we shall be ever with him."[25] Owen then comments:

> And it is an absurd thing for men to esteem themselves Christians who scarce think of Christ all day long; yet some...scarce ever think or speak of him but when they swear by his name.... I wish I did not know more who give evidences that it is a rare thing for them to be exercised in serious thoughts and meditations about him; yea, there are some who are not averse upon occasions to speak of God, of mercy, of pardon, of his power and goodness, who, if you mention Christ unto them, with any thing of faith, love, trust in him, they seem unto

---

18. Owen, *Works*, 7:367–69. Earlier, commenting on the saying, "God is not in all their thoughts" (Ps. 10:4), Owen exclaims, "All atheism springs from a resolution not to see things invisible and eternal." *Works*, 7:354.
19. Owen, *Works*, 7:373–75.
20. Owen, *Works*, 7:377–79.
21. Owen, *Works*, 7:372. Underlined in my edition with a note (undoubtedly Geoff's comment at the time, "we must continually think about eternal things.").
22. Owen, *Works*, 7:379.
23. Owen, *Works*, 7:344.
24. Owen, *Works*, 7:344.
25. Owen, *Works*, 7:344.

them as a strange thing. Few there are who are sensible of any religion beyond the natural.[26]

Providence

"Observe *the especial calls of providence*, and apply your minds unto thoughts of the duties required in them and by them," Owen writes.[27] Provocatively, he urges us to consider that a sudden, unexpected providence involving suffering may be a judgment of God. In such an instance, we must make "a diligent *search into ourselves*, and a holy watch over ourselves, with respect unto those ways and sins which the displeasure of God is declared against. That present providences are indications of God's anger and displeasure, we take for granted. But when this is done, the most are apt to cast the causes of them on others, and to excuse ourselves."[28] Such providences are a call to give ourselves to God:

> God is making wings for men's riches, he is shaking their habitations, taking away the visible defences of their lives, proclaiming the instability and uncertainty of all things here below; and if we are minded to contend with him, we have nothing left to give us rest and peace for a moment but a holy resignation of all unto his sovereign pleasure.[29]

Occasions of temptation

Owen wrote what proved to be the definitive treatment of temptation (*Temptation: The Nature and Power of It*[30]) in 1658, a quarter of a century before his treatment of spiritual-mindedness. In that volume, he defines temptation as "any thing, state, way, or condition that, upon any account whatever, hath a force or efficacy to seduce, to draw the mind and heart of

---

26. Owen, *Works*, 7:345.
27. Owen, *Works*, 7:308. In a marginal note, I have written "e.g. Aberfan," recalling what has become known as the "Aberfan disaster." On the morning of October 21, 1966, more than one hundred thousand cubic meters of coal waste material flowed down a mountainside, engulfing 144 people, including 109 children aged between seven and ten.
28. Owen, *Works*, 7:309.
29. Owen, *Works*, 7:310.
30. Owen, *Works*, vol. 6.

a man from its obedience, which God requires of him, into any sin, in any degree of it whatever."[31]

Once more, Owen—the *pastoral* theologian—emerges to ask the question, How can we turn an occasion of temptation into something that brings God glory when thinking about the nature of the temptation may make it appear more attractive and alluring than it already appears to be? Owen concedes that this is difficult. "There have been instances," he writes, "wherein persons have entered with a resolution to punish sin, and have been ensnared by the occasion until the commission of the sin they thought to punish."[32] It is imperative, therefore, that the mind be brought to contemplate the *guilt* and *power* of sin rather than the sin itself.[33]

In another work, Owen's famous treatment of mortification, he gives the same advice: "*Get a clear and abiding sense upon thy mind and conscience of the guilt, danger, and evil* of that sin wherewith thou art perplexed."[34] We must "load the conscience" with the guilt of the sin rather than contemplate the sin itself.[35] It is just here, at the point of the soul's struggle with sin, that spiritual-mindedness comes into its own. As Ferguson summarizes: "Through it we come to know our own peculiar weaknesses and temptations, and the remedy for them, in Christ's strength and victory, by our contemplation of his love and compassionate care."[36] As a result of engaging in spiritual contemplation of temptations and the providence of God that lies behind such occasions, our faith grows and the contours of the Christian life (cross-bearing and self-denial, as John Calvin made so abundantly clear in Book 3 of his *Institutes of the Christian Religion*) are brought into sharp relief.[37]

Progress in spiritual-mindedness

As I re-read Owen's treatment of spiritual-mindedness, the same volume I read with Geoff on those early mornings in 1974, I noted the places where

---

31. Owen, *Works*, 6:96.
32. Owen, *Works*, 7:313.
33. Owen, *Works*, 7:314.
34. Owen, *Works*, 6:50.
35. Owen, *Works*, 6:56.
36. Ferguson, *John Owen on the Christian Life*, 251.
37. Owen, *Works*, 7:325.

I underlined sections that provided particular help and progress. Among them I noted the following two:

The possibility of self-deception

If spiritual-mindedness is a sign of true and genuine conversion, of spiritual life in the soul of an individual, then what are we to make of its absence? Owen is ruthless:

> But how many of them fall under woful [sic] mistakes! for supposing themselves to be in a gospel state, it proves in the issue that they never entered into it. They were not, it may be, far from the kingdom of heaven, in the same sense as it was spoken of him who never came thither. There is no way to secure an interest in the gospel, as to pardon and mercy, safety and deliverance, but by a growth in grace, holiness, and spirituality; which gives an entrance into the choicest mercies and privileges of it.[38]

Consider how far this view is from those that abound in our time, suggesting an easy-believism that borders on antinomianism and presumption in its crassest forms. For Owen, the admonition of Hebrews 12:14, "pursue…holiness without which no one will see the Lord," is to be taken with the utmost seriousness.

Progress may be slow

This is true in the sense that one Christian differs from another *and* in the sense that the progress of the individual may not be a linear one. Holiness itself is not difficult, Owen insists. After all, Jesus told us, "my yoke is easy, and my burden is light" (Matt. 11:30). The fault lies within us: "The difficulty ariseth not from the thing itself, but from our indisposition unto it and unfitness for it."[39] Then, with a hammer blow, Owen delivers the telling observation: "Some are always beginning at religion, and the beginning of things are always difficult. They design not to be complete in the whole will of God, nor to give all graces their perfect work. They do not with use habituate grace unto a readiness in all the actings of it."[40]

---

38. Owen, *Works*, 7:451.
39. Owen, *Works*, 7:454.
40. Owen, *Works*, 7:454.

Upon that note of "habit" and its importance in gospel sanctification and growth in grace, I am reminded of Geoff Thomas. His half-century of faithful ministry is an embodiment of gospel habit suffused with grace and wisdom. I am immensely grateful to God that, at the threshold of my Christian life and ministry, this spiritually minded servant was placed in my path as an example of Christlike service and godly commitment and passion.

Chapter 12
by John J. Murray

Professor John Murray and the Godly Life

Professor John Murray (1898–1975) was regarded in his lifetime as one of the leading Reformed theologians in the English-speaking world. Dr. J. I. Packer, in a foreword to the latest edition of Murray's *Principles of Conduct*, said: "Had John Murray been blessed with the luminous literary grace of a C. S. Lewis, or the punchy rhetoric of a Charles Hodge, his name would have been put up in lights for the past half century as the finest theologian of our time.... Few have yet appreciated him at his true worth."[1]

He was born on October 14, 1898, in the parish of Creich, which is in the county of Sutherland in the Highlands of Scotland. He was reared by God-fearing parents who, by the time of his birth, had changed their allegiance from the Free Church of Scotland to the newly formed Free Presbyterian Church. After his higher education at Dornoch Academy, Murray served as a soldier in World War I, losing the sight of his right eye. He studied at Glasgow University, where he came to a decision to prepare for the Christian ministry. His church sent him to study at Princeton Theological Seminary in the United States. Within two years of graduating, he was invited back by Casper Wistar Hodge, professor of systematic theology at Princeton, to be his assistant. This he did for one year before joining the faculty of the newly formed Westminster Theological Seminary in Philadelphia. There he taught successive generations of students until his retirement in 1966, when he returned to his native Scotland.

---

1. J. I. Packer, foreword to John Murray, *Principles of Conduct* (Grand Rapids: Eerdmans, 1957), 5. This chapter is adapted from John J. Murray, "John Murray and the Godly Life," *Puritan Reformed Journal* 1, no. 1 (January 2009): 140–55.

The aim of this chapter is to examine the godliness that characterized Murray's life.

The shaping of a godly life

We look first at the major shaping influences of Murray's godly life.

The spiritual life in the parish in which he was brought up
At the end of the eighteenth century, the parish of Creich had been powerfully affected by the gospel. This took place under the ministry of George Rainy. A native of Aberdeenshire, he was inducted as minister of the parish in 1771. According to Donald Sage, he had a struggle mastering the Gaelic language: "In other circumstances this drawback would have been fatal to his usefulness as a minister. But Mr. Rainy was the very model of a sincere, practical Christian; he preached the Gospel more by his life than by his lips."[2] It is said that "over 100 men could openly testify to a personal work of grace and give a reason for the hope that was in them."[3]

The spiritual health of the work in the parish before 1843 depended on four elders. The minister who was called to the newly formed Free Church was the Rev. Dr. Gustavus Aird, later regarded as one of the most distinguished of the Free Church ministers in the Highlands. Eight more elders were added to the session in 1844. They were men of such spiritual caliber that Dr. Aird "often confessed to a sense of utter want of fitness to preside over such a session."[4]

Murray's father, Alexander (or Sandy as he was known), was born at Badbea in 1851. He later recalled how, as a youth, he was able to count "no less than eight prayer-meetings being held on a Saturday evening in an area of three square miles around Badbea."[5] It is no small testimony to the esteem in which the congregation held Sandy Murray that he was ordained to the eldership at the early age of twenty-seven.

---

2. Donald Sage, *Memorabilia Domestica; Or Parish Life in the North of Scotland* (Wick, Scotland: William Rae, 1889), 67.
3. Sage, *Memorabilia Domestica*, 270
4. Iain H. Murray, *Life of John Murray* (Edinburgh: Banner of Truth, 2007), 5.
5. Murray, *Life of John Murray*, 6.

The God-fearing parents in the home

John was nurtured by God-fearing parents. In particular, he was molded by the example of his father. Asked in later life who had been his greatest mentor, he might have mentioned some of the stars in the theological firmament in the seminaries at Princeton and Westminster. Instead, he unhesitatingly named his father. Writing at the time of his father's death in 1942, Murray said: "Though he was my father I may say that there are few men in the Highlands of Scotland whose life and memory was surrounded by such fragrance, and whose life of consistent godliness claimed such veneration and respect." Even in the daily round, the father imparted spiritual counsel to his son. John Murray once told his nephew that "he did not witness a greater intensity of spiritual exercise of soul in any other person, and his very body moved in sympathy with the inner man."[6]

Upon his death, *The Northern Times* wrote of him: "As an elder in his native parish of Creich from the age of twenty-seven until the time of his death in his ninety-first year, he was universally respected, and more than respected, he was revered. The secret of the veneration in which he was held defies analysis. He was a genuine saint, to whom the unseen was closer than breathing, and his religion was as intensely devotional."[7]

In the Murray home at Badbea, there was family worship every morning and evening, with psalm singing, Scripture reading, and prayer. The Sabbath day, after special preparations on Saturday, was observed with family worship, public worship, and private spiritual exercises, such as catechism instruction and the reading of good books. The yearly Communion Season in August, lasting five days, brought godly folk from neighboring parishes to participate in the services. The Murray home, like others, was a center of hospitality and fellowship during the five days.

The correct doctrinal instruction in his youth

John was brought up on the Westminster Shorter Catechism. It was used in the home, the church, and the day school. Learning it was an educational process of priceless value. Archibald Alexander, who founded Princeton

---

6. Murray, *Life of John Murray*, 12.
7. *The Northern Times* (Golspie, 1942).

Theological Seminary, where John was later to study and to teach, was also brought up on the Shorter Catechism. The invaluable role of catechetical instruction in a young child's life is beautifully captured in Charles Hodge's remarks about this important influence in Alexander's childhood, words that could equally be applied to the young Murray:

> The principles of moral and religious truth contained in that sublime symbol, when once embedded in the mind, enlarge, sustain and illuminate it for all time. That God is a Spirit, infinite, eternal, unchangeable in his being, wisdom, power, holiness, justice, goodness and truth, is a height of knowledge to which Plato never reached.... A series of such precise, accurate, luminous propositions, inscribed on the understanding of a child, is the richest inheritance which can be given to him. They are seeds which need only the vivifying influence of the Spirit of life, to cause them to bring forth the fruits of holiness and glory. Dr. Alexander experienced this benefit in its full extent.[8]

The spiritual change that came about in his life

There is no doubt that through the godly example set before him and the teaching imparted to him, John's course of life was set in the right direction. In later life, his wife, Valerie, recalled him expressing the belief that he had known Christ from his childhood. The minister of the Free Presbyterian congregation at Bonar Bridge was Ewan MacQueen. Murray later recalled how, when MacQueen visited the home at Badbea, he would put his hand on the boy's head and say a few words to him affectionately about spiritual things. Murray spoke of those occasions as being accompanied by the first stirrings of spiritual emotion that he could recall.

John was also sensitive about wrongdoing from an early age. There are few incidents recorded of his youth, but one concerns his determination not to tell a lie again. It is clear that during his army service in World War I, spiritual realities were his main concern. Whenever there was opportunity, he would draw aside from his comrades and find some corner where he might read his Bible and pray. He made a profession of faith after returning from his military service.

---

8. Cited in James M. Garretson, *Princeton and Preaching* (Edinburgh: Banner of Truth, 2005), 5.

The characteristics of a godly life
We go on to consider some of the characteristics of Murray's godly life.

His life was characterized by a God-consciousness
Murray was brought up in an atmosphere where the living and true God was a reality. Through a conversion experience, he came to know that God personally. In adult life, Murray was to become an admirer and follower of the Reformer John Calvin. Looking back at his own conversion, Calvin could write, "God subdued my heart to teachableness."[9] Calvin has been described as "a God-possessed soul."[10] The same could be said of Murray. He lived, spoke, and wrote as a man deeply aware of the presence of God.

Writing in later years about piety, Murray said:

> What is piety? It is godliness. Godliness is God-consciousness, an all-pervasive sense of God's presence, of his judgment, of our relation to him and his relation to us, of our responsibility to him and dependence upon him. This God-consciousness is spoken of as the fear of God, the profound reverence for his majesty and the dread of his judgments. This fear of God is not something abstract—it is a filial reverence springing from a relation that has been constituted by redemption in Christ, justification and forgiveness by his grace, adoption in his love.[11]

In Christian conviction, Murray was at one with Calvin. B. B. Warfield claimed that "the central fact of Calvinism is the vision of God." "It begins, it centres and it ends with the vision of God in his glory and it sets itself, before all things, to render God his rights in every sphere of life-activity."[12] Casper Wistar Hodge, Murray's teacher at Princeton, reminds us that "wherever humble souls catch that vision of God in his glory and bow in humility and adoration before him, trusting for salvation only in his

---

9. John Calvin, *Institutes of the Christian Religion*, ed. John T. McNeill, trans. Ford Lewis Battles (Philadelphia: Westminster Press, 1960), 1:li.

10. A. Mitchell Hunter, *The Teaching of Calvin*, 2nd ed. (Westwood, N.J.: Revell, 1950), 296.

11. John Murray, *Collected Writings of John Murray* (Edinburgh: Banner of Truth, 1976), 1:183.

12. B. B. Warfield, *Calvin as a Theologian and Calvinism Today* (Philadelphia: Presbyterian Board of Publication, 1909), 14–15.

grace and power, there you have the essence of the Reformed Faith."[13] That vision permeated what came to be called the "Princeton piety," and it also was at the heart of the "Highland piety" in which Murray was nurtured.

His life was characterized by a covenant-consciousness
Writing in the second half of the nineteenth century, C. H. Spurgeon said that those who understand the covenant have reached the gospel's core and marrow. Sadly, in the first half of the twentieth century in the United Kingdom, covenant theology suffered an eclipse. The neglect was observed by Packer when he said, "In modern Christendom covenant theology has been unjustly forgotten."[14] The turning point can be dated to July 6, 1953, when Murray delivered a lecture on the covenant of grace in Selwyn College, Cambridge, under the auspices of the Tyndale Fellowship for Biblical Research. There is no doubt that the publication of the lecture by Tyndale Press in 1954 marked the beginning of a renewed interest in the subject and marked a significant advancement in the comprehension of the biblical concept of the covenant.

The term *covenant* has to do with the relationship between God and man. How can sinful man stand before the God of transcendent majesty and holiness? The biblical answer is that God has been pleased in His sovereign mercy to enter into covenant with man. In seeking to define it, Murray said: "A divine covenant is a sovereign administration of grace and of promise." It is also "a relationship with God in that which is the crown and glory of the whole process of religion, namely union and communion with God.... At the centre of covenant revelation as its constant refrain is the assurance 'I will be your God and ye shall be my people.'"[15] The pulse and heartbeat of the covenant is its "relational character." "According to this the covenant means that God gives himself to man and man gives himself to

---

13. C. W. Hodge, "The Significance of the Reformed Theology Today," *The Princeton Theological Review* (January, 1922), 13–14, http://journals.ptsem.edu/id/BR1922201/dmd002?page=13 (accessed August 16, 2013).

14. J. I. Packer, "Introduction: On Covenant Theology," in Herman Witsius, *The Economy of the Covenants between God and Man: Comprehending a Complete Body of Divinity* (repr., Escondido, Cal.: Den Dulk Christian Foundation, 1990), no pagination.

15. John Murray, *The Covenant of Grace* (London: Tyndale Press, 1954), 31–32.

God for that full measure of mutual acquaintance and enjoyment of which each side to the relation is capable."[16]

His life was characterized by the fear of God
One of the most profound contributions Murray made to an understanding of the Christian life is his chapter on the fear of God in *Principles of Conduct*. Asking the question, "What is the fear of God?" Murray answers that there are at least two obviously distinct senses in which the word *fear* is used in Scripture. He writes:

> There is the dread or terror of the Lord and there is the fear of reverential awe. There is the fear that consists in being afraid; it elicits anguish and terror. There is the fear of reverence; it elicits confidence and love.... The fear of God in which godliness consists is the fear which constrains adoration and love. It is the fear which consists in awe, reverence, honour, and worship and all of these on the highest level of exercise.[17]

True Christianity may be summed up like this: knowing who and what God is (theology), and embracing a right attitude toward Him and doing what He requires (piety). John T. McNeill, editor of Ford Lewis Battles' translation of Calvin's *Institutes of the Christian Religion*, claims that Calvin's theology is "his piety described at length."[18] Calvin taught that the entire life of Christians ought to be an exercise in godliness.[19] In another place, Calvin said, "He ought to be reckoned a true theologian who edifies consciences in the fear of God."[20]

---

16. Geerhardus Vos, "Hebrews, The Epistle of the Diatheke," *Princeton Theological Review* 13 (1915): 624.
17. Murray, *Principles of Conduct*, 233.
18. John T. McNeill, editorial introduction to John Calvin, *Institutes of the Christian Religion*, trans. Ford Lewis Battles (Philadelphia: Westminster Press, 1960), 1:li.
19. "Exercise thyself to godliness.... This is his proper occupation.... You will do that which is of the highest importance, if you devote yourself, with all your zeal, and all your ability, to godliness alone.... Godliness alone is able to conduct a man to complete perfection. It is the beginning, the middle, and the end, of Christian life." John Calvin, *Commentaries on the Epistles to Timothy, Titus, and Philemon*, trans. William Pringle (Edinburgh: Calvin Translation Society, 1856), 108–109 [1 Tim. 4:7–8].
20. Calvin, *Commentaries on the Epistles to Timothy, Titus, and Philemon*, 283 [Titus 1:1].

John Murray saw the task of theology to be not just conveying ideas to the mind but training the souls of men to obey the Word of God by living a different kind of life. For him, "the biblical ethic is grounded in and is the fruit of the fear of the Lord.... Ethics has its source in religion and as our religion so will be our ethic. This is to say also that what or whom we worship determines our behaviour."[21]

The manifestations of a godly life

The goal of piety, as well as of the entire Christian life, is the glory of God. Having imbibed the teaching of the Shorter Catechism, Murray lived out the superb answer to its opening question:

Q. What is man's chief end?
A. Man's chief end is to glorify God and to enjoy him for ever.

Here we have the objective and subjective sides of Christianity. It is in glorifying God that we enjoy him. Warfield has stated:

> According to the Reformed conception man exists not merely that God may be glorified in him, but that he may delight in this glorious God. It does justice to the subjective as well as to the objective side of the case.... No man is truly Reformed in his thought, then, unless he conceives of man not merely as destined to reflect the glory of God in his own consciousness, to exult in God: nay, unless he himself delights in God as the all-glorious One.[22]

John Owen gives us an excellent definition of true fellowship with God: "Our communion with God consists in his communication of himself unto us, with our return unto him of that which he requires and accepts, flowing from that union which in Christ Jesus we have with him."[23]

Although the obvious fruits of communion with God were seen in Murray's life, he was reticent to speak of his personal experiences. In this he

---

21. Murray, *Principles of Conduct*, 233.
22. Cited in John L. Carson and David W. Hall, ed., *To Glorify and Enjoy God: A Commemoration of the 350th Anniversary of the Westminster Assembly* (Edinburgh: Banner of Truth, 1994), 115.
23. John Owen, "Of Communion with God," in *The Works of John Owen* (repr., Edinburgh: Banner of Truth, 1965), 3:8–9. Language modernized.

resembled his Princeton predecessor, Archibald Alexander. According to Charles Hodge: "He seldom spoke of his own experience or of his methods of religious culture. He lived with God: and men knew he had been on the mount by the shining of his face; but he was not wont to tell what he saw, and he made no record." The attractiveness of this godliness is observed by Packer:

> The experimental piety of the Puritans was natural and unselfconscious, because it was so utterly God-centered, our own (such as it is) is too often artificial and boastful, because it is so largely concerned with ourselves. Our interest focuses on religious experience as such and on man's quest for God, whereas the Puritans were concerned with the God of whom men have experience, and in his manner of dealings with those who he draws to himself.[24]

We can now consider some of the manifestations of that godliness as they were seen in Murray as a Christian, as a preacher, and as a theologian.

As a Christian

Murray's godliness as a Christian was seen, first, in his emphasis on God-honoring worship. The Puritan George Swinnock wrote: "Worship comprehends all that respect which man owes and gives to his Maker.... All that inward reverence and respect, and all that outward obedience and service to God which the word godliness enjoins, is included in this one word worship."[25] True worship is God-centered. It involves fastening our attention on God's glory and grace. If we are to adore that grace and to praise the Lamb, it must be Christ-centered.

Reformed divines have maintained that there are three spheres of worship: private, in the secret place; domestic, in the family circle; and public, in the local church. That model was seen most evidently in Puritan England and in Scotland. Every home was regarded as a church, with the head of the house as its minister. Parents attended to the spiritual nurture of their children. All members of the household were given a time and place to pray

---

24. J. I. Packer, *Among God's Giants* (Eastbourne, England: Kingsway Publications, 1991), 283.
25. George Swinnock, "The Christian Man's Calling," in *The Works of George Swinnock* (Edinburgh: Banner of Truth, 1992), 1:31.

and meditate. "Heart-work" was a priority in preparation for the Lord's Day and for public worship. The Christian Sabbath was "the queen of days." Public worship, according to David Clarkson, is "the nearest resemblance of heaven" that earth knows.[26]

The pattern was clearly evident in Murray's life. Family worship in Badbea was something to be relished. The pattern remained the same throughout his life. The Sabbath day was solemn yet joyful. The five-day Communion season was a rich feast. Such people in such homes contributed greatly to the benefit of the public ordinances. It was heart work that made worship fruitful and God-honoring.

Murray's contribution to congregational worship is recorded by Dr. David Freeman, his minister in Philadelphia: "He appropriated the worship as his own, as though there was no one else in the place. God was before his mind and eyes. He was *intent* on hearing the Word read and preached. I never saw anyone enjoying the singing of praises as he did."[27] The stirring of emotion was seen in him as a member of the congregation; on one occasion, as a communicant at the Lord's Supper, his feelings simply overflowed.

To the end of his life, Murray maintained a love for the Christian Sabbath. The pattern of observance was set in his youth in Creich, and he did not depart from it during some forty years in the United States. Like many of his godly forebears, he refrained from using the word *Sunday*. His observance of the day made him stand out in the Christian circles in which he moved. He did not observe the day in a legalistic fashion, but rather by asking, "How much of this day can I give to my Savior?" In one of the several addresses he gave on the subject, he said, "The rest of the Sabbath is not idleness; it is activity in the sacred exercise of meditation, contemplation and prayer."[28]

Second, Murray's godliness as a Christian was seen in his everyday living. As Murray clearly states in his writings, what and whom we worship determines our behavior. This principle was seen in the lives of the ordinary folk in the parish of Creich. In the words of Iain Murray: "The

---

26. David Clarkson, "Public Worship to be Preferred before Private," in *The Works of David Clarkson* (Edinburgh: Banner of Truth, 1988), 3:194.

27. Cited in Murray, *Life of John Murray*, 93.

28. Murray, *Collected Writings*, 1:227.

Christians of Creich amongst whom the head of Badbea's household was a leader, were as mindful of their relationship to God when farming land or making roads as they were in church." This fear of God gave integration to their daily lives. Their living was all of a piece. There was no distinction between sacred and secular. The daily toil on the land or on the roads was to the glory of God. Piety and hard work went hand in hand. Aird reported to the Royal Commission in 1884, "So far as I remember, I do not know a lazy man in my congregation."[29] Murray eventually came back from scaling the heights of Reformed scholarship to dig ditches, mend fences, and tend to the sheep on the family croft. "As our religion is so will be our ethic."[30]

As a preacher of the gospel
The spiritual quality of Murray's life was also reflected in his preaching and evangelism. "By word and example he insisted that the first need in those called to preach is that they should be religious men: 'Piety must first burn in the individuality of our own hearts and lives. If there is no cultivation of personal piety, the fervour and effectiveness of our ministry will be stultified.'"[31] It is evident from the history of the Christian church that God prepares men first as Christians before they become effective instruments in the ministry of the gospel. In the words of Robert Murray M'Cheyne, "My people's greatest need is my personal holiness," and, "A holy minister is an awful weapon in the hand of God."[32]

There was a further manifestation of his godly character in his passion. The godliness that manifests itself in zeal for the divine glory has passion. Murray said, "To me preaching without passion is not preaching at all." Freeman recalls his preaching: "His whole countenance, his whole being was taken up."[33] He fulfilled the criteria of Dr. Martyn Lloyd-Jones' definition of preaching: "What is preaching? It is theology on fire. And a theology which does not take fire, I maintain, is a defective theology, or at

---

29. Murray, *Life of John Murray*, 10.
30. Murray, *Principles of Conduct*, 231.
31. Murray, *Life of John Murray*, 130.
32. Robert Murray M'Cheyne, Letter to Daniel Edwards, Oct. 2, 1840, in *Life and Remains*, ed. Andrew A. Bonar (New York: Robert Carter, 1856), 211.
33. Murray, *Life of John Murray*, 93.

least the man's understanding of it is defective. Preaching is theology coming through a man who is on fire. A true understanding and experience of the Truth must lead to this."[34]

Murray's godliness was also reflected in the authority with which he spoke. He worked in the God-breathed Scripture texts. He aimed to speak the very words of God. He considered the preacher to be a voice to get inside the hearts and wills of the hearers and motivate them to read and do the Word. Murray, like Calvin before him, had the conviction that the sermon has as its goal the vital confrontation of the hearer with the "face" of God revealed in Holy Scripture. "Man before God's face in preaching" was a watchword of the Genevan Reformer. Murray viewed the sermon as the climax of the worship service. The preaching that convicts man of his need is the very instrument to convey to him the wonders of the grace of God. Without a true appreciation of grace, in response to the full-orbed declaration of it in preaching, there can be no full-orbed doxology in our congregations.

As a seminary professor

It is fitting that Murray studied and taught at Princeton Theological Seminary. From its founding by Archibald Alexander, one of its guiding principles was that a seminary is to be "a nursery of vital piety as well as of sound theological learning."[35] Alexander began a tradition at Princeton that resulted in an easily identifiable "Princeton piety." In the early years of his life, the Presbyterians had shown doctrinal soundness, but they were singularly deficient in experience. In 1788, Alexander read a book titled *The Internal Evidences of the Christian Religion* by Soame Jenyns, which made a profound impression on him. Powerful revivals marked the beginnings and development of Princeton. Dr. Samuel Miller, one of the members of a committee appointed by the General Assembly to plan a theological seminary, summarized the goals in the following words:

---

34. D. Martyn Lloyd-Jones, *Preaching and Preachers* (London: Hodder & Stoughton, 1971), 97.

35. "Act establishing the Seminary," in *A Collection of the Acts, Deliverances, and Testimonies of the Supreme Judicatory of the Presbyterian Church* (Philadelphia: Presbyterian Board of Publication, 1856), 408.

And they do hereby solemnly pledge themselves to the churches under their care that in forming and carrying into execution the plan of the proposed seminary, it will be their endeavour to make it, under the blessing of God, a nursery of vital piety as well as of sound theological learning, and to train up persons for the ministry who shall be lovers as well as defenders of the truth as it is in Jesus, friends of the revival of religion, and a blessing to the Church of God.[36]

Murray shared this concern that a seminary should cultivate piety. At Princeton in its best days, the spiritual ethos of the classroom was strengthened by the total life of the seminary. Warfield, speaking on "Spiritual Culture in the Theological Seminary" in 1903, could observe, "Public means of grace abound in the Seminary."[37] There were not only daily acts of worship, but also a Sabbath morning service in the chapel, a Sabbath afternoon conference on experimental religion, and a monthly concert for prayer. In that spiritual environment, Murray felt very much at home.

However, provision of these means of grace was much less at Westminster Seminary: "Too many tended to look upon Murray's piety as something uniquely his own, whereas in truth it was the genuine fruit of that type of Calvinistic faith which had in other times pervaded whole seminaries and considerable areas of the church."[38]

Walter Chantry, a former student at Westminster, recalls his impressions of Murray:

> Fear of God dominated Professor Murray's classroom. Each period began with prayer from the Professor's lips, which brought all into the presence of an awesome God. Each subject was handled in a dignified and solemn manner that conveyed deep reverence for the Almighty. Professor Murray breathed the attitude that all things in his lectures were holy and majestic. Not a study of the fear of God, but the Professor's visible and audible manifestation of that fear, became a main lesson for his young disciples.[39]

---

36. Garretson, *Princeton and Preaching*, xxii.
37. Benjamin B. Warfield, "Spiritual Culture in the Theological Seminary," *Princeton Theological Review* 2 (1904): 71.
38. Murray, *Life of John Murray*, 137.
39. Cited in Murray, *Life of John Murray*, 93.

Murray stood squarely in the true Princeton tradition of men such as Charles Hodge, whose *Systematic Theology* he used as the class textbook at Westminster. What has been said of Hodge by David Wells could equally be applied to Murray: "We find his work an almost classic realization of the kneeling as opposed to the sitting theologian. He had seen the grace and glory of God and in his *Systematic Theology* he turns to the world to explain his vision."[40] With Murray, there was no such thing as a purely academic study of theology. William Perkins described theology as "the science of living blessedly for ever." Theological understanding and practical piety are inseparable. This is what Murray demonstrated in his life and teaching. This is what he sought to preserve in an age when the two were being put asunder in the church by scholarship.

---

40. David Wells, "The Stout and Persistent Theology of Charles Hodge," *Christianity Today* 18, no. 23 (August 30, 1974), 10.

Chapter 13
by Iain D. Campbell

"The Spirit of God in the People of God": A Celtic Spirituality

It is a great personal privilege to be asked to contribute to this festschrift *for Geoff Thomas on his seventy-fifth birthday. After some period of correspondence, I first met Geoff at a Reformation and Revival Conference in England in 2004, and have been blessed by his friendship, fellowship, and encouragement since.*

I am unlike Geoff in many ways; his stature as a preacher, a reader, and a retainer of information is quite breathtaking; his knowledge of things encyclopedic. But we have this, at least, in common: we are both Celts, both bilingual preachers, and both the products of a history that gives glory to God for His sovereign work in reviving His church from time to time through biblical and doctrinal preaching.

These considerations made it easy for me to choose a theme for this chapter, and I am grateful to the publishers for allowing me to include in this collection the study of a poem, written in Scots Gaelic in the nineteenth century by one of the most prominent of the late eighteenth- and early nineteenth-century Highland evangelicals: Rev. Dr. John MacDonald of Ferintosh (1779–1847). It seems appropriate to honor one redoubtable Celtic preacher with the study of another.[1]

A remarkable ministry

John MacDonald was born in Reay, Caithness, in the north of Scotland in November 1779. He was the son of a leading Christian in the district, whose life is celebrated in one of his son's Gaelic compositions. The schoolmaster of Reay, recognizing the intellectual potential of his young student,

---

1. Part of this chapter was delivered as a lecture at the Banner of Truth Ministers' Conference in Leicester, United Kingdom, in April 2005.

encouraged him in his learning, with the result that MacDonald went to Aberdeen University, where he studied mathematics.

The best biography of MacDonald is also the most uncritical—that by Rev. Dr. John Kennedy of Dingwall, entitled *The Apostle of the North*.[2] Kennedy tantalizes us with the observation that "there is reason to believe that the reading of President Edwards' works was the means of beginning the work of conviction which issued in his conversion to God."[3] Kennedy does not tell us what that reason is, but I think it can be demonstrated that much of the material in MacDonald's hymns bears more than a passing resemblance to Jonathan Edwards's *Religious Affections*. MacDonald's debt to Edwards, the similarity of the themes in their writings, and his popularization of Edwardsean theology all require closer study.

MacDonald's course at Aberdeen was followed by his licensure by the Presbytery of Caithness in 1805. Ordination followed in Berriedale, Caithness, in 1806, when he also married his first wife. He served in Berriedale for only a year, until the Society for Propagating Christian Knowledge (SPCK) presented him to the Gaelic-speaking church in Edinburgh. His work in the Scottish capital from 1807 to 1813 among a Highland diaspora was onerous and difficult, particularly when the need for English services was addressed. He also found himself in demand as a preacher in many different locations.

More important, according to Kennedy, was the fact that MacDonald had an experience of fresh anointing by the Holy Spirit during his time in Edinburgh, which made his preaching more warmhearted and zealous. According to his biographer, "the Lord's people could now testify that he spoke from his own heart to theirs."[4] The change was marked, and afterward MacDonald was noted as a preacher of powerful doctrine and earnest delivery. This was no small element in his being called to the parish of Urquhart, to Ferintosh, in the Highlands of Scotland in 1813.

---

2. John Kennedy, *The Apostle of the North: The Life and Labours of the Rev. John MacDonald, D.D., of Ferintosh* (Glasgow: Free Presbyterian Publications, 1978). See also H. R. Jones, "John MacDonald: Apostle of the North," *Banner of Truth*, no. 443–44 (August–September 2000), 22–39.

3. Kennedy, *The Apostle of the North*, 17.

4. Kennedy, *The Apostle of the North*, 29.

Ferintosh is situated about thirteen miles northwest of Inverness, the Highland capital. MacDonald's grave is worth a visit. So, too, is the famous "Ferintosh Burn," a natural amphitheater in which many open-air services were held in MacDonald's time.

In the parish of Urquhart, MacDonald succeeded Charles Calder and began to labor in what Kennedy describes as "a highly cultivated field."[5] Kennedy is shrewd in his observation that the rich legacy of gospel preaching in the congregation, combined with MacDonald's well-known respect for his predecessor, meant that he could preach elsewhere with a good conscience. He often did; as John Macleod puts it, "though his home was at Ferintosh, it was only the centre of the circle."[6]

However, not everyone appreciated the itinerant nature of his calling. Kennedy relates that a stranger, from a parish whose minister was a Moderate, once met an Urquhart man during one of his minister's long tours. "How is your minister?" the stranger inquired.

"I can't tell you," the Urquhart man replied. "We have neither heard nor seen him for six weeks. It is really too bad that he should be so long away from his own parish."

"Indeed it is," rejoined the other, "but I can suggest to you a plan by which you can have your minister every Sabbath."

"And what is it?"

"Exchange your minister for mine, and I'll engage that he will be left with you for all the Sabbaths of the year."

"Oh, if that's your plan, we will rather stick to what we have."

"If you won't adopt my suggestion," the stranger said, "let me hear no more complaints about your minister's frequent absence. Be thankful that you have a minister of whose services all are anxious to have a share."[7]

---

5. Kennedy, *The Apostle of the North*, 37.
6. John Macleod, *Some Favourite Books* (Edinburgh: Banner of Truth, 1988), 101.
7. Kennedy, *The Apostle of the North*, 38. I relate the anecdote only because it resonates with the many travels that have marked the itinerant ministry God has granted to Geoff Thomas over the years; like MacDonald, he has been a minister "of whose services all are anxious to have a share"!

John Noble provided balance with his observation that while MacDonald's "own people often complained of his frequent absence, yet no sooner did he appear among them and preach, than all their complainings ceased."[8]

Also, as Kennedy observes, "the North needed an evangelist."[9] Many ministers of the period were worldly in their outlook, slothful in their lives, and false in their professions. Kennedy is scathing in his description of Moderate ministers, whom he blames for the spiritual darkness engulfing the Highlands and islands of Scotland at the time. Under the auspices of the SPCK, Gaelic schools were established throughout the region, and an evangelical work was begun through them. MacDonald's evangelistic itineraries were often dictated by the locations of these schools.

Both in Ferintosh and in his wider ministry, MacDonald soon experienced both the bitterness of bereavement as well as the sweetness of gospel blessing. His wife's death in 1814 coincided with his first Communion services at Ferintosh. These were held outdoors, since no building was available to accommodate all who came to them. According to Kennedy, ten thousand were present on the occasion, and MacDonald refused to allow the death of his wife to interfere with the commemoration of the death of the Savior. The blessing on that occasion was repeated often during his life and ministry.

Within Gaelic-speaking Scotland, especially in the Ferintosh years, MacDonald's ministry was richly blessed and eagerly sought. John Morison, a blacksmith on the Isle of Harris, tells this story from 1830:

> Someone came one evening to the smithy where I was hard at work at the anvil and mentioned that Dr MacDonald was come. I tried to subdue my emotion; and I longed for the absence of the messenger; and whenever the messenger had gone I ran to the smithy door and bolted it. I could then, when alone, give scope to my emotions. I danced for joy—danced round and round the smithy floor; for I felt a load taken from off my spirit suddenly. I danced till I felt fatigued; and I knelt down and prayed and gave thanks.[10]

---

8. John Noble, *Religious Life in Ross*, ed. J. K. Cameron and D. Maclean (Edinburgh, 1909), 95–96.

9. Kennedy, *The Apostle of the North*, 38. The reference to "the North" is to the north of Scotland, which I mention only because the sobriquet "apostle of the north" has been attributed to others in church history.

10. Cited in G. Henderson, "Memoir of John Morison," Dain Iain Ghobha, p. xliii.

By any standard, MacDonald was one of the most outstanding, attractive, and singularly blessed preachers in Scottish church history. Following his death in 1847, the Free Church monthly stated:

> Whether we regard Dr MacDonald as a minister of Christ, whose heart glowed with love to the Redeemer, and who therefore felt he could not do too much for the redeemed, as a divine, profound, solid and judicious, as a preacher, powerful, searching, soothing, unmatched except by the first masters of his profession, as a friend, bland, social, cordial and affectionate, he is to be long and much revered.[11]

Although Iain Murray is careful to note, "It would be a great mistake to suppose that such men as MacDonald pioneered in virgin ground singlehanded,"[12] MacDonald's was clearly a remarkable ministry, with Kennedy concluding:

> During three months of each year he preached, on an average, two sermons a day; and in no year of his life in Ross-shire did he preach fewer than three hundred sermons. He preached upwards of ten thousand times during the last thirty-six years of his life; and never delivered an unstudied discourse.[13]

Religious poetry

One of MacDonald's legacies is a rich body of Gaelic spiritual verse, an evangelical hymnody that remains accessible only to readers of Scottish Gaelic, but which is vibrant and full of evangelical piety and experiential theology.[14] These hymns were not designed to be sung in church, but from time to time some verses from MacDonald's hymns are still quoted in Gaelic sermons, and up until a generation or two ago, the standard practice

---

See also A. MacRae, *Revivals in the Highlands and Islands in the 19th Century* (London: Nisbet and Co., n.d.), 93–94.

11. "The Late Dr MacDonald of Urquhart," *Free Church Magazine*, May 1849, 145.

12. Iain H. Murray, *A Scottish Christian Heritage* (Edinburgh: Banner of Truth, 2006), 149.

13. Kennedy, *Apostle of the North*, 119.

14. For a comprehensive review of MacDonald's literary remains, see Rev. Douglas Somerset, "Notes on the Literary Labours of the Apostle of the North," Scottish Reformation Society Historical Journal 2 (2012):147–65.

in many Highland homes on the Lord's Day was to read, and perhaps even sing, some of them.

Most of MacDonald's poetry comes to us in the form of elegies, celebrating the lives and ministries of some of his predecessors or contemporaries, such as Charles Calder of Ferintosh, John Robertson of Kingussie, and John Kennedy of Killearnan. In his study of Gaelic spiritual verse, John Macinnes describes these elegies as "a very effective party propaganda weapon"[15]—in other words, a vehicle for the dissemination of evangelical doctrine. One of the most moving is an elegy for his father, the celebrated catechist of the parish of Reay. It is written in three parts that bear the titles "The Christian on his way to Jordan," "The Christian on the Banks of Jordan," and "The Christian beyond Jordan." A reasonable translation appears in the Free Presbyterian edition of Kennedy's biography.

In the remainder of this chapter, I want to try to capture some of MacDonald's insights by reviewing his poem, "The Work of the Spirit in the Lives of the People of God," which was published in 1845. Macinnes describes this as "a metrical treatise on the work of the Holy Spirit in the souls of believing Christians," and adds: "There is a refreshing absence of the censorious party spirit in this piece. It may not be great poetry, but it is an excellent sermon."[16]

Whether it is great poetry is a very subjective assessment, but it is certainly more than a sermon: it is a remarkable treatment of the work of the Holy Spirit. I will run through the main doctrinal emphases of this poem, which runs to eighty-five stanzas of eight lines. MacDonald introduces his theme by delineating how the work of the Spirit may be recognized in its fruit and in its manner. I include the first stanza here, to inject some Scots Gaelic onto the pages of this *festschrift*:

> O, dheanainn luaidh, nam b'urrainn mi,
> Air obair Spioraid Dhe;
> Mar tha i chaoidh r'a h-aithneachadh
> 'na toradh is na beus.
> 'S fior, tha a freumh tur-fholaicht' uainn

---

15. J. Macinnes, "Gaelic Spiritual Verse," Transactions of the Gaelic Society of Inverness, vol. 46 (1969–70), 342.
16. Macinnes, "Spiritual Verse," 342.

Mar chraoibh 's an talamh sheimh,
Ach innsidh' chraobh le 'toradh dhuinn,
gum bheil aic' bun is freumh.

In English, these lines read:

> *I would speak, if I can*
> *on the work of the Spirit of God*
> *how it is always known*
> *by its fruit and effect.*
> *It is true that its roots are always hidden from us*
> *like a tree in the ground,*
> *but the fruits of the tree will tell us*
> *that it has a foundation and a root.*[17]

The doctrinal point of departure in the composition is the universal fall of mankind in Adam, by which "the work of the goldsmith" has been spoilt (III); this is a rather powerful image of the work of God in the creation of man. We are born into this condition, under the sentence of death, slaves to sin and Satan, and liable to eternal punishment. But God's eternal purpose, from the depths of His love, was to provide a Savior in the person of Christ to secure redemption, and by means of the person of the Holy Spirit to apply that redemption to all the elect.

MacDonald then nuances this, asking: "If Christ died for everyone, as some say, would any sinner suffer the pain of the second death? Would law and justice demand the repayment of debts already cleared?" To this the poet simply says that preachers and people who give place to that form of doctrine are poor indeed (VII). This dismissal of universalism is a fundamental plank to MacDonald's theology.

It is true, he goes on to say, that the gospel call and offer are to be extended to all people without exception, and that all who believe, without exception, enjoy the benefits of Christ's redemption. But while that is true, MacDonald argues, God's eternal decree of election stands. He then makes the important observation that the purposes of God are a great mystery; however, they are a rule of activity for God alone. He did not give us these

---

17. All translations are my own. Roman numerals in the following summary refer to the stanzas of the poem.

secret, mysterious, eternal purposes to be the rule of our obedience: He gave us His Word. That is our warrant for saying to sinners that they must flee to Christ immediately (X).

So the work of the Spirit, in applying redemption to sinners, is a work of grace, and, in its nature, it is the same in every regenerate heart. Although there are differences in Christ's flock, MacDonald says in one of his homely images, all the sheep have the same kind of wool and the same kind of nature. The Spirit's work is hidden from the world and, in part, is hidden even from those who receive its benefits (XIII).

MacDonald goes on to talk of the Spirit bringing conviction of sin, concern for a lost condition, and despair at one's own efforts at reformation. The Spirit wounds before He heals. This wounding, MacDonald says, is sore, but the healing is according to the wounding. It is never the Spirit's intention to leave the soul wounded, but to bring the sinner to Christ. All of this is to the praise of God's grace—just as the salvation our souls need is of grace, so too is the faith that is living and saving.

The poet speaks of a great error going around in his day, one that appeals to fallen human nature: that saving faith precedes regeneration (XXII). He handles this point magnificently. He says that it is true that it is our duty to believe in Christ and to accept His testimony; conversely, it is the guilt of thousands who have heard the gospel that they have never believed. But it is one thing, he argues, to say that it is the sinner's duty to obey God's Word and quite another to imagine that a sinner has the ability to call faith into being. Faith, says MacDonald, is a flower that never grows in the garden of nature; it always requires better soil to give it growth (XXV). Regeneration must precede faith.

In applying the work of redemption, the Spirit unites us to Christ in a bond that nothing will sever (XXVI). He dwells in us, making us His temple, working in us the willing and the doing, sanctifying us by the Word, and enabling us to love Christ. The Word becomes a mirror for us, in which we see Christ. If we can see Christ in all His preciousness in the Word of truth, MacDonald says, that is the work of the Spirit (XXXVIII).

He then delineates the effects of the Spirit's presence in the believer: the Spirit enables the believer to walk in the light of Scripture (XXXIX) and to confess Jesus (XLII). This summary is quite unlike that of the Moderate ministers, who had "ejected Christ out of his dwelling-place." The Spirit enables believers to pray to their Father in heaven (XLVI). Sometimes they pray with a deepening consciousness of God's presence, which MacDonald compares to Jacob's wrestling with the angel at Peniel (XLIX)—he describes the gracious angel as being too strong for Jacob to overcome, yet strengthening Jacob in the act of wrestling with him.

MacDonald laments the disappearance of special seasons of blessing on the people of God in which the Spirit was poured out in a rich measure; days of spiritual summer, he says, have passed into winter (LIII). He reminds us that he is not passing on hearsay but reporting what he himself witnessed (LIV) with regard to spiritual conversion. No one could doubt but that there had been mighty workings of the Spirit in times past.

MacDonald then turns to address the children of God, urging them not to grieve God's Spirit (LXI) lest He withdraw His presence for a time. Not, he says, that the Spirit will ever completely leave the soul in which He has come to dwell, but it is possible that a believer can become like a withered bush whose roots are still alive but whose branches bear no fruit.

In the same poem, he expresses his passion for souls as he addresses the lost: "*O you, the people for whom I care—it is my ardent desire that you close in with my Beloved, before you lie in the dust; for in his love he would gladly pour the Holy Spirit upon you: O, move, flee, join with him—be wise!*" (LXIX). He urges believers to pray earnestly that the dew of heaven will come down in the church, to pray for revival warmth to melt the ice of death, and to pray for breath to blow on the dry bones, the effective breath of God that can remove famine and leanness, and change the very appearance of the church (LXVI–LXVII).

He concludes with an exhortation to preachers (LXXXI–LXXXIII):

> *And you, the ministers of the Lord*
> *Who have been given office in His vineyard,*
> *And who have accepted His Headship in His church,*
> *And who seek the good of the flock;*
> *O! I would exhort you*
> *To feed His own people*
> *And to call sinners to bow before Him*
> *In whom they can trust forever.*

> *The dew of that Glorious Spirit—*
> *May you know it and experience it!*
> *Give Him a dwelling-place*
> *In your own lives particularly.*
> *For He will give you liberty and ability,*
> *That can equip you for your office,*
> *And without His face and fellowship,*
> *Your work is worthless!*
>
> *O, always be like lights,*
> *Shining among the people,*
> *And remember that you are salt*
> *For the earth in which you dwell.*
> *And let the glory of the Redeemer be declared by you—*
> *His love, His death, His victory—*
> *And labour under the dew of the Spirit;*
> *And your labour will have its reward.*

The work of the Spirit, he concludes, flows from and resides in the triune God, and is a work for all eternity (LXXXV).

The contents of this composition should resonate with readers of John Calvin and of Edwards. The fundamental themes of Reformed spirituality are present: fall, redemption, sanctification, and glory. But so are the challenges that face preachers of the gospel in every generation.

What, for example, is the relationship between God's sovereign election and the free offer of the gospel? There can be no discrepancy between them if both are set before us in the Scriptures. The Bible teaches both that God elects His own to salvation and that the invitation of the cross is indiscriminate and free. MacDonald's point of emphasis is that the rule of our faith is not election but revelation, not the secret things, which belong to God, but the revealed things, which belong to us (Deut. 29:29).

It seems to me that a genuine Reformed spirituality is one that happily begins with that fact. Too much discussion of what is spiritual focuses on personal experience and private feelings. The discussion is, to a large extent, very much about ourselves; it is man-centered in orientation and feeling-focused in articulation. But spiritual life should be contoured around the self-disclosure of God in His Word. It is confessional and propositional before it is experiential and emotional.

What is the relationship between faith and regeneration? The gospel presses on its hearers a duty to believe in God, but this does not mean that the ability to respond to that command is within the scope of the sinner's ability.

Faith in Christ, MacDonald argues, is the fruit of regeneration, not its cause. This aspect of the *ordo salutis*, the order of salvation, is no petty theological issue. It brings us to the very heart of our natural condition and our spiritual need. We are commanded in the Word of God to believe in Christ, yet we will not and do not come to Christ until the Father draws us (John 6:44). That does not make the command any less stringent, since we are culpable for the unbelief by which we refuse to yield to the lordship of Christ over our lives.

There is, however, a power that is stronger than the power of sin, and that is the power of God's grace. All that is spiritual in our souls is the reflex of God's prior action and the result of the Holy Spirit's ministry. Preachers do not possess this power, but they are the spokesmen of Christ, whose voices, even as the gospel is heralded, contain the power that will raise the dead and enable them to respond.

And what is the nature of spiritual life? The Holy Spirit is the sanctifier of God's people; He is the Spirit of holiness, and through His sanctifying work the lives of God's people are transformed (1 Peter 1:2). The work of regeneration is evidenced in the continuing work of sanctification.

But the Spirit's work of sanctification goes hand in hand with a spiritual battle, as God's people face sin's temptations, Satan's arrows, and men's hostility. The Spirit's work is uninterrupted, but our experience of it is not. This is a far cry from the overly triumphalistic view of the spiritual life that is often presented in the contemporary church. To be a Christian is not to escape conflict—spiritual life is lived *in* conflict. The promise that the days of our sadness will end (Isa. 60:20) is meaningless apart from the fact that the spiritual life has its share of tears and of battles.

The reason is simple: holiness is the avowed enemy of sin, and death alone brings the end of sin. There is neither perfection before then nor sin afterward. Until then, the ordinary Christian life is a life of struggle. Romans 7 is nothing if not a statement of what it is to engage in that warfare; Paul's cry seeking release from "the body of this death" (Rom. 7:24) is simply a register of the conflict between sin and holiness that is the consequence of the Spirit's work in the heart of God's people.

Conclusion

MacDonald's elegies betray a high view of the work of the ministry, one that demands more than ordinary grace and more than ordinary learning. MacDonald had imbibed the view that Christ Himself furnishes men for the task of the ministry, and that through the ministry His people are taught, sinners are called, and the church is built. When his son was licensed, MacDonald wrote to him:

> The day on which you received your licence constitutes an important date, and inaugurates a new era in your life. The rise or fall of some in Israel may depend on the event which then took place—nay, so far as instrumentality is concerned, the eternity of your hearers may turn upon it. This, I confess, is a solemn, and at times may prove an overwhelming thought. But be strong in your Redeemer; for he is mighty to save and rich in mercy.[18]

In his sovereignty, God uses the preaching of the Word in the gathered congregations of God's people to build up His cause and bless His church. Perhaps we, too, need to recover an emphasis on the preaching of the gospel as the Holy Spirit's instrumentality for the edification of the people of God. Perhaps we also need to recover an emphasis on the *immediacy* of preaching; the great blessings of the past were experienced under the direct sound of the preached Word, not at a distance from it, as happens increasingly as our technologically advanced world allows.

In all of MacDonald's writings, we discover that Calvinism is the best friend of evangelism. When MacDonald's evangelistic preaching is analyzed, it is found to be powerful in its simplicity. Election, foreordination, limited atonement, and supernatural regeneration are all there; and because these elements are there, the free offer of the gospel is there, and it is bathed in a passion for the souls of men, in dependence upon the Spirit, and with a clear end in view: that men will close in with Christ and take Him at His word. In Norman Macfarlane's words: "What sermons! What massive

---

18. Cited in Kennedy, *Apostle of the North*, 153.

doctrines and piercing appeals! He seemed to live with the doctrines of grace as his intimates."[19]

MacDonald was appointed Gaelic moderator of the Free Church Assembly that met in Inverness in 1845. Alexander Beith visited the assembly and sat in on MacDonald's sermon on Acts 17:6—"These that have turned the world upside down are come hither also." In his account of the visit, Beith writes:

> Let us for a moment direct our attention to this remarkable man.... He is before us in full vigour—his massive, robust, firmly-knit person, which has weathered the blasts of nearly seventy winters; his visage glowing and bronzed by the suns of as many summers—surmounted by the dark scanty wig, enclosing a head of finest mold; his clear black eye; his voice of sweetest melody—sweet and powerful, notwithstanding a life-long habit of snuff-taking. Such was Dr John MacDonald, the great Apostle of the North…made what he has become to the Church, not by culture, nor by any stores of knowledge other than the Scriptures, pure and simple, yield.[20]

Perhaps, at last, if we gathered more from a greater association with the Scriptures, along with a greater commitment to confessional theology and a greater dependence on the Holy Spirit of God, we too would know power and blessing in ministry. As we thank God for preachers of the past and the present, let us pray to the Lord of the harvest that by His Spirit He would also raise up such heralds of the gospel for the future!

---

19. Norman Macfarlane, *Apostles of the North: Sketches of Some Highland Ministers* (The Gazette Office, 1900), 6.
20. Alexander Beith, *A Highland Tour* (Edinburgh: Black, 1874), 238–39.

PART IV

Ministry and the Spirit of Counsel and Might

Chapter 14
by Stephen Turner

The Holy Spirit and the Call to the Ministry of the Gospel

Christ has given many gifts to His church, among which are pastors and teachers (Eph. 4:11). He continues to give His people these gifts of leadership today. But how are these gifts of leadership to be recognized? To answer that question, people generally begin by considering the body of the church in which these gifts are to be found. They ask what the church thinks of a particular man in relation to the gifts of pastor and teacher. This process is generally referred to as the "outward" call.

It is hardly surprising that people begin here, since it seems to be a relatively simple matter for the church to assess a man's character and his giftedness according to clear biblical lists, such as that found in 1 Timothy 3. Perhaps it is simply done, yet all the same it is essential to the whole process of a church's appointment of her leaders. The church rightly assumes in following this course of action that since God gifts those He calls and gives gifts appropriate for the tasks to which He calls them, the church may expect to have a degree of confidence in determining whether a man is called to the ministry or not.[1] This "outward" call helps especially to safeguard the church against the possibility of someone rashly taking upon himself a leading role without any reference to the church's will.[2] Men are called to the ministry by the church and to the church.

Yet that is not the end of the matter. Equally critical to the process is

---

1. Edmund P. Clowney, *Called to the Ministry* (Phillipsburg, N.J.: Presbyterian & Reformed Publishing, 1964), 26–31.
2. John Calvin, *Institutes of the Christian Religion*, ed. John T. McNeill, trans. Ford Lewis Battles (Philadelphia: The Westminster Press, 1975), 4.3.10–11.

the man's "personal" or "inward" call, which has to do with his own feelings toward the prospect of engaging in the ministry of the gospel, together with his personal assessment of his abilities. He may be led eventually to a humble confidence as to God's call to him and a desire to make use of those gifts God has given him.

The origins of this inward call are in God Himself: "The internal call is the voice and power of the Holy Ghost, directing the will and the judgment, and conveying personal qualifications."[3] The called man must come through this process with a quiet assurance that Christ has called him to these tasks. The church should share in this confidence in him, having heard him speak of his convictions and inner assurances, and also, very importantly, having seen him faithfully and with spiritual effect engage in lesser but nonetheless vital tasks assigned to him previously.[4]

Both these "outward" and "inward" calls have behind them the very person of Christ Himself, who has given the church His Word and who speaks to and directs His people by His Spirit. An outstanding example of this is the call of Barnabas and Saul in the church in Antioch (Acts 11–13).

The church in Antioch was of significant importance to the missionary movement of the church during the first century. The church is first mentioned in Acts 11: "Now those who were scattered after the persecution that arose over Stephen traveled as far as Phoenicia, Cyprus, and Antioch, preaching the word to no one but the Jews only" (v. 19). But that is not all, because immediately following this remark are words of extraordinary significance: "But some of them were men from Cyprus and Cyrene, who, when they had come to Antioch, spoke to the Hellenists, preaching the Lord Jesus" (v. 20). Luke writes of the outstanding success of the gospel in the city and of Greeks believing along with Jews, so much so that news of these extraordinary developments reached the ears of the church in Jerusalem. The leaders there sent Barnabas to Antioch to see for himself and report back to the people of God. Barnabas' ministry, in turn, led to a great

---

3. Charles Bridges, *The Christian Ministry* (London: Banner of Truth, 1967), 91.

4. For an older view on the outward and inward call, read John Gill, *A Body of Divinity* (Grand Rapids: Sovereign Grace Publishers, 1971), 862–66. For a contemporary view, read Dave Harvey, *Am I Called?* (Wheaton, Ill.: Crossway, 2012), 17–64, or Darrin Patrick, *Church Planter* (Wheaton, Ill.: Crossway, 2010), 29–40.

many more believing. His passion for the work in that city constrained him to pay a visit to Tarsus to solicit the help of Saul, whom he had met previously in Jerusalem soon after the latter's conversion (9:27). Saul returned with him to Antioch and worked alongside Barnabas for a full year while they taught great numbers of people. This is an account of something truly momentous; a very large, growing church with both Jewish and Gentile converts taught by two men of considerable ability.

Then, importantly, we are told of the compassion of the church and its concern for believers in other places (11:27–30). The church sent these same two leading men, who had come to them from outside Antioch, to accompany a gift the church had collected for the help of believers in Judea.

This concern for others beyond their city should not be overlooked when we consider a watershed moment in the life of the church, recorded in Acts 13:1–4. In this section, we have the account of the church sending out her first missionaries. Here we see the interaction of the Holy Spirit with the church in Antioch and the call of Barnabas and Saul to the ministry of the gospel. The church in Antioch, under the Holy Spirit, thus became the center of the missionary movement to the Roman world.

The central importance of the Holy Spirit to the call

The Holy Spirit is seen here to command and to call His church. Luke has already shown the Spirit being sent from God, filling the Lord's people with Himself, and exerting powerful effects upon the believers (Acts 1:8; 2:4, 17, 38; 4:8; 6:5). The Holy Spirit is Lord (5:3–4). He gives direct words of guidance to His people (8:29; 10:19, 20; 11:12).[5] The Holy Spirit in Acts is clearly a person, a divine and sovereign person.

We need to give attention to Acts 13:1–4 and underscore the facts mentioned by Luke: the gathering of Antioch's leaders, their worship and spirituality in fasting, and their placing their hands on the newly appointed missionaries and sending them off. The Holy Spirit is key to understanding all of these events. He is at the center of the story.[6] His work in calling the

---

5. Wayne Grudem, *Systematic Theology* (Grand Rapids: Zondervan, 2000), 642–44.
6. Gordon Fee, *Paul, the Spirit and the People of God* (Peabody, Mass.: Hendrickson, 1996), 59–62.

men was prior to anything the church did. His authority was indisputably greater than theirs. He directed the church to set apart for Him two men whom He had called: "Now separate to Me Barnabas and Saul for the work to which I have called them" (v. 2b).

The priority of the Spirit's calling, as opposed to anything the church did at this juncture, is underlined in that the reader has already been informed of the events recorded in Acts 9—Saul's arrest by Christ's call and command. The Holy Spirit's call to Barnabas and Saul was of the same kind and had the same authority behind it as Jesus exerted when He called Saul on the road. The Holy Spirit called them to the same mission to which Christ called Saul. The Spirit was given the last word as well, after the church had obeyed Him and "sent them off," for Luke's account of the call goes on to say that the two of them were "sent out by the Holy Spirit" (Acts 13:4).

The words Luke uses to describe the church sending and the Spirit sending are not the same so that we might not miss the point—the Spirit's authority is preeminent over against that of the church. The church merely set the men free at the Spirit's command, but the Spirit sent them off. He is the Lord and Master of the church, guiding and directing His people. He is "the missionary of the Trinity."[7] He ordains. He sends. This is a significant emphasis in Acts (see 8:29, 39–40; 10:19–20; 11:12; 16:6–7; 20:28). What human being or group of human beings would dare command the church in this way? Yet the church is not left out of the picture, despite the Spirit's overwhelming power.

The church's role in the call

It was to this church, which was so singularly impacted by the Spirit, that Barnabas and Saul (now called Paul) returned, because it was there that "they had been commended to the grace of God for the work which they had completed" (Acts 14:26). Those words refer to the occasion recorded in 13:1–4. Barnabas and Paul's report, their ascription of all their success to the glory of God, and their subsequent long stay with the church are then mentioned. Later, Paul and Barnabas were sent on another mission from

---

7. Michael Horton, *The Christian Faith* (Grand Rapids: Zondervan, 2011), 556–60.

the church—this time for discussion with the apostles and elders in Jerusalem (15:2). Again, they returned to the sending church (15:30). Then, once again, for the final time, Paul was sent, "commended by the brethren to the grace of the Lord" (15:40). The church in Antioch was a sending church.

On the occasion we are considering in chapter 13, the Spirit spoke to the church in Antioch while her leaders, her prophets and teachers, were worshiping God and fasting: "As they ministered to the Lord and fasted, the Holy Spirit said…" (v. 2a). Here is a picture of a spiritually minded and focused church. These activities of worship and fasting suggest their deep desire to hear God's voice.

Surprisingly, there was no discussion in the church as to the suitability of the two men. The Spirit is the authority in the church. The Spirit determines whom He will use. "This is not the picture of a Church discussing the fitness of men for the doing of any particular work. There is a sense in which it would be perfectly accurate to say that the Church had no voice in the selection of these men. The choice was not left to the Church. The choice was based upon a prior fact in the activity of the Spirit: 'Separate Me Barnabas and Saul for the work whereunto I have called them.'"[8] However, that is not to say the church in Antioch had no view on their suitability. By this stage, they were confident of the qualities of the men whom they sent, having already entrusted them with responsibility in the matter of the gift (Acts 11:30).

No mention is made in the passage as to how the Spirit spoke. A word spoken by a prophet seems like the most obvious means of conveying such clear instructions.[9] Prophets may cease, but the Lord is able to be as clear now with regard to His directions as He was then. For those of us in more "ordinary" circumstances, John Calvin's remark stands in regard to the election of men to the ministry of the church: "[The Lord] alone should rule and reign in the church as well as have authority or pre-eminence in it, and this authority should be exercised and administered by his Word alone."[10] Humble attention to His Word will lead us today to the right man. The

---

8. G. Campbell Morgan, *The Acts of the Apostles* (London: Pickering & Inglis, 1965), 239.

9. John Chrysostom, *Acts of the Apostles* (Oxford: Library of Fathers, 1866), 386.

10. Calvin, *Institutes*, 1053.

voice of the Spirit in the Word of God has been and must always be the paramount indicator to the church of the Spirit's will in regard to the suitability of a man for the ministry. The Bible must be reverently consulted by leaders and members of the church as they consider anyone aspiring to the ministry. A church that approaches the matter of the call to the ministry as a church intent on hearing the voice of the Spirit in His revealed Word is a church that will hear His voice and be confident of knowing His will.

However, the church in Antioch was characterized by still other commendable aspects. Everything we see here speaks of their togetherness; they were together in worship and together in obedience in sending the men off. Also, the prophets and teachers were together as a leadership. It has been truly said of this account in Acts 13 that "the missionary enterprise had its birth in a united prayer meeting of church leaders."[11]

Yet another aspect of the church in Antioch strikes the reader. The church was called to definite action and obedience by the Spirit, and it obeyed Him. This stands out in the text. The Spirit commanded them, "Separate to Me...." The church then obeyed: "Then, having fasted and prayed, and laid hands on them, they sent them away" (Acts 13:2–3).

Oneness and obedience combine to make for a striking picture of a church thoroughly involved in this matter of the call of Barnabas and Saul. After fasting, praying, and setting their hands on them, they separated these members from the church without delay. In this physical way, they demonstrated their oneness as a congregation and especially their determination as leaders and members to obey the intention and will of the Holy Spirit. The laying on of their hands obviously did not qualify Barnabas and Saul for the work ahead of them, since the Spirit had qualified them by gift and calling, "but by this means they expressed their fellowship with the two and their recognition of the divine call."[12] These two outstanding men were called in a church conspicuous for its unity and spirituality.

The man and the call to the ministry

What of the men themselves? What were their thoughts in regard to this

---

11. J. Oswald Sanders, *Effective Prayer* (London: OMF, 1988), 21.
12. F. F. Bruce, *The Acts of the Apostles* (London: The Tyndale Press, 1956), 254.

great moment in their lives? Nothing of an overt nature is said in Acts 13 on this matter because, as I have been arguing, the emphasis is on the Spirit rather than on the men and the church. But did that mean that neither Barnabas nor Saul participated in this event? On the contrary, every indication is that they were already strongly committed to the work of the gospel.

For example, Barnabas had traveled to Tarsus for the express purpose of bringing Saul back to Antioch to help meet the enormous needs of a church that was growing exponentially (Acts 11:25). The two of them then settled down to teach the church: "So it was that for a whole year they assembled with the church and taught a great many people" (v. 26). It is hardly surprising that the church then appointed these two outstanding men to accompany their gift to the believers in Judea (v. 30). On fulfilling that task, these two men then responsibly returned to their home church (12:25). They next appear in Acts 13:1–4 as part of the leadership to whom the Holy Spirit spoke as they gathered to worship and fast. These were men who were already heavily involved in the work of the ministry of the gospel at the time when the Spirit commanded the leaders to set them apart for Him. They were evidently men who had set their hearts on engaging in this work, as true leaders in the church should. "The first sign of the heavenly calling," says Spurgeon, "is an intense, all-absorbing desire for the work."[13]

They were men, however, who did not hold up their hands for recognition in the church. This was not the way of these apostles or of the church in Antioch in general. The church appointed them to the task of accompanying its gift to Judea (11:25) and the Holy Spirit appointed them for this great missionary task. An eagerness to serve should not be equated with a confidence in claiming leadership. When referring to Paul's words in 1 Corinthians 1:1, Calvin says this of Paul: "If so great a minister of Christ dare not claim authority for himself to be heard in the church—save on the ground that he has been ordained to it by the Lord's command and faithfully carries out what has been committed to him—what shamelessness

---

13. C. H. Spurgeon, *Lectures to My Students* (London: Marshall, Morgan & Scott, 1969), 26.

will it be in any mortal devoid of one or both of these, to claim this sort of honor for himself?"[14]

This same humility toward God should be evident in any called man throughout his lifelong ministry. This ought to be the case because, while the man is called by the Spirit at the commencement of his ministry, there is an ongoing call by the Spirit as he serves. The power of the Holy Spirit's call lives on in his heart. He lives under it. He hears it through the years. It sounds in the ears of his heart when he is immersed in the struggles of his life as a servant. He cannot escape its living power. The Spirit continually refreshes His original call. The man who is led by the Spirit responds through the years of his ministry with that same humility of heart and gratitude that he knew when he first heard his Lord calling him.

The call to the ministry today

The Holy Spirit must be central to the whole process of the call to the ministry today. The man who is the subject of that call, together with the church of which he is a part, must be ready to accept the Spirit's will and listen to and obey His directions. The Holy Spirit leads. The man of God follows His lead. The true church follows His lead.

Before He calls men to the ministry, Christ calls them to Himself.[15] They are called to know Him, to love Him, and worship Him with their bodies and souls. To be even more specific, the church is called to death since it is called to the cross of Christ.[16] Christ's man is called to die: "The Christian life is a life of crucifixion (Gal. 2:19)."[17] In a word, he is called "to daily service."[18] The Christian servant is Christ's slave. The slave of Christ is called to die daily for Christ's sake, among Christ's people, and in Christ's world.

Leadership in the church, and in particular the appointment of leadership, had supremely to do with the Holy Spirit in the early church. The Holy Spirit has not changed in His role in the church or in His authority

---

14. Calvin, *Institutes*, 1062.
15. Clowney, *Called to the Ministry*, 5–7; Harvey, *Am I Called?*, 36–39; Patrick, *Church Planter*, 21–27.
16. Clowney, *Called to the Ministry*, 13.
17. Dietrich Bonhoeffer, *The Cost of Discipleship* (London: SCM Press, 2003), 231.
18. Clowney, *Called to the Ministry*, 21.

and right to direct the Lord's people and their leaders. He is the beginning and the end. The man may aspire to serve, but that is not the end of the matter. Likewise, the church's leadership may meet to weigh up the needs and hopes of the church, but their subsequent decisions do not have the final word. The end of the matter is the Holy Spirit and His will. Everything our churches do in regard to the call to the ministry—and, for that matter, any endeavor we plan to take up—must be seen by our practice as well as by our public confession and private, heartfelt acknowledgment to have the Holy Spirit at its center.

When this is not the case, there may be serious consequences. First, the church will likely be misled in the choice of her leaders, mistaking the powers of personality and youth for giftedness of the Spirit. This mistake is all too common today. Second, Christ must of necessity be less glorified and His body less built up in spiritual maturity if the church assumes a dominant role despite being dependent on Him for life and gifts. Third, the man who is the subject of the call will inevitably have a far less solid confidence in the Lord's help for his ministry than might have been the case had the church from which he is sent devoted itself to worshiping the Lord and knowing His will in regard to their sending him.

A clear, declared recognition of the Holy Spirit's role in directing and guiding His church, and in particular in appointing leaders for the tasks He sets, is the key to better approaching the call to the ministry today. And it is the key to addressing what is now of serious concern to the church—the dearth of young men applying for the ministry. The church needs to rediscover the role of the Spirit in this regard. He is Lord. He is the same One who directed the church in its earliest days, as outlined in Acts. Therefore, let us go to Him now as a church, as leaders, as young men, and ask Him to both reveal His will to the church and lead the church into new days of missionary enterprise, of leadership, and of courage. Let us begin our discussion of the subject of the call to the ministry with the Holy Spirit. In the matter of the call to the ministry, let us ask for the Spirit when we pray about the ministry, as Jesus counseled us to do in Luke 11:13.

I have been a pastor for nearly forty years and am able to say, without hesitation, that over the years neither I nor the churches of which I have been a pastor have asked for the Holy Spirit and His leading as we should have done. And I'm sure I am not unusual in this regard.

Young men, if you are considering the ministry, ask for the Spirit. Churches, challenged by the tasks ahead and the needs of God's people, ask for the Holy Spirit to be present as He was, so powerfully and so wonderfully, in Antioch. Could it be said that their worship on that occasion was indicative of their usual life and practice? Or were they worshiping as they did because they had a deep, pressing sense of concern for far-away peoples who had never heard of Jesus? Either way, the Antioch church is a fine example to us of how we ought to submit to the lordship of the Holy Spirit in the matter of the call to the ministry today.

Chapter 15
by Conrad Mbewe

The Empowering Work of the Holy Spirit

I live in Africa. When we think of power, especially spiritual power, we think in terms of casting out demons, healing the sick, doing all kinds of miracles, and even raising the dead. The fact that these feats occurred during at least three epochs in biblical history makes a lot of people conclude that they ought to be occurring even today. That, they say, is the empowering work of the Holy Spirit.

Sadly, this view not only fails to see the primary purpose that these extraordinary works of the Holy Spirit among the people of God were meant to achieve, but it also fails to put in place God's primary concern across history. God wants to glorify Himself through conforming sinners to His image. This is what the Holy Spirit came to do.

Thus, in dealing with the Holy Spirit's empowering work, we are primarily concerned to show how He enables us to go from being sinners to being saints, and how, through us, he helps others to go from being sinners to being saints. The Holy Spirit is not only God's advocate in us, but He is also the One who empowers us to be like God and to do God's will.

The specific areas in which the Holy Spirit empowers us in order to achieve this are varied. In this chapter, I will look at four of them. All I seek to do is to illustrate the way in which the Holy Spirit empowers us in each of these areas.

In sanctification

The Holy Spirit's work of assistance is inseparably connected with His indwelling and sanctifying work. Octavius Winslow says the "one most important feature in the work of the indwelling Spirit is the sanctification of the believer."[1] Our chief pursuit must always be conformity to the image of the Lord Jesus Christ.

Closely connected with this is the Holy Spirit's work of strengthening us with power in the inner man. In this way, He empowers us to mortify the flesh and to become more and more like Christ. That is why, in his letter to the Ephesians, immediately after speaking about being given understanding and wisdom, the apostle Paul goes on to speak about our being strengthened by the Spirit, and especially that we might know this power at work within us:

> the eyes of your understanding being enlightened; that you may know what is the hope of His calling, what are the riches of the glory of His inheritance in the saints, and what is the exceeding greatness of His power toward us who believe, according to the working of His mighty power which He worked in Christ when He raised Him from the dead and seated Him at His right hand in the heavenly places. (Eph. 1:18–20)

Later, Paul adds that he prayed, "that He would grant you, according to the riches of His glory, to be strengthened with might through His Spirit in the inner man" (Eph. 3:16).

The Spirit strengthens us with power in the inner man. Commenting on Paul's use of the word translated as "strengthened," James I. Packer observes that "Christ gives strength (*endunamoo, dunamoo, krataioo*), so that the Christian becomes able to do what left to himself he never could have done."[2] We know something of inward stamina, of moral energy, because of the Holy Spirit.

In Ephesians 3:20, we read, "Now to Him who is able to do exceedingly abundantly above all that we ask or think, according to the power that works in us, to Him be glory in the church by Christ Jesus to all generations, forever and ever. Amen." The point here is quite clear: There is a great power at work within the saints, power through which God will bring glory to Himself.

---

1. Octavius Winslow, *The Work of the Holy Spirit* (Edinburgh: Banner of Truth, 1984), 105.

2. J. I. Packer, *Keep in Step with the Spirit* (Leicester: Inter-Varsity Press, 1985), 23.

This power is a moral energy. It is there for the mortification of the flesh. In Romans 8:13, Paul says, "For if you live according to the flesh you will die; but if by the Spirit you put to death the deeds of the body, you will live." Putting to death the misdeeds of the body will and can be done only by the Holy Spirit's empowering.

In prayer and worship
One area in which the Holy Spirit empowers us is in prayer and worship. Romans 8:26 says: "Likewise the Spirit also helps in our weaknesses. For we do not know what we should pray for as we ought, but the Spirit Himself makes intercession for us with groanings which cannot be uttered." Benjamin B. Warfield notes that the direct teaching of this passage is that "the Holy Spirit, dwelling in Christian men, invites their petitions, and thus secures for them both that they shall ask God for what they really need and that they shall obtain what they ask."[3] Similarly, in Romans 15:30, as Paul appeals for prayer from the saints, he says, "Now I beg you, brethren, through the Lord Jesus Christ, and through the love of the Spirit, that you strive together with me in prayers to God for me." He appeals to them using two sources of inspiration for prayer: one is the lordship of Jesus Christ and the other is the love of the Spirit. The love that the Holy Spirit had given them for Paul and the work of God in which he was engaged ought to inspire them to labor in prayer with him. The love of the Spirit inspires us to pray! That is something all of us experience whenever we hear of a beloved saint of God under sore affliction—our hearts soar up to God in prayer. Even when you are spending time alone with the Lord in prayer, you literally wrestle on behalf of that saint in prayer to God.

Ephesians 2:18 says, "For through Him we both have access by one Spirit to the Father." Here Paul is talking not only about prayer but about the whole of worship, the whole of our vertical relationship with God. We have access to God through this one Spirit. He enables us to offer adoration, confession, thanksgiving, and supplications to God the Father through the name of our Lord Jesus Christ.

---

3. Benjamin B. Warfield, *The Person and Work of the Holy Spirit* (Amityville: Calvary Press, 1997), 55.

Ephesians 6:18 says we should be "praying always with all prayer and supplication in the Spirit, being watchful to this end with all perseverance and supplication for all the saints." When Paul speaks about praying in the Spirit, he is not saying we should break out in tongues on all occasions. Rather, he is saying we need to pray in the strength and empowering of the Spirit on all occasions. Remember, the context in Ephesians 6:10–20 is that of spiritual warfare. We need God's power to enable us to stand in the day of evil, and Spirit-inspired prayer is a major means to this end. In the same vein, Jude 20 says, "But you, beloved, building yourselves up on your most holy faith, praying in the Holy Spirit."

Finally, Philippians 3:3 says, "For we are the circumcision, who worship God in the Spirit, rejoice in Christ Jesus, and have no confidence in the flesh." This refers again to the whole area of worship. We worship God by the Holy Spirit's empowering. Here are six specific ways in which the Holy Spirit helps us in the area of prayer and worship:

(1) *The Holy Spirit empowers us to form proper views of the spiritual object of prayer and worship.* The answer to question 1 of the Westminster Shorter Catechism—"The chief end of man is to glorify God and to enjoy Him forever"—is a statement that the Holy Spirit burns into us as a living reality. As a result of this, when we go to the place of worship, we do not go to enjoy ourselves or to feel good, but we go to render that which is pleasing to God. We go to offer sacrifices of praise to Him because He is worthy. We are persuaded that our worship must have as its objective God's honor and glory rather than our own pleasure. When we go to pray, the Holy Spirit empowers us to realize that prayer is pre-eminently meant for the realization of God's moral will—His good, pleasing, and perfect will—in this world and in our lives. So when we go to pray, our chief concern is not for another pair of shoes, a bigger house, a better job, or more appetizing food. Rather, it is primarily this: "Hallowed be Your name, Your kingdom come, Your will be done on earth as it is in heaven" (Matt. 6:9b–10). That is our first concern; only after that do we concern ourselves with "give us this day our daily bread" (v. 11). The Holy Spirit burns that priority into us. One of the ways in which we can know that the Spirit of God is leading us in this realm of prayer is that we feel that all our needs are insignificant compared to this, that God might be honored and glorified in answer to our prayers.

(2) *The Holy Spirit empowers us to have wisdom in laying our petitions before God.* Hardly ever will a true child of God spend his time before the presence of God asking for things to be spent upon his lusts and passions. Hardly ever! Those who are carnal are often prayerless, because they know that the types of activities they want to engage in are not the types they can talk to God about. Thus, their prayer lives are very weak. It is always the same old prayer: "Lord Jesus, we thank you for waking us up in the morning and for looking after us today and we're looking forward to a good night's rest. Amen." However, a Christian who is walking with God prays about every circumstance in his life, and his prayers about these circumstances are full of spiritual wisdom. The Spirit empowers us to pray aright in that way. We do not know what we ought to pray for, but the Spirit enables us to pray aright. And sometimes it is even with groans that words cannot express (Rom. 8:26).

(3) *The Holy Spirit empowers us in waiting patiently for God's answer.* We do not fret or complain, but we know something of waiting patiently upon the Lord. We refuse to rush God or to take shortcuts. We do not abandon the morality that God's Word demands to find our own answers to our prayers. We say: "I would rather die than make a shortcut. I will wait upon God." The Holy Spirit not only enables us to wait patiently for God's answer, but also to wait patiently for God's answer in God's own way. Therefore, we learn to say from the depth of our hearts, "May Thy will be done." We say this not as a little appendage to a prayer, but as something we really mean. Ultimately, we want God's will, not our own.

(4) *The Holy Spirit empowers us to pray beyond our felt needs and to reach our real needs.* The true saint of God, therefore, puts his emphasis on that which is his real need in the eyes of God. Winslow notes:

> A believer may not know his real condition, his absolute need. There may be a secret declension in his soul, the enfeebling and decay of some spiritual grace, the slow but effective inroad of some spiritual enemy, the cherishing (like Achan) of some forbidden thing, the feeding of some worm at the root of his holiness—and all the while he may remain ignorant of the solemn fact. And how is he to know it unless someone teaches him? And who is that teacher but the Spirit?[4]

---

4. Winslow, *The Work of the Holy Spirit*, 186.

Think for a moment of the testimony that Paul gives in 2 Corinthians 12 concerning the thorn in the flesh. He pleaded with the Lord about it, that it should be taken away from him. However, Paul came to see the greater purpose of God in permitting this messenger of Satan to harass him. When he first prayed, pleading with the Lord three times, it was more to do with his felt need for relief. However, he was enabled to see his real need—his sanctification. Listen to him in verse 7: "And lest I should be exalted above measure by the abundance of the revelations, a thorn in the flesh was given to me, a messenger of Satan to buffet me, lest I be exalted above measure." The Spirit enabled him to pray beyond his felt needs, so he was able to joyfully accept this thorn in his flesh.

(5) *The Holy Spirit inspires prayer itself.* As we saw earlier, Paul asked the Romans, "through the love of the Spirit, that you strive together with me in prayers to God for me" (Rom. 15:30). The Spirit stirs up within us a spirit of prayer and supplication. James Buchanan, elucidating this notion, writes:

> The grace of the Holy Ghost, then, is indispensable, if we would maintain the spirit and enjoy the exercise of prayer; but we must ever remember, that in this, as in every other part of his work, he acts by the use of means, and in a way that is wisely adapted to the rational and moral nature with which we are endowed. He acts upon us, not as mere machines, but as moral agents; and by various considerations and motives, he teaches and disposes us to pray. Every part of his work as the Spirit of grace has a tendency to prepare us for this exercise; for whether he acts as a reprover, convincing us of sin,—or as a sanctifier, subduing our corruptions, or as a comforter, giving us peace and joy in believing, or as a teacher, enlarging our views of divine truth, and confirming our faith in it, all the operations of his grace are subservient more or less directly to the exercise of prayer.[5]

(6) *The Holy Spirit empowers us to plead Christ's atoning blood and efficacy.* When we are before God in prayer and we say, "In the name of the Lord Jesus Christ," that is not merely a little appendage to our prayer. No! It is real to us. We know that it is only by the merits of our Lord Jesus Christ—by His righteousness—that we can find acceptance in the eyes of God. It

---

5. James Buchanan, *The Office and Work of the Holy Spirit* (Edinburgh: Banner of Truth, 1984), 271–72.

is only on the basis of Christ's shed blood on the cross that our prayers can prevail in God's presence. It is only as Christ, who is at the right hand of God, perfects our worship and prayers that they become acceptable to God. So, as we say, "In Jesus' name," or "For Jesus' sake," we have within our hearts a sense of confidence that it is only in Him that our prayers will truly prevail. This confidence is by the empowering of the Spirit. It is a conviction that only the Spirit can give.

In Christian service
A third area in which the Holy Spirit empowers us is in service. He enables us in two ways:

(1) *The Holy Spirit empowers us by giving us gifts and abilities.* Paul, teaching about spiritual gifts, says: "Therefore I make known to you that no one speaking by the Spirit of God calls Jesus accursed, and no one can say that Jesus is Lord except by the Holy Spirit. There are diversities of gifts, but the same Spirit.... But the manifestation of the Spirit is given to each one for the profit of all.... But one and the same Spirit works all these things, distributing to each one individually as He wills" (1 Cor. 12:3–4, 7, 11). The gifts that we have as individuals are all given to us by God's Spirit.

Acts 2:4 says, "And they were all filled with the Holy Spirit and began to speak with other tongues, as the Spirit gave them utterance." Notice that the Spirit enabled them. It is not that someone was thumping and shaking them, and telling them: "Come on, loosen your tongue, loosen it! It's coming, just loosen yourself a little more." Tongues were not being cranked out of people. Rather, the Holy Spirit enabled them to speak. There was no struggling. We do not struggle to receive gifts, do we? There was no need to toil away, as if they were trying to start a car that had broken down. It just flowed. It was an empowering.

By the way, these tongues were not a kind of gibberish that no one could understand. We are told in the verses that follow:

> And when this sound occurred, the multitude came together, and were confused, because everyone heard them speak in his own language. Then they were all amazed and marveled, saying to one another, "Look, are not all these who speak Galileans? And how is it that we hear, each in our own language in which we were born? Parthians

and Medes and Elamites, those dwelling in Mesopotamia, Judea and Cappadocia, Pontus and Asia, Phrygia and Pamphylia, Egypt and the parts of Libya adjoining Cyrene, visitors from Rome, both Jews and proselytes, Cretans and Arabs—we hear them speaking in our own tongues the wonderful works of God" (Acts 2:6–11).

The disciples were speaking in known languages they did not know how to speak. They were enabled to speak in all these different languages by the Holy Spirit.

Romans 12:6–8 says: "Having then gifts differing according to the grace that is given to us, let us use them: if prophecy, let us prophesy in proportion to our faith; or ministry, let us use it in our ministering; he who teaches, in teaching; he who exhorts, in exhortation; he who gives, with liberality; he who leads, with diligence; he who shows mercy, with cheerfulness." The words "gifts differing according to the grace that is given" refer to the fact that the Spirit gives us enabling, which not every person has. Not everyone can do what a particular believer can do. He deliberately and uniquely fits us for the realm of service in which He places us. The least that any Christian can do for himself is to know what his abilities are, and then to get down to business to use them for the sake of the body of Christ and for the extension of God's kingdom.

(2) *The Holy Spirit empowers us by making us effective.* The Spirit does not give us gifts and leave us to use them according to our own strength; rather, He comes alongside and enables us to bear fruit to the glory of God. In 1 Corinthians, Paul says: "And I, brethren, when I came to you, did not come with excellence of speech or of wisdom declaring to you the testimony of God. For I determined not to know anything among you except Jesus Christ and Him crucified. I was with you in weakness, in fear, and in much trembling. And my speech and my preaching were not with persuasive words of human wisdom, but in demonstration of the Spirit and of power, that your faith should not be in the wisdom of men but in the power of God" (1 Cor. 2:1–5). He adds in 2 Corinthians: "And we have such trust through Christ toward God. Not that we are sufficient of ourselves to think of anything as being from ourselves, but our sufficiency *is* from God, who also made us sufficient as ministers of the new covenant, not of the letter but of the Spirit; for the letter kills, but the Spirit gives life" (2 Cor. 3:4–6).

Paul is saying that the fruit of our ministry is the fruit of the Holy Spirit working in and through the gifts He has given us. As we see people coming to new life in Christ, repenting from sin and putting their faith in Him, it is not because of anything special about us. As we see real spiritual fruit in our ministry, it is the Spirit Himself empowering us, making us competent and effective.

We need to learn something of pleading with God in prayer for His empowering. How can I, as a pastor of a church, be content with preaching week after week, year in and year out, without seeing souls being converted or growing in the things of God? I cannot simply sit back and say, "I am at least faithful in my preaching and teaching." No! As a preacher, I should be pleading with God every week, saying: "If Thou wilt not bless me, I will not go forth this day. Lord, as I mount that pulpit, as I begin to speak, grant that apart from my own words there might be the accompaniment of the Spirit's power, so that men and women might be convicted of their sin, that the discouraged might be encouraged and inspired, that we might know something of the wrenching of sin from the hearts of your people and a birthing of a real pursuit after holiness. Speak through me so powerfully that the people of God might know God has spoken!" O that we would plead with God until we begin to notice heads bowing low, cheeks becoming wet, and loud cries coming from hardened sinners and backsliders!

In times of suffering

Fourth, the Holy Spirit also empowers us in the realm of persecution and suffering. He does so in at least two ways:

(1) *The Holy Spirit empowers us by giving us courage and boldness.* In Acts 4, we read of a time when the church was under intense persecution. The apostles were arrested, told to stop preaching Christ, and were finally dismissed. When they got to their own people, they reported all that had been done to them at the hands of the chief priests and the elders. Luke records that upon hearing this, the whole company of believers raised their voices together in prayer: "Now, Lord, look on their threats, and grant to Your servants that with all boldness they may speak Your word, by stretching out Your hand to heal, and that signs and wonders may be done through the

name of Your holy Servant Jesus" (Acts 4:29–30). Then we are told: "And when they had prayed, the place where they were assembled together was shaken; and they were all filled with the Holy Spirit, and they spoke the word of God with boldness" (v. 31). Even as they were under persecution, because of being filled with the Spirit, the disciples went about preaching the gospel courageously and boldly in the face of suffering.

(2) *The Holy Spirit empowers us by giving us the right words to speak.* When we are in the heat of pressure, with no time to formulate self-defense speeches, the Holy Spirit gives us the actual words to speak. In Matthew 10:17–20, the Lord Jesus Christ said to His disciples:

> But beware of men, for they will deliver you up to councils and scourge you in their synagogues. You will be brought before governors and kings for My sake, as a testimony to them and to the Gentiles. But when they deliver you up, do not worry about how or what you should speak. For it will be given to you in that hour what you should speak; for it is not you who speak, but the Spirit of your Father who speaks in you.

We see a clear example of this in the book of Acts:

> And it came to pass, on the next day, that their rulers, elders, and scribes, as well as Annas the high priest, Caiaphas, John, and Alexander, and as many as were of the family of the high priest, were gathered together at Jerusalem. And when they had set them in the midst, they asked, "By what power or by what name have you done this?" Then Peter, filled with the Holy Spirit, said to them, "Rulers of the people and elders of Israel: If we this day are judged for a good deed done to a helpless man, by what means he has been made well, let it be known to you all, and to all the people of Israel, that by the name of Jesus Christ of Nazareth, whom you crucified, whom God raised from the dead, by Him this man stands here before you whole. This is the 'stone which was rejected by you builders, which has become the chief cornerstone.' Nor is there salvation in any other, for there is no other name under heaven given among men by which we must be saved." Now when they saw the boldness of Peter and John, and perceived that they were uneducated and untrained men, they marveled. And they realized that they had been with Jesus (Acts 4:5–13).

Peter preached this conscience-piercing sermon without any premeditation; it was not a written-out sermon! The Holy Spirit gave him the words he spoke. The disciples were unschooled, ordinary fishermen, but they were speaking with great boldness in the midst of the men who graced the corridors of power in their day. And there was no sign that they were trying to piece together a few apologetics discourses. They charged the men before them with sin, declaring that they had participated in the crucifixion of the Righteous One of God. The apostles told them, "Dear sirs, that same Jesus whom you crucified—you builders, you master architects of Israel—He is the only one by whom all men everywhere in Israel and across the globe must be saved."

Often this empowering work of the Holy Spirit takes place in the midst of persecution. The Holy Spirit enables us to serve Him in order to meet the need of the hour. He gives us the gift. He gives us the effectiveness. He gives us the courage and boldness. And He gives us just the right words so that our service redounds to God's glory alone. To borrow the words of Paul, "But we have this treasure in earthen vessels, that the excellence of the power may be of God and not of us" (2 Cor. 4:7).

Conclusion

The point in all these illustrations is not to give an exhaustive list. Rather, it is to show that it is the Holy Spirit who works within us both to will and to do according to God's good pleasure (Phil. 2:13). When we learn that, it ought to humble us in every respect, whether it is in terms of our ability to pray aright; to have a right focus in our worship; to produce much fruit in service; to withstand persecution; to stand in the realm of suffering; or to find the right words in all that we are going through; whether it is the fact that we have an above average knowledge of God, His person, His purpose, and His works; or whether it is the fact that we have known something of His inward strengthening, the inward maturity in the things of God. All of this comes to us by the Spirit out of the abundance of His grace. Without Him, we can do nothing.

Putting it a little differently, when we see a brother who has fallen in sin; a brother who looks at church as a place to display his carnality; a believer who does literally nothing in church and knows nothing of being the means of the conversion or building up of any soul; a saint who is always biting his tongue whenever he is called upon to speak on behalf of the cause of Jesus Christ; or a believer who is still struggling with the ABCs of salvation, and still weak in his walk, we need to learn to say, "There go I, but for the grace of God." It will keep us humble. That proud, self-confident Christian who is always laughing at the weaknesses and inabilities of others does not know as he ought to know.

But this truth also ought to make us confident (but not self-confident). When we look at others who are far ahead of us; who seem to have an air of spirituality when they are in the place of worship; who, when they open their mouths to pray, make us feel as if we have never prayed before; who, when they are leading the worship service, seem to take us into the Holy of Holies; whose abilities far outstrip ours; who are more effective than we are in their own ministries; who are courageous and bold in their work for the Lord; who, in the midst of persecution, seem to be able to say the right words; whose knowledge of the truth of God far exceeds ours; and who are full of the fullness of God in every way, we should not despair. We should be able to say: "I can do all things through Christ who strengthens me. By His Spirit, the sky is the limit."

This double—apparently contradictory—response must come to us as we consider seriously the Holy Spirit's empowering work. We are to be humble, yet confident. Can you testify of this in your Christian life? You must never rest content with a Christianity that is devoid of the Spirit's empowering. This is part of the process of sanctification, and if you are not growing in this then there must be something seriously amiss in your life. May you be a person who seeks the Holy Spirit's empowering in all aspects of your walk with Christ.

Chapter 16
by Austin Walker

The Supply of the Spirit of Jesus Christ and Apostolic Ministry

For I know that this will turn out for my deliverance through your prayer and the supply of the Spirit of Jesus Christ.
—PHILIPPIANS 1:19

Paul endured suffering for Christ from the very beginning of his ministry. When he confounded the Jews in Damascus after his conversion, they plotted to kill him. He escaped under cover of night when the disciples in the city let him down through the walls in a large basket (Acts 9:23–25). In 2 Corinthians 11:22–33, boasting of his infirmities, he catalogs many of his experiences of suffering as an apostle of Jesus Christ, culminating in his escape from Damascus. He wrote that letter about AD 57. By the early 60s, Paul was a prisoner in Rome and still suffering for the cause of Christ. While in prison, he wrote the Prison Epistles, Philippians included.[1] How was it possible for this man to undergo such repeated trials, almost constant and extremely varied sufferings, and yet not be overwhelmed and destroyed by them in his body and spirit? How, on the contrary, was he able positively to exclaim, "for to me, to live is Christ, and to die is gain" (Phil. 1:21)?

By extension and implication, we should also ask how it has been possible for the church of Jesus Christ to survive for a further two thousand years, often facing various kinds and degrees of persecution. Furthermore, how is it possible for any preacher to sustain a long and faithful biblical ministry, facing foes within and without? A substantial part of the answer

---

1. See D. Edmond Hiebert, *An Introduction to the New Testament*, three-volume collection (Waynesboro, Ga.: Gabriel Publishing, 2003). The sections discussing the dating of 2 Corinthians and Philippians are found in vol. 2, 146–47, 290–92.

is found in the words of Philippians 1:19: "your prayer and the supply of the Spirit of Jesus Christ."

The situation facing the apostle in Rome

Paul knew that he had been appointed for the defense of the gospel (Phil. 1:7). He also knew that the Philippians were very concerned about what was happening to him while he was in Rome. There was an unusual bond between the church in Philippi and the apostle that had been established when Paul first visited the city and preached the gospel there (Acts 16:11–40). They knew how he had been "spitefully treated" while there (1 Thess. 2:2). They had given hospitality to Paul and his companions, and when he had left, they had sent material help on more than one occasion to supply his needs (Phil. 4:10, 14–17).

Paul wrote to assure them that despite what he was experiencing in Rome, everything had "actually turned out for the furtherance of the gospel" (1:12). Such an outcome was probably the very opposite of what they expected and perhaps, in the details, even what the apostle anticipated. He was persuaded, however, that one factor had controlled what had happened to him: namely, the advance of the gospel. That was no chance happening. He had been appointed by God to that end, and that included all his current trials and afflictions. God ruled in His sovereign power and wisdom, and the apostle was persuaded that the advance of the gospel would not be hindered by events in Rome.

Nevertheless, the situation Paul was facing was serious. On the one hand, he was facing the frustrations and perplexities arising from the sins of envy and strife, the result of selfish ambition. He was a prisoner in Rome, and some rival preachers were taking advantage of his circumstances and rubbing salt into his wounds. They were preaching Christ, but out of very impure motives. Thinking that Paul had been removed from the scene by his imprisonment, these men indulged in a form of oneupmanship, aiming to get as far ahead of the apostle as they possibly could. By so doing, said Paul, they aimed to "add affliction to my chains" (1:16). They interpreted Paul's imprisonment as weakness and could not understand how such an incapacity could ever be an opportunity for the advance of the gospel. However, the picture was not as gloomy as it might have been, for there were also in Rome those who preached Christ with sincere and pure motives.

We might think that Paul would have been so distressed by this insincere group of preachers that he would have seen it as a severe hindrance to the progress of the gospel. But Paul was of a decidedly different opinion. These men were certainly operating with wrong motives, but his imprisonment *had* turned out for the advance of the gospel. He was eager to convey that to the Philippians. The very fact that he was in prison meant that Paul, in chains for Christ, was being spoken of in wide circles—the whole palace guard—and the preaching of the gospel had received fresh momentum. His testimony to Christ and the increased boldness of other disciples to bear witness greatly heartened him. Thus, Paul was full of joy because, whatever the motives might be, Christ was being preached and the gospel was being advanced.

On the other hand, Paul was facing the prospect of death. He did not know what the outcome of his trial before the Roman authorities would be. Despite this uncertainty, he remained calm and was able to calm the fears of the Philippians. Whether he lived or died, he was able to face the outcome with patience and fortitude. It appears from Philippians 1:7 that he had already faced one judicial review of his case with a favorable outcome, and he seemed fairly confident that he would finally be released and would see the Philippians again—a desire that was fulfilled. However, he knew that he would not be ashamed either way: "Christ will be magnified in my body, whether by life or by death" (1:20).[2]

How was Paul able to face these uncertainties and the prospect of death with such calm? How was he able to respond so positively to those who actually aggravated his sufferings by their spirit of rivalry? It would have been very easy for Paul to become preoccupied with them, to raise his hackles in self-defense, and then denounce them. Instead, he responded in a very different manner. He knew he was appointed for the defense of the gospel, and that would involve facing issues like this. However, he did not

---

2. J. Gresham Machen, *The New Testament: An Introduction to Its Literature and History*, ed. W. John Cook (Edinburgh: Banner of Truth, 1976), 175–78, provides a brief but helpful construction of events in Rome.

just knuckle down and, in cold blood, accept that this situation was the result of the sovereignty of God. Rather, he recognized that the outcome depended on the prayers of the Philippians and the supply of the Spirit of Jesus Christ.

A profound personal statement

J. Gresham Machen draws attention to the "intimacy and mutual confidence which existed between the church and its founder."[3] Paul was writing to the Philippians in intimate personal terms. Having spoken of his joy that Christ was preached whatever the motives may have been (v. 18), he moved on to speak of his anticipated joy regarding his own deliverance and the magnifying of Christ, regardless of the outcome of his trial. There is nothing detached or casual about the apostle's personal statement. He could not be certain about the outcome of his trial in Rome, but he was certain about his personal role in that outcome—it was to show "an enlarged, life-size Christ to all who care to look, a Christ fully displayed in every dimension and capacity of Paul, a Christ, 'magnified in his body.'"[4]

By speaking in this manner, Paul set a pattern for every Christian who is determined to walk in his footsteps. Everything in Paul's life was geared toward preparing for the day of Christ, who is "the key of all history and of personal history…the deciding factor in every Christian choice."[5] In facing the uncertain future, every Christian is to make the magnifying of Christ his single controlling concern.

It was not arrogance or presumption that led the apostle to speak in verse 19 with such confidence about his deliverance. He began with, "For I know…." He was fully persuaded that he would be delivered and vindicated, and that Jesus Christ would be glorified, whether he lived or died. Caesar's court would make its decision, but Paul was not ultimately in Caesar's hands. Discharged from prison or not, he knew that he had been divinely appointed for the defense of the gospel. He knew that the Lord

---

3. Machen, *The New Testament*, 173.
4. J. A. Motyer, *The Richness of Christ: Studies in the Letter to the Philippians* (London: InterVarsity Fellowship, 1966), 36.
5. Motyer, *The Richness of Christ*, 37.

Jesus Christ would not fail him, so that he would end up ashamed and abandoned in disgrace. The motives of some men were evil, but he could never impute evil motives to his faithful, sovereign Lord and Savior.

Job is mentioned only once by name in the New Testament, in James 5:11. However, the best commentators are persuaded that Paul here was echoing Job's confidence expressed in the Septuagint (the Greek version of the Old Testament): "This will turn out for my deliverance" (Job 13:16). Peter T. O'Brien concludes that Paul applied Job's words to his own situation because he, like Job, was confident of his final vindication by God.[6]

There remains a question as to whether the deliverance to which Paul refers was his present plight as a prisoner facing a human court or his ultimate vindication in the heavenly court. Many of the early church fathers, Chrysostom included, understood Paul to be referring only to temporal deliverance before a human tribunal. John Eadie cataloged the historical consensus of exegetical opinion, though he himself was persuaded Paul was not referring to a temporal deliverance.[7] Likewise, O'Brien concludes that the deliverance spoken of here "usually refers to the final deliverance of the believer at the last judgment…final eschatological salvation…deliverance from the coming wrath of God…and the endowment with the divine glory."[8] Paul used the normal New Testament word for "salvation" (translated "deliverance" by the New King James Version). Although the word is used to refer to the final salvation in other passages, the context of verse 19 suggests that Paul may have had in mind both his vindication before a human court and his final vindication before God.[9]

However we understand this deliverance, it is very clear that the apostle had a well-grounded, long-term, settled conviction. His trust was firmly in Christ. He was completely confident of his future, envisaging his personal enjoyment of salvation ultimately in the day of Christ. Nothing of what was

---

6. Peter T. O'Brien, *The Epistle to the Philippians: A Commentary on the Greek Text* (Grand Rapids: Eerdmans, 1991), 108–9.

7. John Eadie, *A Commentary on the Greek Text of Paul's Letter to the Philippians* (Birmingham, Ala.: Solid Ground Christian Books, 2005), 42–44.

8. O'Brien, *The Epistle to the Philippians*, 109–10.

9. Sinclair B. Ferguson, *Let's Study Philippians* (Edinburgh: Banner of Truth, 1997), 26.

happening in Rome—"this" in verse 19 refers to the situation in which he found himself—dented his ambition to attain to it.

Here, surely, is something instructive for every generation of Christians and especially preachers of the gospel. No one ever has any reason to fear the outcome of events. Pressures and setbacks come from every direction; some of them are very unpleasant and most of them are unexpected. But Paul believed in God's sovereignty. He was persuaded he was appointed for the defense of the gospel. When circumstances seem to conspire against us, it is all too easy to act as if the Lord has lost His crown and been dethroned. But Paul remained confident, undeterred by difficult circumstances. He was calm, drawing comfort and strength from his "earnest expectation and hope" (v. 20).

But what is the origin of this hope and how is it maintained in the daily pressures of living as a Christian? Paul had a ready answer that he believed with the same kind of confidence.

The sufficiency of the intercession of the Philippians and of the Spirit of Jesus Christ

Paul was firmly persuaded that his deliverance would be accomplished through the intercessory prayers of the Christian church in Philippi and the supply of the Spirit of Jesus Christ. He believed in human means as well as divine means. These means were closely related, for both expressed complete dependence on God. The way Paul wrote shows this. Both "prayer" and "supply" are governed by one preposition ("through") and are connected by a single definite article. By writing in this manner, Paul intended his readers to understand that the supply of the Spirit was the answer to the intercessory prayers of the church.[10] The outcome was certain—he would be able to stand firm and be faithful to Christ during his temporal trials, and finally he would attain salvation in the day of Christ. Sufficiency is invested in both these means, a sufficiency that is of God.

The term "prayer" refers to a need and is used in the New Testament of

---

10. Motyer says that the two thoughts of intercession and supply are bound so closely together by the apostle that we could, without violence, translate the Greek, "your prayers and the consequent supply..." (Motyer, *The Richness of Christ*, 51).

prayer that is addressed to God, particularly a petition or a supplication. It is pre-eminently the language of faith and of dependence on God alone. If a Christian is going to stand firm and live for Christ rather than be dragged under by the riptides of events and circumstances, he needs help. The apostle once again is our pattern. He was in need, so he urged the Philippians to plead with God on account of his circumstances. For the apostle, such intercessory prayers were never incidental. He, on the one hand, constantly prayed for the Philippians (1:3–11), and, on the other hand, he often wrote to urge others to intercede for him.[11] For the apostle, such prayers were never incidental or mere formalities. Instead, they were a vital means of participation, or fellowship, in the struggle for the advance of the gospel. Paul was appointed for the defense of the gospel, but he did not expect to be successful in that defense apart from the constant intercession of the churches of Christ.

In verse 19, "prayer" is singular, suggesting that Paul was making a very specific request of the corporate body of believers in Philippi. He wanted to see Jesus Christ magnified, whether he lived or died. He desired to be finally vindicated on the great day of Christ. If that was to happen, the specific help he required was nothing less than the "supply of the Spirit of Jesus Christ." Some translations speak of the "help" or the "provision" of the Spirit, but neither of those terms accurately conveys the full meaning of the word used here. The New King James Version renders the word "supply," and J. A. Motyer notes that this "'supply' has a 'plus' element in it; it is the 'full, sufficient supply.'"[12]

When the Lord Jesus Christ sends His Spirit, we are not to think of the Spirit's influence as if it were a trickling stream that might dry up at the first sign of drought. In the Mediterranean world, with its hot, dry

---

11. For example, Rom. 15:30–32; 2 Cor. 1:11; Eph. 6:19; Col. 4:3; 1 Thess. 5:25; 2 Thess. 3:1–2; Philem. 22.

12. Motyer, *The Richness of Christ*, 51. J. B. Lightfoot translates the noun as "bountiful supply." See J. B. Lightfoot, *Saint Paul's Epistle to the Philippians* (London: Macmillan, 1869), 89. Most of the commentators give two or three examples of the use of the word in the Greek-speaking world. In marriage contracts, it was used to refer to the provision for a spouse; in medical language, it was used of the ligament that acts as a support; in the Athenian theater, it was used to describe the provision that the leader of the chorus made for the members.

summers, such streams are common. But Paul's picture is one of abundance, of a perennial river like the Nile. This river flows through deserts in its northernmost section, but for centuries its abundant waters have provided the basis for the civilizations that have thrived in Egypt. Paul asked the Philippians to pray for the abundant, perennial supply of the Spirit of Jesus Christ—the same Spirit who rested on Christ and gave Him power to carry out His messianic ministry. He received the Spirit without limit or measure (John 3:34).

There are some important differences between the supply of the Spirit that was given to Christ and that which is given to believers. For example, in the Messiah, the Spirit dwelled in utter fullness and power, and He met with no resistance of any kind because the Lord's heart was always without sin. In believers, even in a man like the apostle, sin remains. However, that does not mean that the Spirit's power in a believer is reduced to something that is inferior or ineffectual. The exalted Lord Jesus sends His Spirit (also described by Christ as "the Spirit of your Father") to empower His servants, and He does not keep them as paupers.

The words Jesus spoke in Matthew 10:16–20 (cf. Mark 13:11; Luke 12:11) have a direct bearing on the apostle's circumstances. Christ prophesied how His disciples would be brought before governors and kings for His sake. He stressed that they were not to worry about how or what they should speak, then gave this reason: "For it will be given to you in that hour what you should speak; for it is not you who speak, but the Spirit of your Father who speaks in you" (vv. 19–20). Was this promise in the mind of the apostle as he wrote from prison, awaiting his trial before Caesar? Did the Philippians also recall this promise as they prayed for him? Perhaps Paul recalled the occasion in Jerusalem when Stephen was martyred. Luke recounted the abundant supply of the Spirit given to Christ's faithful witness that day—Stephen was "full of the Holy Spirit" (Acts 7:55).

Because of the close bonds of love between him and the Philippian church, Paul knew that they were praying for him and would continue to do so. He was confident that he would receive an abundant measure of the Spirit to support him in his weakness and to overcome any fears and anxieties, so that he would magnify Christ in his body and then finally stand vindicated and saved in the day of the Lord Jesus. Of immediate significance to the apostle was the fact that he had been appointed for the defense of the gospel. Therefore, in complete dependence on the supply of the Spirit, he would speak wisely, boldly, faithfully, and without shame as he testified to Jesus Christ before the great men of the Roman Empire. He would be enabled to do so because of the effectual prayers of the Philippian church.

A question remains as to whether "the supply of the Spirit of Jesus Christ" refers to the Spirit who was supplied to Paul (the objective genitive) or to the abundant help given by the Holy Spirit to Paul (the subjective genitive). Either is possible. J. B. Lightfoot comments that "the language... will bear both meanings well, and that therefore any such restriction is arbitrary. 'The Spirit of Jesus' is both the giver and the gift."[13] These more technical questions should not be allowed to obscure the fact, aptly and tersely captured by Sinclair Ferguson, that Jesus Christ "reserves the best of his gifts for the time of our greatest need; of that Paul was certain."[14]

Implications for Paul, minsters of the gospel, and the church

The Holy Spirit's abundant supply was essential to Paul's ministry

Paul could not have functioned as a faithful apostle of Christ apart from the work of the Holy Spirit in answer to the prayers of the Philippians. To be appointed for the defense of the gospel in this hostile world and left to his own devices and power would have totally overwhelmed him. The way in which he responded to those preachers driven by selfish ambition (vv. 15–16) is evidence of the work of the Holy Spirit in his mind, will, and emotions. He handled that situation with restraint, not repaying evil for evil, and with commendable magnanimity. Furthermore, rather than being driven by selfish ambition, he had a very different perspective. He saw the good effects his imprisonment was having. The gospel was advancing in Rome and Christ was being preached (albeit in pretense as well as in truth), so he was able to rejoice, and would continue to do so (v. 18).

He was also persuaded that the Holy Spirit would enable him boldly and faithfully to testify to the Lord Jesus Christ before the Roman tribunal and that Christ would be magnified in his body whether he continued to

---

13. Lightfoot, *Saint Paul's Epistle to the Philippians*, 89.
14. Ferguson, *Let's Study Philippians*, 27.

live or suffered death. Christ Himself had specifically promised the help of the Holy Spirit for that very situation.

Finally, Paul was possessed by an overriding confidence in his future vindication before the heavenly court. Space does not permit us to detail the work of the Holy Spirit in connection with that hope. A few examples must suffice. The New Testament speaks of believers being sealed with the Holy Spirit of promise, who is given to us as a down payment of our inheritance (Eph. 1:13–14); God, who raised the Lord Jesus Christ from the dead, gives life to our mortal bodies through the Holy Spirit who dwells in us (Rom. 8:11, 23; cf 1 Cor. 15:45; 2 Cor. 4:16–5:11); and the work of the Spirit is intimately involved in the process of salvation that leads to the obtaining of the glory of our Lord Jesus Christ (2 Thess. 2:13–14).

The Holy Spirit's abundant supply is essential to every minster of the gospel
Every preacher of the gospel is as dependent on God and the abundant supply of the Holy Spirit as was the apostle Paul. Philippians 1:19 in its context gave us three aspects of the Spirit's work. Whether ministers are dealing with people who have insincere motives, are required to be faithful to Christ while enduring prison and the prospect of facing hostile authorities, are aiming to live as Christians with a constant, vibrant expectation and hope of final salvation, or are experiencing any of the myriad other demanding situations in a minister's life and ministry, dependence on the supply of the Spirit is essential.

In a sermon on this text, Charles H. Spurgeon, speaking of the act of preaching, declared:

> It is the *sine quâ non* [the essential condition] of a ministry from God that it should be in the power of the Spirit.... [He] must teach us the truth and then guide us as to which truth is to be spoken. Then the Holy Spirit must inflame the minister. The man who never takes fire, how is he sent of God? He who never glows or burns, what knows he of the baptism of the Holy Ghost, which is also the baptism of fire. Pray, therefore, for the supply of the Spirit! Without the Spirit every ministry lacks that subtle, I was about to say indescribable, something which is known by the name of *unction*. Nobody here can tell what unction is. He knows that the Spirit of God gives it and he knows

when it is in a discourse and when it is absent. Unction is in fact the power of God.[15]

Do those of us who are ministers of the gospel set about our work in this apostolic manner—in complete dependence on the abundant supply of the Spirit of Jesus Christ? A man of God is nothing without the Spirit of God.

The prayers of the church are essential to the faithfulness of every true minister
In the same sermon, Spurgeon devoted considerable time to explaining why and in what ways the congregation is to pray for its minister. He was following the apostolic precedent laid down by Paul. The apostle was thinking not simply of individual prayers, but the prayers of the corporate body of believers in Philippi. Recall how the believers in the church in Jerusalem "raised their voice to God with one accord" (Acts 4:24). The result was remarkable: "they were all filled with the Holy Spirit, and they spoke the word of God with boldness" (v. 31b). Paul was urging the church to which he was writing to pray in a similar manner for the supply of the Spirit. He knew that all his goals, hopes, and expectations would come to nothing without the prayers of the church. Such intercession and supplication is indispensable for the furtherance of the gospel. Do we have men of the caliber of the apostle? Are we members of churches with the capacity to pray like the Philippians?

Early in his London ministry, Spurgeon complained:

> When Zion travails, she brings forth children; when Zion is in earnest, God is in earnest about his work; when Zion is prayerful, God blesses her. We must not, therefore, arbitrarily look for the cause of our failure in the will of God, but we must also see what is the difference between ourselves and the men of Apostolic times, and what it is that renders our success so trifling in comparison with the tremendous results of Apostolic preaching. I think I shall be able to show one or two reasons why our holy faith is not so prosperous as it was then. In the first place, *we have not Apostolic men*; in the second place, they *do not set about their work in an Apostolic style*; in the third place, we have *not Apostolic churches* to back them up; and in the fourth place, we have

---

15. C. H. Spurgeon, "The Minister's Plea," in *The Metropolitan Tabernacle Pulpit: Sermons Preached and Revised by C. H. Spurgeon, during the year 1873* (Pasadena, Texas: Pilgrim Publications, 2002), 19:609.

not *the Apostolic influence of the Holy Ghost* in the measure which they had it in ancient times.[16]

Are these observations and complaints still valid? If so, ought we not as ministers and churches to seek the mercy of God, humble ourselves in fresh repentance, and set ourselves in renewed dependence on God to pray for the supply of the Spirit of Jesus Christ? According to the apostle, the furtherance of the gospel depends on such action.

---

16. C. H. Spurgeon, "Gospel Missions," in *The New Park Street Pulpit*, 6 vols. (1892; repr., Grand Rapids: Baker, 1994), 2:177–84. It can be read at http://www.spurgeon.org/sermons/0076.htm

Chapter 17
by Robert Oliver

An Elizabethan Cameo: The Ministry of Edward Dering

By any consideration, the reign of Elizabeth I (1558–1603) was one of the most remarkable eras in English history. Great figures emerged in church and state as the kingdom emerged from weakness and uncertainty to become a significant player in European affairs. The list of eminent Elizabethans includes politicians, writers, poets, artists, adventurers, and, most important of all, men and women of God.

Elizabeth, one of the most erudite of sovereigns and a very skillful politician, has to be seen as a moderate Protestant who wanted a church that would draw together men and women from as wide a religious spectrum as possible. She promoted the structured services of the restored *Book of Common Prayer* and discouraged too much preaching. Private initiatives, especially among the lower clergy, were not encouraged.

Coming to the throne after the bitter persecutions of Mary I (1553–1558), when it must have appeared that the cause of the gospel in England was lost, Elizabeth had to turn to men who had been exiled to the great centers of European reform for leadership in her Church of England. These men had experienced a more thorough Reformation than had been possible in the brief reign of Edward VI (1547–1553). They had also been exposed to some of the finest biblical exposition of the day in centers such as Geneva and Zurich. In England, they were never able to secure the reform of church structures that many of them desired, but they were able to establish a powerful tradition of preaching and pastoral care. These men were nicknamed "Puritans" or "Precisianists." Of them, Professor A. G. Dickens writes:

Throughout Elizabethan England Puritan preachers dominated the pulpits, even though many of them were intermittently engaged in disputes with their bishops. As their sermons show, their preaching ability and their numbers had no equivalent in pre-Reformation or mid-Tudor England.[1]

A significant figure among these was Edward Dering (1540–1576), although the facts that his life was short and his ministry was carried out early in the reign have resulted in neglect in subsequent centuries. His relatively few writings were seldom reprinted after the end of Elizabeth's reign, to the loss of later students of Puritanism. Recent study confirms that he was an important figure in these years.

We are indebted to the late Professor Patrick Collinson for rescuing Dering's memory and pointing out that his short career can too easily be underestimated. Collinson considered Dering to be "the archetype of the puritan divine, whose life and works were a model for the many who would come after him in the seventeenth century."[2] Although Collinson has recounted something of Dering's public ministry, his development and the nature of his spirituality remain to be investigated.

The Derings of Surrenden-Dering

A little to the south of the North Downs in Kent, separated from them by the Vale of Holmesdale, is the arc of the Greensand Hills, historically marking the boundary of the Weald of Kent and Sussex. On this ridge, some six miles west of the market town of Ashford, is the village of Pluckley, with its parish church dating from 1093. About a mile to the east of the church was the manor house of Surrenden, which survived until the middle of the twentieth century. The manor property passed into the hands of the Dering family in the reign of Henry II (1154–1189). Later acquisitions secured extensive lands in the parish of Pluckley and beyond. Successive generations of Derings lie buried in the parish church of St. Nicholas, where their

---

1. A. G. Dickens, *The English Reformation*, rev. ed. (London: Fontana, 1972), 428.
2. Patrick Collinson, *A Mirror of Elizabethan Puritanism: The Life and Letters of 'Godly Master Dering'* (London: The Dr Williams's Trust, 1964), 2. In his magisterial work, *The Elizabethan Puritan Movement* (London: Jonathan Cape, 1967), Collinson sets Dering in the context of the wider movement.

wealth enabled them to restructure the Lady Chapel in the south aisle in the fifteenth century. This subsequently became known as the Dering Chapel. From the Pluckley churchyard in one direction can be seen the Weald, originally the great forest known to the Anglo-Saxons as Anderida. It was still heavily wooded in the sixteenth century. In the other direction stretch the North Downs, along which runs the historic Pilgrims' Way from Winchester to Canterbury. Pluckley lies within the diocese of Canterbury, and the archbishop is the patron of its parish church.

By the middle of the sixteenth century, the manor had become known as Surrenden-Dering and the head of the family was John Dering, who had married Margaret Brent of the adjoining parish of Charing, where the Brents were significant landowners. John and Margaret had five sons, of whom Edward was the third. Since John died in 1550, Margaret must have been responsible for much of Edward's education, possibly assisted by his elder brother Richard, who was the heir to the Dering estate. He must have shown sufficient promise to be sent to Cambridge, where his progress was outstanding.

Years of persecution

Edward was born in the later years of Henry VIII, who had broken away from the papacy but retained Roman Catholic theology and practices, with the one significant exception that he gave permission for the publication of an English translation of the Bible.

During the reign of Edward VI, more radical changes came. Services were conducted in English, the Roman Catholic Mass was replaced by a Reformed Communion service, and the gospel was preached. However, this flowering of Reformed thought and practice was short. Edward died of tuberculosis in the summer of 1553 and was succeeded by his Roman Catholic half-sister, Mary I, who was resolved to restore the old order, including submission to the papacy. To achieve this, she devoted the last three years of her reign to bitter persecution of Protestants. Almost three hundred died at the stake, fifty-four of whom were from Kent, more than from any other English county.

The fearful sentence of death by burning was not new in Kent. The county had long been a center for the Lollards, the followers of John Wyclif, who met in secret for Bible reading and prayer at a time when possession of the Bible in England was a capital offense. Occasional investigations in the fifteenth century led to Lollard trials that indicated that there were at least two Lollard centers, one in the villages around Tenterden and the other near Wye. There may well have been others. The Derings would have known that shortly before the Reformation broke out in Europe, John Brown of Ashford was burned on Whitsunday 1517 for the offense of denying the real presence of the body of Christ in the Eucharist.

Between 1555 and 1558, heresy trials and executions became much more common. Local officials in Kent were keen to hunt out the "heretics." The Derings had some family connections with the village of Rolvenden, whose vicar, John Frankesh, was one of four who were burned in July 1555, including the vicar of Adisham, near Canterbury. Frankesh was denounced by Richard Thornden, who had professed Protestantism as vicar of Tenterden, but as dean of Canterbury actively persecuted his erstwhile associates. As far as is known, there were no martyrs from the parish of Pluckley, but six months after the death of Frankesh, a weaver from Tenterden and six women were burned, including Agnes Snoth, a widow from the adjoining village of Smarden.

Career at Cambridge

Edward must have entered Christ's College, Cambridge, during Mary's reign, but there is no evidence that his religious opinions caused difficulties with the establishment at that time. It is possible that during this period, like so many of his countrymen, he was able to change his creed with each change of monarch. It is also possible his religious convictions were as yet unformed. Having graduated with a bachelor of arts degree in 1560 after the Protestant Elizabeth had ascended the throne, he proceeded to earn a master of arts in 1563, followed by a bachelor of theology in 1568. From 1560 until 1570, he was a fellow of his college. When Elizabeth visited Cambridge in 1564, Edward was chosen to celebrate the occasion with a Greek oration. His scholarly reputation won him a somewhat grudging tribute from Archbishop of Canterbury Matthew Parker, who called Dering "the greatest learned man (so thought) in England."

Some time around 1560, Edward's Puritan convictions matured. Dates are not clear, but his fellowship at Christ's College preceded by several years that of the more famous Puritan Laurence Chaderton. Collinson has some interesting comments on the Puritanism of this college, "which it owed to a succession of tutors." While a number of other colleges at both Oxford and Cambridge were involved in vociferous protests against clerical dress and ceremony, quieter but equally significant developments were taking place at Christ's:

> Here there grew a puritan tradition moderate in its reaction to those ceremonies and church order which are usually represented as the main ground of puritan protest, but passionately indignant against the practical inadequacies of the Elizabethan Church and above all against its pastoral deficiencies. It was a tradition established and begun, in all probability, by Dering himself. It was continued by Laurence Chaderton who became a fellow in 1568 and who soon gave up ordinary tutorial responsibilities in order to devote himself wholly to his plans for harnessing the university more effectively to the supply of preaching ministers for the Church at large.[3]

The preacher

In 1567, Dering was appointed Lady Margaret preacher at Cambridge, and also at that time he became a member of the archbishop's household, where he may have been a chaplain. In November, Parker appointed him rector of Pluckley. He seems to have been non-resident and appointed a curate for the parish. Edward Hasted's list of the rectors of Pluckley includes the abbreviation STP, which stands for *"Professor Theologiae Sacrae"* ("Professor of Sacred Theology").

By 1570, non-residence must have given him a guilty conscience, for in that year he denounced the practice in what has become his best-known work, a sermon preached before Elizabeth in the Chapel Royal. It cost him the queen's favor and probably that of the archbishop, if he had not already forfeited it. However, he still had prominent friends at court who

---

3. Collinson, *A Mirror*, 7.

undoubtedly gave him a measure of protection for a time. A letter to his brother Richard explains:

> For my lord of Canterbury I have been once with him, but I mean not to go the second time. My Lord of London is a good man. I am often with him. I have seen in him such tokens of a good spirit, that I reverence him in my heart and will serve him in Christ in all things.[4]

At this time, Dering was living in the diocese of London and had a good relationship with the bishop, Edwin Sandys, who had been one of the Protestant exiles in Mary's reign, spending most of his time abroad in Strasburg and Zurich. The year 1570 brought Roman Catholic rebellion in the north of England and Elizabeth's formal excommunication and deposition by Pope Pius V. The government had plenty on its mind and hence was probably not disposed to stir up a hornet's nest by proceeding against an increasingly popular London preacher. Surprisingly, Dering was a chaplain to the duke of Norfolk, who was implicated in the Northern Rebellion and eventually paid for it with his life. Dering served the duke along with John Foxe, the martyrologist. There survives a letter from Dering to Norfolk in which the preacher reproaches himself for a lack of faithfulness:

> And now my Lord I beseech you, pray for me, and humbly upon my knees I ask you hearty forgiveness wherein I have not done as it became me touching you. You know how in my time I have persuaded you from your wicked servants, from your popish friends and from your adulterous woman. But alas, my Lord, your high calling hath bridled my words. I could not speak as I should. My words were too soft to heal so old a disease. Why should I have tarried in your Lordship's house except these evil things had been amended? This bearing with your evil was the greatest evil I could have done you. And I beseech you, forgive me, and God for his mercy's sake shall make me strong that hereafter I shall not fear to reprove the sinner, and God shall forgive you your dullness of spirit that could not be moved with a little counsel.[5]

---

4. Cited in Collinson, *A Mirror*, 7.
5. Edward Dering, "Letter to the Duke of Norfolk" (London, 1590), in *Certain godly and comfortable Letters, full of Christian Consolation, Written by M. Ed Dering unto sundry of his friends And now published for the profit of the Church of God*, annexed to his *XXVII Lectures or Readings upon Part of the Epistle to the Hebrews*, in *Works* (facsimile, USA, np,

Collinson quotes an unpublished letter from Dering that suggests that before the Duke's execution, Dering believed that Norfolk had repented and that Dering acknowledged the duke as a brother in Christ.[6]

Clearly Bishop Sandys was impressed with Dering. He appointed him as a divinity lecturer in St. Paul's Cathedral, where he preached a series of twenty-seven lectures on the epistle to the Hebrews, reaching 6:6 before the queen intervened to stop him at the end of 1573. He was forbidden to preach any more in the queen's dominions. He had carefully avoided politics in the Hebrews lectures, but the government clearly thought that he was giving too much encouragement to the Puritan party. To his brother Richard, he wrote on December 24, 1573:

> DW on Friday last as I was about to preach forbade me in her Majesty's name, so I stand now forbidden, not by the Bishop, but by our Princess, whom I beseech God to make a happy governor in his Church, and many years to give peace unto his people. If we prayed as we should, God would make perfect the good work he hath begun and make us see the peace of Jerusalem all the days of our life.[7]

Dering was already suffering from tuberculosis. From then on, he concentrated on writing and publishing his lectures on Hebrews, prefacing these with a letter to the queen. He also composed prayers for godly households and engaged in lengthy pastoral correspondence, encouraging the faithful to hold fast their profession. Shortly before his public ministry ended, he married Mrs. Anne Locke, widow of a wealthy London merchant. Years before, Anne had been a correspondent of John Knox, and Knox had stayed with her family in the reign of Edward VI. Anne and Knox had been fellow exiles in Geneva. Anne was an erudite Protestant lady who had translated and published in English the sermons of John Calvin on the prayer of Hezekiah. In her second husband, she found a man

---

nd). Dering's spelling has been modernized in this chapter, but quotations are otherwise as given in the *Works*. The *Works* of Dering were published in 1590, and "more at large" in 1597 and 1614. The latter, full editions are not paginated, so Dering's writings will not be cited by page number.

6. Collinson, *A Mirror*, 13.

7. Dering, "Edward Dering to Richard Dering" (November 19, 1570), in *Godly Letters*.

who showed something of Knox's boldness in dealing with monarchs and with a similar vision for his own land.[8]

Dering kept corresponding with his friends until shortly before his death, which took place at Thoby Priory in Essex on June 26, 1576. His life had been short, but he was remembered long as one of England's proto-Puritans. His works were eagerly read until replaced by those of more famous writers. It remains to examine his legacy.

The sermon preached before the queen

Dering came to prominence when he preached a remarkable sermon[9] before Queen Elizabeth I in the Chapel Royal on February 25, 1569/70.[10] His text was Psalm 78:70:

> He chose David his servant also, and took him from the sheepfolds, even from behind the ewes great with young took he him: to feed his people in Jacob, and his inheritance in Israel. So he fed them according to the simplicity of his heart, and guided them by the discretion of his hands.

Collinson described the sermon as the occasion when Dering "took the Queen to task in the most outspoken Lenten sermon she ever heard."[11]

Dering showed from the psalm that the tribe of Ephraim lost precedence in Israel to Judah because of its sin, "in which we learn not to abuse God's mercies, lest they be taken away from us as from the tribe of Ephraim they were." Moving to a consideration of King David, he showed that God had raised him from the lowly position of a farmer's son who looked after the sheep and, in spite of all obstacles, had raised him to the throne. Although he did not specifically state it, Dering's implication was

---

8. Fascinating details about Anne Locke can be found in volume 4 of Lewis Lupton, *A History of the Geneva Bible, Travail* (London: The Olive Tree, n.d.), 19–24.

9. Dering, "A Sermon preached before the Queen's Majesty the 25th Day of February, 1569," in *Works*.

10. By modern reckoning, the date would be 1570, but in Tudor times, the year numbers changed on Lady Day, March 25, so printed versions carry the date 1569.

11. Patrick Collinson, "Dering, Edward (c. 1540–1576)," in *Oxford Dictionary of National Biography*, ed. H. C. G. Matthew and Brian Harrison (Oxford: Oxford University Press, 2004), 15:872–74.

that Elizabeth had had the same experience. Like King David in early life, she had been unlikely to rise to prominence. She was the youngest of Henry VIII's children and had never expected to succeed to the throne as long as there was a prospect that Mary would have children. During Mary's reign, her life had been in real danger. Mary had never really trusted her and on one occasion had sent her to the Tower. Dering emphasized the overall godliness of King David and declared that that had been the secret of his success as king. Then he showed from Hebrew history how often the abuse of God's mercies led to great and severe judgments.

Running through the sermon are frequent reminders of God's goodness to England.

> How plentiful at this day are God's mercies and benefits poured out upon us, both upon our Queen and upon her people. How mightily doth he defend us in so many dangers. How sit we here in safety when the world is in an uproar.... These good blessings of God are signs of his great mercy.

But, Dering stressed, there was no ground for complacency:

> We will return to our purpose and learn of a princely prophet what is a prince's duty, *he must needs feed Jacob and Israel*, that is that Kings must be nurse-fathers and queens must be nurses unto the Church of God. Unto this end they must use their authority, that God's children may learn virtue and knowledge.

David actively promoted godliness. Deploring the spiritual blindness of the emperor, European kings, and, above all, the pope, better things were required from England. Above all else, preaching must be encouraged. God sent Levites out among the tribes of Israel. Christ sent the apostles to preach and to teach. "Oh that our ministers were such as Moses prayed for," Dering said. "Then no doubt God would bless them according to their request and confound their adversaries that rise up against them."

Turning to the plight of a nation where this was not so, he cried:

> Christ said: *Pasce, pasce, pasce,* Feed, feed, feed: This charge he hath given even as we love him, so to see it executed. Say what we will say, and the more we say it the more impudently we shall lie, if we say we love him, while we keep not his commandments. Would to God we were wise to understand it. Christ said *they are the salt of the earth,*

and what shall be done with them if they can season nothing? Christ said, *they are the light of the world*, and what heap of miseries shall they bring with them if they themselves be dark? Christ said, *they be the watchmen*: and what case shall the city be in, if they do nothing but sleep, and delight in sleeping.... They are the pastors, and how hungry must the flock be, when they have no food to give them? They are the teachers, and how great is the ignorance, where they themselves know nothing? They are the evangelists, or messengers of glad tidings: how little hope have they, and how little faith, whose messengers cannot tell what the Lord saith?

Dering moved on to show that he was painting a picture of the English clergy in general and to argue that the queen's indifference was augmenting the evil:

Look upon your ministry, and there are some of one occupation, some of another: some shake bucklers, some ruffians, some hawkers and hunters, some dicers and carders, some blind guides and cannot see, some dumb dogs and cannot bark. And yet a thousand more iniquities have now covered the priesthood. And yet you in the meanwhile that all these whoredoms are committed, you at whose hands God will require it, you sit still and are careless, let men do as they list.

To deal with the problem, Dering urged the queen to ensure that patrons were fulfilling their responsibility of appointing suitably qualified men and ensure that the bishops dealt with the abuses of pluralities and non-residence. Above all, they must deal with men "who say they are learned and can preach, and yet do not, that are (as I said) dumb dogs, and will not bark, bridle at least their greedy appetites, pull out of their mouths those poisoned bones, they so greedily gnaw upon."

He warned the queen:

Let these things alone, and God is a righteous God, he will one day call you to your reckoning. The God of glory open your eyes to see his high kingdom, and enflame your heart to desire it.... Then shall we end these short and evil days with gladness. And when Christ shall appear to judge the quick and the dead, we shall stand at his right hand, in the number of his elect, and hear that last and happy sentence that never shall be called back again: *Come ye blessed of my Father, and possess the Kingdom which is prepared for you from the beginning of the world.*

No preacher had ever dared to address a Tudor monarch so forcibly. The queen never forgot and never forgave. That Dering enjoyed the measure of liberty that he did in the remainder of his short career suggests that he had sympathizers in high places. The printed version of the sermon passed through sixteen editions in Elizabeth's reign, a record for any single sermon at that time; possibly some were printed overseas. The demand indicates something of the strength of the growing Puritan constituency.

There was no suggestion that Dering believed that England was a covenanted nation, as was Israel. Nevertheless, the sermon shows that he believed that the providence of God was at work in a marked way in England. The allusions to God's goodness are there. They appear even more strongly in his prayers.

Great blessings clearly entailed great responsibilities. The queen and her ministers had a duty to promote true religion, but the work had to be carried on by preaching.

The vital importance of preaching

By speaking in the way that he did, Dering risked his future as a minister of the gospel and possibly his personal liberty. The sermon, however, was an expression of a deep-seated conviction that a faithful preaching ministry was essential for the future of Christianity in England and, indeed, for the well-being of the kingdom. There had been a decade of freedom from Rome. Protestant services had been re-introduced in the English language. But without a preaching ministry, all the gains of recent years would be lost. The people must be fed. The queen, however, was not desirous of too much preaching. The routine of the prayer book services, with the addition of sermons read from the approved *Book of Homilies*, would suffice for most parishes. Dering's cry, "Feed, feed, feed!" indicates that he knew that the homilies could never meet the needs of a spiritually destitute people.

Apart from the lectures on Hebrews that Dering delivered a little later, the only other Dering sermon to have survived is one he preached at the Tower of London, about three months before the famous one before the queen. This earlier sermon gives us some understanding of what Dering perceived to be the needs of an ignorant people.

The Tower was a state prison and a garrison center. There were also civil servants working there. The congregation was very different from the one that assembled in the Chapel Royal.

Dering preached on the bread of life from John 6. He carefully explained that the references to the bread of life could not be teaching directly on the sacrament of the Lord's Supper, which had not been instituted at the time when the Savior delivered this memorable discourse. This gave Dering an opportunity to show that the teaching of transubstantiation that lies behind the Roman Catholic Mass is a blasphemous superstition. Ranging through Scripture, he gave examples of figures of speech used by the various biblical writers and demonstrated that they were never intended to be taken literally. As in his sermon before the queen, he used biblical illustrations, as well as a few from classical literature, to drive home his points. The burden of the sermon was to bring his hearers to a personal faith in Jesus Christ. That is the true feeding. Christ gives a spiritual life that is sustained by faith. But for that faith to be given, there must be a sense of need. The world does not want what the gospel offers because it is "so drunken with these transitory vanities. They never felt what the things are that abide for ever. He never tasted of Christ that hungereth and thirsteth after vain glory."[12]

Prayerful use of Scripture

To understand the secret of Dering's faithful ministry, it is necessary to examine his walk with God. He was sustained by a belief that he was doing the will of God even when he was condemned by powerful figures of the church and state. How did he receive this faith? Dering knew that a mere hearing of the text of Scripture was not enough. The Word must be applied by the Holy Spirit. Something of his conviction may be seen in a prayer he regularly used before his lectures on Hebrews:

> O Lord God, which hath left unto us thy holy Word to be a lantern unto our feet, and a light unto our steps, give unto us all thy Holy Spirit: that out of the same Word, we may learn what is thy holy will

---

12. Dering, "A Sermon preached at the Tower of London, by M. Edward Dering, the 11 December, 1569," in *Works*.

and frame our lives in all holy obedience to the same, to thy honor and glory, and increase our faith through Jesus Christ our Lord. *Amen.*

In common with other Puritan pastors, Dering was concerned to promote family religion. He published a *Catechism* with a collection of prayers for families, titled *Godly Private Prayers for Householders.* These were intended to help godly householders in their meditations, and they also could be read at family devotions. They provide us with some insight into the workings of Dering's own heart. He taught his readers that they were to approach Scripture with prayerful preparation:

> Give me grace, most merciful Father, that for so high a treasure among us, I may be thankful, reverently embrace, accept and esteem the same, as the most precious jewel upon earth; be therein confirmed most strongly, that all things therein contained, be most certainly and undoubtedly true, not by any mortal man, but by thy most Holy Spirit in man, penned and written to the comfort and benefit of man, that I may most humbly, lowly and with high reverence, submit myself thereto as becomes thy eternal Majesty.[13]
>
> Lighten my understanding, most dear Father, with thy Holy Spirit, that I may learn, clearly conceive and understand the things therein contained, which no mere mortal man can conceive, than those that have learned of thee and whom thy Holy Spirit dost lighten and instruct. Guide me dear Father with thy Holy Spirit, that having understanding of the mysteries therein contained, I may be fully established, and confirmed in the true knowledge of thee, my Father, and of thy beloved Son, Jesus Christ, my Lord and Savior, thoroughly in conscience persuaded that I have my full and perfect salvation and life everlasting in him, and through his atonement made through his death and passion: that I do not vainly abuse the knowledge of thy most sacred word to satisfy vain curiosity or brag of knowledge, but only to the relieving of my hungry and wounded conscience, to the loosing of my fettered soul, and appeasing of my sorrowful heart, that I may to the end of my life, walk in sincerity of heart before thee, my heavenly Father, in the comfort of thy dear Son, my Savior, upholden by the merciful power of the Holy Ghost, to thine everlasting praise and glory, world without end, Amen.[14]

---

13. Dering, "Prayer to be confirmed in the Knowledge of God's Word," in *Works.*
14. "Prayer to be Confirmed in the Knowledge of God's Word, in *Works.*

Dering's prayers

Dering's *Godly Private Prayers for Householders to Meditate Upon, and to Say in their Families* were undoubtedly a reflection of his own prayers, indicating the issues that weighed most heavily with him and above all indicating the nature of his relationship with God.

These prayers are suffused with reverent confidence, enabling the reader to listen to this sixteenth-century preacher wrestling with God for blessing on the cause of Christ. He uses a variety of addresses for God in the same prayer. In "A Confession of Sin with Faith and Repentance," he comes to a "Merciful and Heavenly Father," aware that he is a child in the heavenly family, and so he says "we prostrate ourselves before thy Majesty." The concept of kingship is always there; several times he addresses God as "thy Majesty." At other times he addresses God as "Heavenly Father" or "Most merciful Father," and on at least one occasion as "most dear Father." He is fully conscious of the greatness and glory of God, but he also knows that God is never so distant that He is unaware of the hopes and fears of His children.

While Dering rejoices in the access he has to God, he does not forget the sin that separates us from God and that must be confessed. He acknowledges "our heinous offences" and declares "we feel ourselves laden with a huge company of horrible sins." The term *horrible* occurs several times in his confession of sins. In "A Morning Prayer for Families," he confesses "naughty and corrupt love." He becomes more specific as he asks his heavenly Father to "chase away from us all rancour and malice, all pride, envy, disdain, uncharitableness, unkindness, whatsoever is contrary to that love, whereof thou hast given us a lively example in our Savior Jesus Christ."

Dering knew how to combine confession of sin with faith and repentance:

> O merciful and heavenly Father, we thy servants do humbly prostrate ourselves before thy Majesty, acknowledging here in thy sight our heinous offences, committed against thy Majesty, seeing and beholding thy heavy wrath against them. We feel ourselves laden, O Lord our God, with a huge company of horrible sins, whereof the very least conceived in thought is sufficient to throw us down to the everlasting burning lake.

He develops this theme, but does not stay there:

In heaven, earth or hell, we see none able to sustain the weight of them, but even [only] thy dearly beloved Son, Jesus Christ, who in mercy infinite and compassion endless, hath sustained and overcome that endless punishment due unto them. In him therefore, in him, most merciful Father, and through him we come to thee, being fully assured according to thy promise that thou wilt accept and take that full recompense, which he thy dear Son hath made for us, as a just ransom for all the sins of all those who with a true faith take hold of him. In him therefore we see thine anger towards us appeased, thy wrath satisfied, and our debts paid.

All hindrances must be removed. Referring to the work of the Holy Spirit, Dering prays, "by the coming of the selfsame Spirit...scatter in us all the night of ignorance and forgetfulness of all those things that pertain to the fuller and clearer knowledge of thy truth."

At all times, Dering is careful to set all his worship in the context of eternity. In "An Evening Prayer for Families," after thanking his heavenly Father for His recent acts of lovingkindness, he continues praising God, "especially for that old and ancient love, wherewith thou hast loved us before the beginning of the world: for that also thou hast called us by the voice of the holy gospel in that good time thou hast appointed for us." After continuing to ask for immediate grace, he concludes his evening prayer by praying that "whensoever it shall please thee to call for us, we may willingly go unto thee as children to their dear Father, strangers to their own country, and members to their own Head: and so much the gladder, by how much thou Lord art better than all the men in the World, and the Kingdom thou hast prepared for us, better than all the kingdoms thereof."

Heavenly mindedness is always present in Dering's prayers, but he is aware of the needs of this world, so he includes "A Prayer for the Estate of the Whole Church." He prays for "thy whole true and Catholic Church and every member thereof." He rejoices that "God has caused to vanish the dark and misty clouds of ignorance and superstition," a reference to the Reformation. But he sees the need to ask God, "by thy Holy Spirit to touch the hearts of men, that they may embrace that thy high treasure sent among us." He asks that "simple hearts" may no longer be deceived by "that man of sin, which so proudly exalteth himself above all that is called God." He is mindful of the blessings now enjoyed in his land:

> Forasmuch as it has pleased thee in mercy above all nations of the earth, to pour down the sweet showers of heavenly grace upon this our English nation abundantly, in more plentiful wise watering the same with the gifts of thy Holy Spirit, in promoting the gospel and overthrowing idolatry, we pray thee to continue thy favour toward the same and utterly root out all remnants, relics and monuments of idolatry.

Dering's relationships with Elizabeth were difficult, but he did not cease to pray for her and to encourage others to do so also, "acknowledging thy mercy in placing over them a godly Princess, then may everyone in their callings walk in all true and humble obedience unto thee and for thee without resistance, tumults, insurrections, conspiracies or rebellions."

When he could no longer preach, Dering went on praying for the ministry of the gospel and teaching others to do likewise:

> Those pastors that thou hast given us, it would please thee to increase the number of them: those that have fallen asleep and carried away with the corruptions of the times, thou wouldest awake, letting them understand the charge thou hast committed unto them, the trust thou hast put them in, and the account that thou wilt take at their hands. Be gracious, O Lord, unto this land of ours, and enter not into judgment with the horrible sins of it, namely the corruption and light esteeming of thy word, so many years offered unto us, and we being trusted withal: so many nations better than we being passed by, that would have brought forth the fruit thereof more than we have done: and we not only have brought forth no good fruit, but rotten and unsavoury to provoke thy Majesty withal. Notwithstanding all these our sins, it would please thee in that love wherewith thou hast first loved us, when we hated thee, and in that long patience wherein thou hast hitherto born with us, and dost yet bear, and tarriest for our repentance, our hearts being effectually touched with thy Holy Spirit, striking those rocky hearts of ours, making them soft and meek to receive the print of thy Holy Word, and the seal of thy blessed Spirit, writing with thy finger thine own Laws in them, so that thou mayest read thine own hand.[15]

---

15. "An Addition to the Former Morning Prayer as time and leisure shall allow," in *Works*.

Dering's correspondence

After Dering was banned from preaching, he continued to minister by writing books and letters, and these give us insights into his godly character. Shortly after he gave his famous sermon before the queen, Dering wrote to his brother Richard, who seems to have been appalled by Edward's rashness. In the letter, Dering tried to help his brother spiritually:

> Good brother Dering, here follow me. You shall be a good deal richer than you already are: study the Scripture, read books, be able to reason in your faith. Especially and above all have a lively feeling of God, that you may think more vile of all the glory of the world, than of the dust of the earth. You know that we must all perish, and you must walk the way of all flesh: our good parents, Father and Mother they are gone before.[16]

At this stage, he seems to have been unsure of Richard's spiritual state:

> You are my eldest brother, and you know not how glad I should be to see you go before me in religion. God hath given you neither a light head nor little understanding. If you would apply yourself unto knowledge, you should then reap the fruit of your labour in more gladness of heart than yet you can imagine. Begin once a little, and taste how sweet the Lord is, and you shall feel the riches of his joy, and say happy be the time that I ever knew it.[17]

Edward emphasized the joys of Christianity in dealing with his brother. He also showed how the sense of the presence of God and the proximity of eternity gave an urgency to his appeals and helped to explain his fearlessness in the presence of the queen and the great figures at court:

> And for Master S[ecretary, William Cecil, the queen's secretary] or for any other of such high calling, I love them in the Lord, even as I love my own soul while they and I shall live. Though I bear the loss of worldly things, yet by the grace of Christ I will never lose a good conscience, and though they be angry with me, I will not leave to pray for them, and commit my cause unto God. He will one day multiply his

---

16. Dering, "Edward Dering to Richard Dering" (November 19, 1570), in *Godly Letters*.
17. Dering, "Edward Dering to Richard Dering" (November 19, 1570), in *Godly Letters*.

grace, where he hath well begun, and they shall I trust be thoroughly taught, whom God hath already so well instructed.[18]

Writing to Richard a year or so later, he seemed more confident of his brother's spiritual state and asked for his prayers because he had been forbidden to preach. Richard seems at this time to have lacked assurance, so Edward wrote:

> I will pray for you, that your eyes may have perfect and pure light to see the loving countenance of the Lord, which is better than life: so you shall be happy in the days of your vanity. And when nature makes you to…walk in the way of the world, then shall you reap the fruit of your labour, and say with gladness, *Lord lettest thou thy servant depart in peace.*

An undated letter to his brother John shows his concern for his wider family:

> I thank you good brother, for your letter, and for your care of my recovery, but most of all that you show a good testimony of your mind, that the fear of God doth dwell in you; of this I am glad. For I know how earnestly I desire it, and I see how unfeignedly you are brought unto it.

After exhortations to persevere in the faith, he continued, referring to his mother's brother and his family:

> I beseech God to bless my good uncle Brent, and make him now to know, which in his tender years he could not see: for the world was then dark and we were blind in it; but since we have been lightened with the gospel of the Lord Jesus, and so much more earnestly now we must pray that it may be unto us the gospel of health and we may increase in the knowledge of the mystery of it. And that the Lord may open his gracious countenance revealed in it to my Aunt, that she may also make a blessed change, to leave vain imaginations of her own mind, which are full of ignorance, and learn Scripture, which can make known unto her the living God. And commend me heartily to them both, to whom I wish as to myself.[19]

---

18. Dering, "Edward Dering to Richard Dering" (November 19, 1570), in *Godly Letters*.
19. "Edward Dering to John Dering," no date, in *Works*.

Dering continued writing letters of spiritual counsel to his friends, notably a number to members of the Kentish gentry, whom he had known from childhood. These included a number to Mistress Killigrew, sister-in-law to Lord Burghley and wife of Henry Killigrew, a government servant. A number of letters are preserved in the *Works*. Others remain in manuscript, some in the Kent County Archives in Maidstone. There were no doubt many more that remained in private hands but have disappeared.

The letters that remain give us many insights into the life of a remarkable man whose short ministry played an important part in teaching the Word to the first generation of Englishmen after gospel preaching was restored under Elizabeth. These early Puritans did not mold the Church of England in the way that they had hoped, but they helped to establish a well-taught people whose influence, out of all proportion to their numbers, was to continue for many years to come.

Chapter 18
by Gary Benfold

Passion and the Spirit's Sovereignty in the Thinking and Evangelistic Preaching of Martyn Lloyd-Jones

> *Above all, realise that if you are a child of God, it is because God has determined it, and what He has determined about you is certain and safe and sure. Nothing and no one can ever take you out of His hands, or make Him forgo His purpose in respect to you. The doctrine of the eternal decrees of God before the foundation of the world! He knew me. He knew you. And our names were written in the Lamb's Book of Life before the world was ever made, before you and I or anybody else ever came into it. Let us bow before His Majesty. Let us humble ourselves in His holy presence.*[1]
>
> —D. MARTYN LLOYD-JONES

Martyn Lloyd-Jones was asked on one occasion in a BBC TV interview why, if his message was true, so few believed it? He responded, "Ultimately, this is the will of God."[2] This response shows beyond doubt that Lloyd-Jones believed in the sovereignty of God—and much more. As Graham Harrison put it, "Others might theorize about the sovereignty of God: he believed it and rested in it!"[3]

He believed, too, in the vital necessity of Scripture, the only Word of the living God. Very many published volumes of his sermons (he is said to be the best-selling Welsh author ever, in any genre), all of which include careful "unpacking" of Bible texts or passages, together with the availability of more than sixteen hundred individual recordings of sermons with the

---

1. D. M. Lloyd-Jones, *God the Father, God the Son* (London: Hodder and Stoughton, 1996), 102.
2. Iain Murray, *The Fight of Faith*, 632.
3. Graham Harrison, "A Man Sent by God," *Evangelical Magazine of Wales* 20, no. 2 (April 1981): 47.

same characteristic, give testimony to the reality of that confidence. At a time when preaching seemed, to many, to be in terminal decline (at least in the UK), it was largely due to the influence of Lloyd-Jones' ministry that sustained, serious, systematic expository preaching began to be revived in the churches.

The relationship between "Word" and "Spirit" in Christian ministry is a subject of ongoing debate. What attracts less attention, however, is the place that the *manner* of preaching plays in its effectiveness. It is a part of the question of the relationship between God's sovereignty and human responsibility, or God's use of means in accomplishing His purposes. In this chapter, therefore, I want to look at just one ingredient of the act of preaching by considering the passion with which Lloyd-Jones preached his evangelistic sermons, and then asking, given his convictions about God's sovereignty, why he felt such passion was necessary or appropriate.

An overview of Lloyd-Jones's life and ministry

First, for the sake of those who are unfamiliar with the life and ministry of "The Doctor," let me offer a brief outline.

Born in Cardiff in December 1899, Lloyd-Jones's intellectual gifts were recognized early, and he trained as a medical doctor at St. Bartholomew's Hospital (Bart's) in London. By the age of twenty-four, he was chief clinical assistant to Sir Thomas (later Lord) Horder, the King's physician. Already at this date, however, he was feeling the pull of Christian ministry, having been converted to Christ sometime around 1923. He said of this conversion that the "Holy Spirit quickened me and wakened me to the realization of certain profound and vital truths taught in the Bible."[4]

So, in 1927, he became minister of Bethlehem Forward Movement Mission (Sandfields) in Aberavon, a poor mining and steel-working district of South Wales. The General Strike of 1926 was a recent and painful memory; its effects were still being felt, and poverty and hardship were endemic. However, this unpromising situation was to be the scene of eleven years of remarkable ministry, with results such that Iain Murray describes

---

4. Quoted in John Brencher, *Martyn Lloyd-Jones (1899–1981) and Twentieth-Century Evangelicalism* (Carlisle: Paternoster, 2002), 11.

the years around 1930 as a time of "revival."[5] The blessing was not confined to Aberavon; Lloyd-Jones's itinerant ministry in Wales on weekdays led to him being described as "the modern Moody for whom we are waiting."[6]

After his removal to London and the famous pulpit of Westminster Chapel in that city, his pattern of evangelistic preaching continued. Every Sunday evening it was his custom to preach directly to those who were not converted. His midweek ministry continued, too—and once again, those sermons were largely evangelistic in purpose, up to and beyond his retirement in 1968, only coming to an end shortly before his death on March 1, 1981. (Indeed, it was as a result of his itinerant preaching at a meeting in Sheffield, South Yorkshire, in 1973 that I was converted.) It is important to realize that, while he is primarily remembered as a Bible teacher of considerable ability and power, in his own eyes Lloyd-Jones was an evangelist.[7]

He once said that "the most fatal blunder of all; and certainly the commonest,"[8] was that of assuming that everyone listening to a sermon must be a Christian. Although he rarely made personal or autobiographical references in his *preaching*, he described in his *lectures* to ministry students at Westminster Seminary[9] how, for many years, he had been a regular church attender while completely mistaken as to his spiritual state. Therefore, he said, he would argue for "an absolute rule without any hesitation whatsoever" that there should always be one evangelistic sermon each week in every church. A failure here, he said, would produce a congregation of cold, hard Pharisees—religious, harsh, and self-satisfied.

As I hope to show, Lloyd-Jones's preaching was passionate. This chapter aims to examine his understanding of God's sovereignty in salvation and

---

5. Iain H Murray, *The First Forty Years* (Edinburgh: Banner of Truth, 1982), 203.

6. Quoted in Murray, *The First Forty Years*, 326. "Revival" in this sense—the sense in which Lloyd-Jones always used the word—is not an organized evangelistic campaign, but a time of special blessing from the Spirit of God. During such a time, many people are converted, while those who are already Christians become aware of a deeper, more powerful sense of God in their lives. Lloyd-Jones puts the effect on believers first because "you cannot revive something that has never had life."

7. See D. M. Lloyd-Jones, *Old Testament Evangelistic Sermons* (Edinburgh: Banner of Truth, 1995), vii.

8. D. M. Lloyd-Jones, *Preaching and Preachers* (London: Hodder and Stoughton, 1971), 46.

9. This series of lectures was published as *Preaching and Preachers*; see previous note.

then to consider the Doctor's passionate delivery in the light of that. We will first examine his teaching on the Holy Spirit's sovereignty in salvation. Then we will consider his style of preaching, looking particularly at one notable sermon. Finally, we will study how well his doctrine and his passionate manner fit together, attempting briefly what C. H. Spurgeon said he would never attempt: the reconciliation of friends.

The sovereign Spirit

With so many volumes of his sermons readily available, including volumes on Ephesians 1 and on Romans 8, it would be possible to outline Lloyd-Jones's understanding of God's sovereignty in conversion from several different sources. I have chosen, however, to focus on just one source.

For three years, beginning in 1952, Lloyd-Jones devoted his Friday night meetings at Westminster Chapel to a series of lectures on great Christian doctrines.[10] In these lectures, he set out his understanding of the work of the Holy Spirit in conversion.

First, he argues, the Holy Spirit always works through the Word of God:

> Now there are many people who claim that He works directly.... Not at all! The Holy Spirit always uses the word: "This is the word which by the gospel is preached unto you," says Peter (1 Peter 1:25). "Being born again," says Peter, "not by corruptible seed, but of incorruptible, by the word of God, which liveth and abideth for ever" (1 Pet. 1:23).[11]

The Doctor then proceeds to spell out what the Spirit does through the Word. First, He reveals the great love of God to sinners in general. Second, He presents and offers salvation in Christ, stating the facts about Christ, the record of the life, death, resurrection, and resurrection appearances of the Lord. This is what preaching does: it proclaims these facts and explains them. Third, the Spirit calls men and women to repentance because of these facts, and finally calls them to faith in Christ.

---

10. Published as *Great Doctrines of the Bible* (Wheaton, Ill.: Crossway, 2003) and previously in three volumes.
11. Lloyd-Jones, *Great Doctrines of the Bible*, Kindle edition, location 6370.

All of this, Lloyd-Jones says, is the Holy Spirit's general work, and He does it wherever the gospel is proclaimed. This is the general call of the gospel; it is done from the Scriptures, by the church and its people, and is the work of the Spirit. But it saves no one. The "general call" goes out both to those who respond and to those who do not respond. If anyone is to be saved, there is more to be done, and it must also be done by the Holy Spirit:

> We have seen also that the Holy Spirit is concerned about giving the general call of the gospel, and we emphasised that it is a call that is given to all, to those who remain unbelievers and to those who become believers.... So the question at once arises: Why this difference? And in dealing with the work of the Holy Spirit, of necessity we have to face that problem.[12]

Lloyd-Jones then outlines five different historical understandings of the Spirit's work in conversion: the Pelagian answer (wherein man is born neutral and can believe God's Word or reject it: "The Holy Spirit does nothing within the person at all"[13]); the Semi-Pelagian (wherein love for God originates in individuals, but we need the assistance of the Holy Spirit); the Arminian (wherein "the Holy Spirit gives sufficient measure of grace to everybody born into this life to accept and to believe the gospel");[14] the Lutheran (wherein "grace is again operating in all men and women...[but] men and women have the capacity to resist the operation of God's grace"); and, finally, the Reformed (wherein "the Holy Spirit of God does a work in those who are saved which He does not do in those who are not saved").[15]

It is this last view that Lloyd-Jones owns as his own, and he goes on to expound it in the following chapter, "Effectual Calling." He defines effectual calling as that work "that the Holy Spirit does to those who become believers, and only to them, in order to apply the work of redemption."[16]

He says further:

> This, then, is something that is quite obvious. We can say that in addition to the external call there is this effectual call, and that what

---

12. Lloyd-Jones, *Great Doctrines of the Bible*, Kindle edition, location 6413.
13. Lloyd-Jones, *Great Doctrines of the Bible*, Kindle edition, location 6427.
14. Lloyd-Jones, *Great Doctrines of the Bible*, Kindle edition, location 6438.
15. Lloyd-Jones, *Great Doctrines of the Bible*, Kindle edition, location 6449.
16. Lloyd-Jones, *Great Doctrines of the Bible*, Kindle edition, location 6391.

makes anybody a saved person and a true Christian is that the call of the gospel has come effectually.[17]

Characteristically, he goes on to say, "Let me give you some scriptures that establish that," and then quotes Romans 8:28–39, 1 Corinthians 1:2, 1 Corinthians 1:23–24, and 1 Peter 2:9–10 before concluding, "Now it is obvious therefore that in these people the call has been effectual; that is the teaching of these scriptures."[18] He then shows that the difference between the "general" call and the "effectual" call is that the general call is simply external, but the effectual call is an internal, spiritual call—and again, he gives Scripture proofs.

It is inevitable that we should ask: Why does the Spirit effectually call some and not others? It is not that some resist and others do not: Lloyd-Jones' whole point is that we *all* resist until the Spirit intervenes. As the hymnwriter Josiah Condor wrote:

> 'Tis not that I did choose Thee,
> For, Lord, that could not be;
> This heart would still refuse Thee
> Hadst Thou not chosen me....
>
> 'Twas sovereign mercy called me,
> And taught my opening mind;
> The world had else enthralled me,
> To heavenly glories blind....[19]

For Lloyd-Jones, and for Reformed theology generally, the answer is in the plan of God—indeed, in an eternal covenant, or agreement, between the persons of the Trinity:

> There can be no question at all but that the Scriptures teach that before the foundation of the world a council with respect to man took place between the three Persons of the Trinity—the Father, the Son, and the Holy Spirit. And there in that eternal council they seem very clearly to have divided up the work of redemption, so that we can

---

17. Lloyd-Jones, *Great Doctrines of the Bible*, Kindle edition, location 6566.
18. Lloyd-Jones, *Great Doctrines of the Bible*, Kindle edition, location 6580.
19. From the hymn "'Tis Not That I Did Choose Thee" by Josiah Conder, 1789–1855.

describe the Father as the originator, the Son as the executor and the Holy Spirit as the One who applies what the Son has achieved.[20]

This eternal covenant involved the Father giving a people to the Son:

> The next step in this compact, or covenant, between the Father and the Son was that God the Father gave God the Son this people whom He would raise at the last day. Read, for instance, John 6, and you will find that our Lord constantly refers to that and He says He must not lose anything that God has given Him.... But further, we see that God not only gave Him the people, He also gave Him a certain work to do with respect to them. Again in John 17 we read, "I have glorified thee on the earth: I have finished the work which thou gavest me to do" (v. 4). So the Father, in eternity, gave the Son a certain work to do and then, having given it, He sent Him to do it.[21]

Here Lloyd-Jones is expounding, in outline, a Reformed or Calvinistic understanding of the work of redemption: an eternal covenant, a people given to the Son by the Father, a work accomplished by the Son for those people, and the Holy Spirit working in the world to call those people to faith in Christ:

> It is a perfect plan, and it was all perfect before the very foundation of the world. God had mapped it out in eternity, and then had put it into operation in this world of time. You cannot read the Bible without noticing in a very particular way the time element. Everything that has happened up till this moment has happened according to God's plan and programme.[22]

Here, then, we have a man convinced of a glorious work of God, planned and accomplished once for all, but applied by the Holy Spirit in due time to all whom the Lord our God calls. And this man is a preacher. So how does he go about proclaiming this work of God, and particularly to those who do not yet believe it? How does he *preach*, and in particular, how does he preach *evangelistically*?

---

20. Lloyd-Jones, *Father and Son*, 217.
21. Lloyd-Jones, *Father and Son*, 218–19.
22. Lloyd-Jones, *Father and Son*, 219.

Passionate preaching

Famously, Lloyd-Jones argued that preaching is "Logic on fire! Eloquent reason!" and went on to say: "A theology which does not take fire…is a defective theology.… A man who can speak about these things dispassionately has no right whatsoever to be in a pulpit."[23] Yet his opening words in most of his sermons gave no hint of the fire to come.

Lloyd-Jones's characteristic way of opening a sermon—certainly in his Westminster years—was to say, "The verse to which I would like to draw your attention is to be found…," followed by the necessary Bible reference. It is hard to imagine a more mundane beginning, or one that so comprehensively breaks the "rules" or "accepted practice" of homiletics. He did not begin with a contemporary reference or a story, still less with a joke or quip. There was not even any significant variation in his opening sentence. However, this formulaic opening made the point clearly at the beginning that the preacher was not going to be giving his own ideas. Instead, he was going to be talking about what the Bible means. Quietly and undramatically, therefore, it called for a paradigm shift in the attitude of the listener.

Next, if he was not recapping a previous week's sermon, he typically would move on to an analysis of the present-day situation, and begin to show how the text or passage was relevant. This was his introduction, and he described it as a medical approach: a physician working with his patient so that the patient might be persuaded of the need for treatment. He often gave an unusual amount of time to these introductions, and they should not be regarded as unimportant preliminaries. My doctoral research on Lloyd-Jones's Acts sermons[24] identified occasions when around a third of a sixty-minute sermon was given to introduction. A similar pattern can be seen in many of his earliest published sermons, the evangelistic sermons from Aberavon.[25]

Many hundreds of Lloyd-Jones's sermons are now in print, and many hundreds more are available in recorded form. The sermon published as

---

23. Lloyd-Jones, *Preaching and Preachers*, 97.
24. The sermons are published as *Authentic Christianity*, 6 vols. (Edinburgh: Banner of Truth, 1999–2006).
25. D. M. Lloyd-Jones, *Evangelistic Sermons at Aberavon* (Edinburgh: Banner of Truth, 1983).

"Sound an Alarm,"[26] singled out by Murray as having a major effect when Lloyd-Jones preached it in Cardiff on New Year's Day 1957, is a typical example and worth examining. Fewer than twelve years after the end of the Second World War, the Suez Crisis seemed likely to plunge Britain into the third major war of the century, and Murray comments that it was "an evening marked by an unusual solemnity in the congregation."[27]

The sermon was based on Isaiah 22:8–14 ("And in that day did the Lord God of hosts call to weeping and to mourning," v. 12a). Let us note first a passage from the introduction. It takes for granted habits of Bible reading that could not be assumed today, but also serves as the "hook" to catch attention:

> Thus it comes to pass that as you are reading through your Bible suddenly you come across a passage and you say: "Well, that might have been written today, it is an exact description of what is happening at the present time!" Precisely, says the Bible, because all the changes that have taken place in the human race are entirely on the surface; they are mere changes in appearance and in clothing and in externals. Man *qua* man remains exactly what he has always been.... Very well, let us look at it and see what it has to tell us. Here, I say, is the Word of God to any individual in this congregation who is in trouble or distress, it is the Word of God to the whole world immersed and involved as it is in all these alarums and trials and troubles, of wars and rumours of wars, and the horrible possibility of yet worse things to come. Let us then listen to it, and pray God that He will give us his grace.[28]

Following such an introduction, Lloyd-Jones proceeded with a devastating logic; if anyone doubted on first reading that the passage was "an exact description of what is happening at the present time," he could not doubt it for long. First, he showed that God had removed the "covering" that prevented the people of Judah seeing what had really happened, taking away their blindness. In the same way, God had, in Lloyd-Jones's own time, opened the eyes and removed the optimism of "every person who is

---

26. Lloyd-Jones, *Old Testament Evangelistic Sermons*, 208–23.
27. Iain H. Murray, *The Fight of Faith* (Edinburgh: Banner of Truth, 1990), 336.
28. Lloyd-Jones, *Old Testament Evangelistic Sermons*, 209–10.

capable of thinking at all."[29] As in Judah, he said, it had become clear that the British people's sin had undermined the spiritual strength of the nation and of individuals. Then he examined how Judah had tried—frantically and futilely—to put things right, but without coming to terms with the real problems. Again this was applied to the United Kingdom and to the world at large. He showed the reason that all efforts had failed—a blindness to the moral and religious problems at the root of the current situation—and went on to press home the profound and radical character of the problem. All of this preceded a passionate call to repentance:

> Repent and acknowledge and confess your sin to God, and obey Him when He tells you to believe in His Son, Who died for you and your sins, and to follow Him whatever the cost, and you will find yourself saved, you fill find yourself at peace with God, with a new life, a new nature, and a new outlook upon everything. Fear of death will go, fear of the judgment will go. Having gone back to the Maker, to the Fashioner and Designer, you will find yourself a new man.
> This is essentially an individual message. Nations do not turn to Christ together, but individuals do; and as individuals do in large numbers, nations are influenced....[30]

This outline and these extracts do not do justice to the sermon. Even on the printed page, however, it is hard to miss the passion of the preacher's words. This is true again and again in his published sermons, and especially in his published evangelistic sermons. But hearing the recordings made at the time makes it even more clear, revealing a passion that may begin as a low growl before rising in volume and pitch to a powerful peroration, as if the preacher would compel his hearers to abandon their godless and ungodly worldviews, see the logic and power of the gospel, and close with Christ immediately. No one to my knowledge comes as close to the Doctor's own famous definition of preaching—"logic on fire"—as Lloyd-Jones himself.

Reconciling friends

Now the question becomes clear: If God by His Spirit effectually (and irresistibly) calls to Himself those He has chosen before the foundation of the

---

29. Lloyd-Jones, *Old Testament Evangelistic Sermons*, 211.
30. Lloyd-Jones, *Old Testament Evangelistic Sermons*, 223.

world, what is the point of passionate preaching? Indeed, what is the point of preaching at all, or of any form of evangelism?

It is, of course, possible to emphasize the sovereignty of God to an extent that the Scriptures simply do not allow. If God is so completely sovereign, having infallibly chosen for salvation a vast host that no man can number, who "not only may be saved, but are saved, must be saved, and cannot by any possibility run the risk of being anything but saved"[31]—then why do we need to do anything at all? It leads to the famous caricature: "Sit down, young man; when God is pleased to convert the heathen, he will do so without your help or mine!"

On the other hand, we may notice that Scripture emphasizes human responsibility not just in accepting the message but in preaching the message, too, to a very high degree: "how shall they hear without a preacher?" (Rom. 10:14b). Thus, we may conclude that God is not fully sovereign, and even may be frustrated at the way in which so few respond to the gospel, and so few of those who do respond go on to proclaim the gospel.

Lloyd-Jones, in common with other Reformed theologians and preachers, avoided both extremes. For example, he insisted:

> *All the decrees of God are unconditional and sovereign.* They are not dependent in any sense on human actions. They are not determined by anything that people may or may not do. God's decrees are not even determined in the light of what he knows people are going to do. They are absolutely unconditional. They do not depend upon anything except God's own will and God's own holiness.[32]

He goes on, however, to say:

> But—and I want to make this quite clear—that does not mean that there is no such thing as cause and effect in life. That does not mean that there are no such things as conditional actions. There is such a thing in nature and in life as cause and effect—yes. But what this doctrine says is that every cause and effect, and free actions, are part of the decree of God Himself. He has determined to work in that particular way. God has decreed that the end which He has in view

---

31. C. H. Spurgeon, quoted in Iain H. Murray, *The Forgotten Spurgeon*, 2nd ed. (Edinburgh: Banner of Truth, 1973), 77.
32. Lloyd-Jones, *God the Father, God the Son*, 98 (emphasis in original).

shall certainly and inevitably be brought to pass, and that nothing can hinder or frustrate it.[33]

Biblical preachers, and biblical Christians, know very well that God is absolutely sovereign; they give thanks for it in their prayers. They know, too, that God is sovereign in the salvation of individuals, and regularly pray that God would save their friends and family members, as J. I. Packer pointed out more than five decades ago.[34] But biblical Christians know other things, too. For example, they know that God holds individuals responsible for the choices that they make. God tells Ezekiel that "if anyone hears the trumpet but does not take warning and the sword comes and takes his life, his blood will be on his own head. Since he heard the sound of the trumpet but did not take warning, his blood will be on his own head. *If he had taken warning, he would have saved himself*" (33:4–5, emphasis added). It makes no difference to the point I am making here whether we see this as referring merely to a military situation or to eternal salvation itself (although I would certainly include the latter). Both the sovereignty of God and the responsibility of individuals are taught in the Bible—even, as Packer points out, side by side. (He quotes as his example Luke 22:22: "the Son of man goeth [to His death], *as it was determined*: but *woe unto that man by whom he is betrayed!*"[35])

Here, then, is the ultimate and theological answer: the God who ordains the end also ordains the means. God, who has planned the salvation of a multitude, has also ordained how it will happen. We must not allow our understanding of God's absolute sovereignty to drive out of our minds and doctrines the equally biblical truth of our responsibility to believe the gospel ourselves and to present it to others.

The passion of Lloyd-Jones in preaching is in part explained by the magnificence, depth, and beauty of the truths he was proclaiming: how could these things possibly be handled coldly? But it is not the only answer, or even the main answer. God has appointed means; there is cause and

---

33. Lloyd-Jones, *God the Father, God the Son*, 99.
34. J. I. Packer, *Evangelism and the Sovereignty of God* (London: InterVarsity Press, 1961), 14–15.
35. Packer, *Evangelism and the Sovereignty of God*, 22. Emphasis added in the Scripture quotation.

effect. To use a very simple illustration, if your neighbor's house catches fire, you must tell him. But if you want him to believe you (in the middle of the night, when he is warm and comfortable, and there are lots of apparent incentives for him to stay where he is), you will not be measured, quiet, and polite in your tones, but urgent and passionate. The soul's danger is greater by far than that of a body in a house fire.

Human beings who need to be saved by God's almighty grace and the wonders of the gospel are more likely (speaking "as a man"[36]) to be saved through a passionate exposition and explanation of that gospel than through a dispassionate proclamation. Lloyd-Jones knew the reality of hell, so his passion was not false or forced. But he knew the importance of persuasion, too—and so he did not restrain his passion. "Knowing therefore the terror of the Lord, we persuade men" (2 Cor. 5:11a).[37] It is a lesson that many preachers need to learn.

How, then, should we learn from this, and from Lloyd-Jones? Let me plead for the following:

First, I plead that we give urgent consideration to re-establishing in our churches a regular, and preferably weekly, opportunity for evangelistic preaching. In both the United States and the United Kingdom, as I understand things, it is a dying practice, and many reasons are given for it. But we are not reaching our cultures. The masses of people are outside our churches, and many of those in the churches hear no clear, regular explanation of what they must do to be saved. We may not simply say, "The elect will be saved, and the rest will perish." Though it is true, it is our God-given responsibility to work urgently and to plead passionately for the salvation of souls.

Second, I plead that we give urgent consideration therefore to the *manner*, and especially the *passion*, of our preaching. We believe that only a whole-hearted response to the gospel message can save our hearers from eternal doom. Surely, when we preach, it ought to sound like that? Exegetical accuracy is necessary, but it is not enough. Verbal clarity is necessary,

---

36. Romans 3:5.
37. The King James Version, cited here, is right; the Greek has no "try to" as in the New International Version.

but it is not enough. Interesting illustrations are helpful, but they are not enough. We do mean what we say, and we *must*—surely—sound as if we do.

When I was converted almost forty years ago, I had a very good unconverted friend who was much brighter than I and—in those teenage years at least—very cynical. When I began to preach, I would often imagine him in the congregation and ask myself, even if he were not persuaded by what I was saying, whether he would have to admit that it was an accurate explanation of the text in front of us. Then I would ask: Even if he did not believe it himself, would it be obvious to him that I believed it, and that I believed passionately that it mattered? Surely, nothing less will do.

Contributors

Gary Brady is pastor of Childs Hill Baptist Church, North West London, England, UK.

Paul Levy is pastor of The International Presbyterian Church, Ealing, London, England, UK.

Carl Trueman is the Paul Woolley professor of church history at Westminster Theological Seminary, Philadelphia, and pastor of Cornerstone Presbyterian Church, Ambler, Pennsylvania, USA.

Sam Waldron is Academic Dean and professor of Systematic Theology at the Midwest Center for Theological Studies, and a pastor of Grace Reformed Baptist Church, Owensboro, Kentucky, USA.

Joel Beeke is president and professor of Systematic Theology and Homiletics at Puritan Reformed Theological Seminary, and a pastor of the Heritage Netherlands Reformed Congregation, Grand Rapids, Michigan, USA.

Fred Malone is pastor of First Baptist Church, Clinton, Louisiana, USA.

David Jones is pastor of Mount Stuart Presbyterian Church, Hobart, Tasmania, Australia.

Ian Hamilton is minister of Cambridge Presbyterian Church, England, UK.

Sinclair B. Ferguson recently retired from being the senior minister of the First Presbyterian Church in Columbia, South Carolina, USA, and now resides in Scotland, from where he exercises an international itinerant, conference, and teaching ministry.

Michael A. G. Haykin is professor of church history and biblical spirituality and Director of The Andrew Fuller Center for Baptist Studies at Southern Baptist Theological Seminary, Louisville, Kentucky, USA.

Derek W. H. Thomas is the senior minister of the First Presbyterian Church in Columbia, South Carolina, USA.

John J. Murray is a retired minister in the Free Church of Scotland (Continuing) living in Glasgow, Scotland, UK.

Iain D. Campbell is minister of Point Free Church of Scotland, Isle of Lewis, Scotland, UK.

Stephen Turner is pastor of Shore Baptist Church, Auckland, New Zealand.

Conrad Mbewe is pastor of Kabwata Reformed Baptist Church, Lusaka, Zambia, Africa.

Austin Walker is a pastor of Maidenbower Baptist Church, Crawley, West Sussex, England, UK.

Robert Oliver is a retired Baptist minister and church history lecturer (London Theological Seminary) living in Bradford-on-Avon, Wiltshire, England, UK.

Gary Benfold is pastor of Moordown Baptist Church, Bournemouth, England, UK.